TOGETHER WE ROARED

TOGETHER WE ROARED

ALONGSIDE TIGER FOR HIS EPIC TWELVE-YEAR, THIRTEEN-MAJORS RUN

STEVE WILLIAMS AND EVIN PRIEST

wm

WILLIAM MORROW

An Imprint of HarperCollins*Publishers*

HarperCollins books may be purchased for educational, business, or sales promotional use. For information, please email the Special Markets Department at SPsales@harpercollins.com.

FIRST EDITION

Library of Congress Cataloging-in-Publication Data has been applied for.

ISBN 978-0-06-341870-7

25 26 27 28 29 LBC 5 4 3 2 1

Steve Williams

To my lovely wife, Kirsty. Thank you for your unwavering support through all the good times, and the not-so-good times. I couldn't have done it without you.

So many people made this journey an incredible one. But it would never have happened without Butch Harmon and Mark O'Meara recommending me for the job.

Evin Priest

For Laura, Karen and Tim, who believed in me.

For the great golf writers who believed in our profession.

For Benny and Cannizzaro, who believed spending time with me on tour was a good idea.

CONTENTS

AUTHORS' NOTE

Tiger Woods frequently uttered a five-word phrase that would make caddie Steve Williams grin at his boss's chances of winning that week. "The course fits my eye," Woods would remark about happy hunting grounds on the PGA Tour, such as Bay Hill Club and Lodge in Orlando—where he won the Arnold Palmer Invitational a record eight times—and Firestone Country Club in Akron, Ohio. He won there eight times, too. He didn't always win after saying it, but "out of the 63 PGA Tour titles he won with me, an overwhelming majority came after he'd told me that, and sometimes he even said it publicly," Williams, Woods's bagman from 1999 to 2011, recalls. Woods used the motto days before some of his most *important* victories: before his drought-breaking major win at the 1999 PGA Championship at Medinah No. 3; when Williams first caddied for Woods at Augusta National earlier that year; and before the 2002 U.S. Open at Bethpage Black, which was the first municipal golf course to ever host America's national championship.

Williams knew there was more meaning than simply Woods enjoying the course's design. "What it meant to me was, if there was any tension or anxiety in his swing in the days or weeks leading up, it was gone when he said those words," Williams recalls. "I knew he felt comfortable with every shot the course demanded, and that allowed Tiger's instincts to shape the ball to kick in. Technical thoughts went out the window."

As you will find in these pages, the way Woods and Williams communicated with each other was unlike any player-caddie partnership in golf's history. It was the cornerstone of their relationship. Language is the answer to a commonly asked question: *Why did Tiger Woods and Steve Williams win so much together?*

Their dialogue began with a dubious phone call to Williams's hotel room in early 1999, and their conversations were initially complicated by Williams's hilarious refusal to buy, or use, a cell phone in the late 1990s, even as cell phone ownership soared. Even after Woods purchased one for his caddie in the early 2000s, the pair continued to write special handwritten messages of encouragement and constructive feedback to each other. Their verbal interactions were legendary—from Williams learning what Woods meant when he said he did a "Nolan Ryan" on the course, to mottoes they shared, like "Fast pay makes fast friends."

Sometimes, Williams took information from something as simple as body language, which Woods would use to have Williams ask people to politely leave him to practice in solitude, or it could be with his eyes. "I would always look at Tiger's eyes on any approach shot, or recovery shot, because I could read his intentions," Williams says. Ironically, in the end, a lack of open discussion when their partnership was on the rocks in 2011 was what expedited their split.

Communication was also the inspiration for why Williams and I decided to write *Together We Roared*. We both felt there was an obvious hole in the legacy of Woods and Williams and how their story had been told; there had never been a definitive account of their whirlwind 12 years together. Certainly not one that exclusively zoomed in on how their combination produced 13 major championship wins, as well as six runners-up and two third-placings at golf's four biggest events. Put simply, one of the greatest partnerships in the history of sports didn't have its own book. Until now.

Williams and I began to relive his time with Woods through a podcast during the COVID-19 pandemic, called *Chasing Majors*. We had so much fun revisiting their success, major by major, that we decided a book was the only medium that could deliver the richness and depth it deserved. We also felt it needed to be written in the third person to allow Williams to focus on recalling his deepest and most vivid memories during extensive interviews. For *Together We Roared*, we sat down for approximately six months' worth of weekly and twice weekly interviews, which indicated one thing: there were so many stories about caddying for Woods that he'd never told. The other important reason for a third-person retelling was the room that created to include more than just Williams's memories: there are countless interviews with other champion golfers, such as Mark O'Meara, Chris DiMarco, Adam Scott, Stuart Appleby and Ian Baker-Finch, as well as other caddies. It also gave us the ability to include extensive research through newspaper archives, magazines and databases to paint a broad, immersive picture. We hope this book takes readers inside the room, and on the green, with Woods and Williams with fly-on-the-wall detail. *Together We Roared* is supercharged with nostalgia.

Williams and I wanted to write this book because Woods is one of the most mysterious figures to have ever played professional sports. And although he was intensely protective of his privacy, a lifestyle Williams had to adopt, Woods and Williams were very normal and humble people. At least Woods was as close to normal as a person could be with his global fame. *Together We Roared* gets to the heart of their normalcy; they were two friends, two knuckleheads, who respected and trusted each other, traveling the world winning historic golf tournaments. Through Williams's relationship with Woods, fans will see a human side of the superstar not previously explored—such as their handwritten notes, well-timed phone calls, gifts and thoughtful gestures. It was also evident through Woods's constant gratitude for Williams's caddie work. Despite Woods's superhuman achievements and golf shots, his robotic pursuit of Jack Nicklaus's record 18 major wins and his stoic and cryptic relationship with media, Woods showed people in his inner sanctum, like Williams, that he had a caring, intellectual, curious and relatable side.

Together We Roared also offers behind-the-scenes insight to the pulsating moments that fans can never relate to but simply admire for their brilliance: the underappreciated significance of their first major win together, the 1999 PGA Championship; the discussions in between shots during the 2000 U.S. Open at Pebble Beach; cradling the claret jug on the private jet ride home from Scotland after the 2000 Open Championship at St. Andrews; what Williams said that made Woods break down in tears as he won the 2006 Open at Royal Liverpool, his first major win after the passing of his father, Earl; and the heart-stopping, stomach-churning moments and dialogue during the 2008 U.S. Open as Woods won his 14th major on a broken leg at his beloved Torrey Pines South Course in San Diego.

One of the many quirks of Woods and Williams's correspondence was that Williams kept handwritten notes from each hole, round, tournament and season that they worked together. *Together We Roared* leans on some of those never-before-seen statistics, like the stretches of consecutive holes Woods played without three-putting a green. Readers will also gain valuable insights into how Williams compiled that data, which in the 1990s and 2000s came well before the official numbers were assembled in one place. Williams's records of fairways hit, greens hit and total putts for a round occasionally differed from the tour's data. That was because Williams was realistic in navigating Woods around a golf course; sometimes his ball sat inches off the green, or fairway, but Woods had successfully hit the zone or side he was aiming at. In Williams's mind, that was target hit.

Another incredibly rare feature of *Together We Roared* is a collection of photos from Williams's shrine to his accolades with Woods in the billiards room of his home in Auckland, New Zealand. There are flags from the final green at each of the 13 majors Woods won with Williams, and almost all are signed by the superstar. Some even have historic messages of praise for Williams about his performance that week. There are also never-before-seen photos, such as the 2005 Ford GT Woods gifted Williams after a memorable PGA Tour win, as well as the staff golf bags Woods used in 1999 and 2000 that he also gave to Williams.

Together We Roared doesn't skirt around tricky subjects, such as Woods and Williams's icy split in 2011, which was followed by two instances of controversial remarks Williams made about his former employer. While this book mentions Woods's 2009 extramarital scandal, it doesn't dwell on it out of respect for Woods and his family, and it only looks at that time through the lens of the effect it had on Woods's working relationship with Williams. In the end, this book allows Williams to reflect, with hindsight, on the 12 years they spent—from 2011 to 2023—without speaking. And how they reconnected. *Together We Roared* is about so much more than just the headlines; it's about friendship. It is a love letter to a special bond and arguably the greatest player-caddie partnership in golf history.

When sports fans think of Woods and Williams, they usually have a similar set of questions:

-What was it like to have a front-row seat to Woods?
-What was it about their dynamic that yielded 13 majors and more than 80 wins worldwide?
-How suffocating was the pressure of caddying for arguably the greatest golfer ever?
-How much of an adrenaline rush was it to tell Woods exactly what club, distance and type of shot to hit in the crucial moments of the world's biggest and oldest golf tournaments?
-What was it like to be in the inner sanctum of true greatness?
-How close did they become as friends?
-Why did they split up, and have they talked since?
-After all these years, what does Williams think about their historic run?

Together We Roared endeavors to answer those questions, once and for all.

We hope that you'll find this book is one more message from Williams to Woods. And, perhaps, that it's the most important of them all.

TOGETHER WE ROARED

CHAPTER 1

DAWN THIRTY

The hotel room phone rang around 8 P.M. on Tuesday, March 2, 1999, in Miami Beach, Florida. Its tinny, high-pitched buzz was particularly annoying for veteran golf caddie Steve Williams, an early riser who didn't appreciate late-night calls at the best of times. Certainly not the day after he'd landed from a 20-hour, 8,000-mile journey from Auckland, New Zealand. Williams was slumped over the bed, half asleep but trying to stay awake until nine in an attempt to thwart jet lag. Normally, he'd stay at the house of his boss, golf star Raymond Floyd, in nearby Indian Creek Island, but it was full of guests. They were in town to watch Floyd play his home event, the PGA Tour's prestigious Doral-Ryder Open.

Reluctantly, Williams picked up the phone. After all, it *could* be important.

"Steve . . . Hey, it's Tiger Woods!" an excited, young voice said.

"Bob, f— off, mate. I'm going to bed," Williams responded. Annoyed, but chuckling at the accuracy of the imitation, Williams hung up. He thought it was a prank call by his friend in Oregon, Bob Garza. Williams had a house in the SunRiver Golf Club community in central Oregon, where Garza was one of the club's golf professionals. He did an outstanding Woods impression.

The phone rang again. "Steve, it really *is* Tiger. You got a minute?"

Crunch. Williams slammed the phone down again, more forcefully.

It rang a third time.

"Steve, it's Tiger! Please don't hang up!" the exasperated voice said. "I've split with my caddie. I'd love to talk to you about possibly working for me."

Williams's stomach sank; maybe it *wasn't* Garza. Maybe it *was* Woods. Feeling silly about hanging up, twice, on the world number one golfer, Williams apologized instantly and arranged to meet Woods as soon as the Doral tournament was finished. (Years later, Woods would remember the awkward phone calls when he met Garza face-to-face during a practice round at the 2002 New Zealand Open. Williams had arranged for Garza to play a practice round with Woods, who said to a starstruck Garza, "So, *you're* the guy who can take off my voice?")

In March 1999, Woods had split with his caddie of two and a half years, popular bagman Mike "Fluff" Cowan. Cowan was a colorful character who wore a handlebar mustache and would often hold up burning cigarettes while a golfer sized up a shot so that the smoke would indicate wind direction. As Woods's caddie, he was so recognizable that fans sought his autograph and he even appeared in TV commercials for ESPN and for the World Golf Village Renaissance St. Augustine Resort in Florida. But Woods wanted a caddie with a lower profile.

Woods had asked his longtime swing coach, Butch Harmon, about a replacement and he recommended Williams. Harmon had befriended the Kiwi during his time looping for former world number one Greg Norman, then a student of Harmon's. Woods also sought advice from his close friend, mentor and Isleworth neighbor, PGA Tour pro Mark O'Meara. O'Meara had won two majors in 1998, the Masters and the British Open, and he, too, suggested Williams. O'Meara respected Williams's work ethic, which he'd observed during his stints caddying for Norman and before that, Ian Baker-Finch, in the 1980s. Woods phoned Floyd, whose career was winding down, and asked permission to approach the Kiwi.

After Woods's call, Williams spent the ensuing week wrestling with the excitement of the opportunity and the nerves of the challenge. He also had to stay present, given he still had a job to do with Floyd at Doral. Williams would need to save his homework for the evenings at Doral, given he didn't know too much about Woods's game, other than his prodigious power off the tee and that he was tipped to become one of the greats. "Google didn't exist, and every aspect of caddying was old-school," Williams recalls. "I felt a bit of tension that week waiting for our meeting."

During one of the rounds at Doral, Williams visited a portable toilet and accidentally dropped his yardage book—a type of map for caddies with distances on it—into the blue sanitary water. When he didn't have the book for Floyd's next shot, Williams had to tell him about the accident. Floyd laughed and said, "Your mind is elsewhere, Steve."

On Monday, March 8, Williams drove three and a half hours north up I-95 to Woods's house in Orlando. At the gates to Isleworth Country Club, a gated community within Windermere, 14 miles southwest of Orlando, Williams was asked to show his driver's license to security. He weaved through streets of multimillion-dollar homes en route to Woods's house: a gorgeous, oak-lined property on a cove on Lake Bessie. Woods's neighbors included baseball legend Ken Griffey, Jr., Los Angeles Lakers center Shaquille O'Neal and Hollywood star Wesley Snipes.

Williams felt the drive into Isleworth had a sense of both grandeur and seriousness, but he had to suppress a laugh moments later when Woods, 23, answered the door in Nike gym apparel and invited Williams inside, but said he was finishing a war mission on a video game.

Williams sat quietly for five minutes on the world number one golfer's couch, thinking how strange the situation was. He was about to be interviewed for a job with an athlete many were predicting would single-handedly change the game of golf and become a cultural force unto himself. That much seemed likely when he'd won the 1997 Masters by 12 shots and broken down everything from scoring records to racial barriers in a globally celebrated moment. But here that superstar was, leaning half off the couch and tapping away furiously on a controller during a first-person shooter game. Williams, 35, had been an amateur caddie since childhood, and a globe-trotting professional bagman since 1978. But he hadn't seen anything like this. Williams was fascinated that Woods, young, famous and as talented as a golfer could be, was playing video games. One link Williams *could* make between the video games and golf was the intensity Woods was showing the TV; his small talk could not break Woods's focus. Woods eventually turned the TV off and explained to Williams that he was looking for a new, full-time caddie. "Tiger said, in no uncertain terms, that he was going to break Jack Nicklaus's record of 18 major wins and he needed a caddie who was willing to work as hard as he would to help him achieve that goal," Williams recalls.

The relationship between a pro golfer and a caddie was arguably the most unique in sports, and Woods was about to expose that dynamic better than any golfer in history. That a global superstar in an individual sport would need a sidekick was akin to tennis icons Andre Agassi and Serena Williams needing a staff member to stand behind the baseline and pull out a different racket for every single shot. And if that consigliere had to also use the wind, court surface and other variables to advise the tennis player on whether to hit a backhand slice or a topspin forehand. Woods had to get this dynamic right or risk falling short of his infinite potential. A caddie could help enhance his talent, or with the wrong call, cost him major championship wins. In addition to carrying the clubs, providing details on wind direction and distance to a target, some caddies were expert readers of the slope on putting greens. They could save their player multiple strokes—and therefore hundreds of thousands of dollars in prize money—by advising which direction a putt would break to within millimeters, and how hard to hit it. Caddies played the role of a sports psychologist, too. When their player was stressed, they used tactics to distract them in a productive way, such as telling the golfer to reenact an incredible shot they had executed in the past to steady the ship. Conversely, if their golfer was in contention to win, and adrenaline levels were surging, it was the caddie who needed to adapt. They factored in the extra energy and speed associated with trying to win a golf tournament and would suggest a club, or a shot shape, that was going to prevent the player from sending an approach shot flying way past their target.

Golfers spend upward of five hours during each round sticking mainly to themselves and not conversing much with their playing partners. Their minds could also wander during practice, with countless hours spent beating balls on a driving range. Caddies were a source of companionship. If a golfer was wildly popular or famous, caddies also acted like bodyguards among excited fans. It was hard to fathom Woods needed help, but he did.

"That first meeting with Tiger was about getting to know each other and whether this was worth pursuing," Williams says. Woods asked what Williams enjoyed doing in his spare time, which was racing saloon cars on a dirt speedway, playing sports and exercising. He'd also grown up playing a high level of rugby. Woods was intrigued by the racing, impressed with Williams's daring side, given professional golf was not very high-octane. "He could also tell I was a lone wolf, like him," Williams says. What was evident to Williams was that Woods was a nice guy with a sense of humor. The former was going to be important considering the hours, days and months they'd spend side by side, while the latter would be essential in relieving tension in high-pressure moments on the course. And there would be plenty if Woods's plan to eclipse Nicklaus's majors tally materialized. "If I said yes, I knew it would be an extremely demanding job. Tiger was similar to Norman in his burning desire to win; a good week was victory. No other result mattered. That's extremely hard to do in golf."

Williams thought Woods's insatiable hunger for winning bordered on superhuman. Yet everything else about their initial meeting, namely the endearing modesty of the house relative to the other mansions in Isleworth, suggested he was an Average Joe. Well, maybe a Significantly Above Average Joe. That dichotomy stood out to Williams. Isleworth was a very wealthy neighborhood, but Woods's mansion, while impressive, was down to earth relative to his neighbors'. There weren't any decadent, shiny pieces of art or crazy-expensive furniture or ridiculous statues.

Williams's boss from 1989 to 1999, Floyd, was at a very different stage in his life. He was 56, playing on the seniors' tour, and had won four majors (1976 Masters, 1969 and 1982 PGA Championship, 1986 U.S. Open) in a decorated career. Floyd lived in a palatial mansion on the ultra-exclusive Indian Creek Island near Miami Beach, which overlooks Biscayne Bay. Spanish singer Julio Iglesias once listed an eight-acre waterfront lot there for $150 million while former Miami Dolphins coach Don Shula and retired NFL quarterback Tom Brady have also been Indian Creek Island property owners.

Williams asked Woods what he was up to after their meeting, to which he responded, "I'll just practice, then wash my car." Williams was shocked that someone with his profile and wealth would wash his own car. Woods seemed like a regular guy, albeit with an irregular talent. Williams loved washing cars and, while he didn't know it at the time, it would quickly become a mutual hobby between the two.

Williams laughs, remembering he originally needed 24 hours to say yes to Woods's offer. In fact, before Woods had phoned his Miami Beach hotel room the previous week, Williams planned to retire in 2000 and he'd already told Floyd. He wasn't going to leave the industry entirely because his dream was to establish a national caddie academy to nurture future generations of loopers. Had he followed through with retiring on tour, Williams would have passed up one of the greatest jobs in history. Williams knows it sounds ludicrous in hindsight, but after his initial meeting with Woods he did have legitimate doubts.

"Tiger's job offer was exciting, but also daunting because he'd won one major and when he said he wanted to break Jack's record, I thought, *You have 17 more major wins just to equal it*," Williams says. He was anxious thinking about the level of work required, the microscope he'd be under and the pressure that would undoubtedly build. Williams also knew his life would never be the same. He was intensely private and reticent, an old-school Kiwi who was about to become the most famous caddie in history, whether he liked it or not. While he weighed up his options that Monday, Williams phoned several people, including Baker-Finch, who in addition to being close friends with Williams had known Woods since he spent two days playing with the 16-year-old phenom at Isleworth at the end of 1991. Hughes Norton, who would later become Woods's first agent at IMG, phoned the Australian star and asked him to show the recently crowned U.S. Junior Amateur champion around Isleworth with O'Meara. "In '91, Tiger was a skinny kid with a big smile, hit the ball a long way and had a tremendous amount of confidence, but he was also incredibly respectful and humble," Baker-Finch recalls. "For years, he'd remind me, 'Hey Finchy, you shot 64 that day at Isleworth and kicked my ass!' I continued to play a lot of golf with him in '95 and '96 while he was still an amateur. As his game developed, I thought he was going to be something extraordinary. In '99, when Steve called me, I told him he still had a lot left in the tank as a caddie. I said 35 was too young to retire. This was his chance to become one of the greatest caddies in history."

Williams also called his great friend and fellow caddie Fanny Sunesson. The Swede had looped for Nick Faldo and helped the English golf great win four majors in nine years. She told Williams what he was already thinking: it was too good an opportunity to pass up. "So, I said yes," Williams says.

Williams called Woods the following morning, Tuesday, March 9, and said, "I'd love to come and work for you." He was encouraged by Woods's enthusiastic response, which he finished by saying, "I'll see you at Bay Hill," which meant the Arnold Palmer Invitational. Williams also called Woods's agent, IMG's Mark Steinberg, and told him the good news. Later that morning, IMG issued a statement via fax machine. "TIGER WOODS HIRES STEVE WILLIAMS AS HIS CADDIE" was the headline. Woods hiring Williams was seen as the wunderkind taking control of his own career and team; in 1997 he'd demanded that Harmon help him overhaul his golf swing despite winning the Masters with it, while he'd also split with his previous agent, Norton, in 1998, and with Cowan, his caddie, in 1999.

Later that week, Williams also received a call from Woods's father, Earl. Earl, 67, wanted to offer advice on caddying for his son and Williams instantly appreciated Earl's opening remarks that the New Zealander didn't need to be told how to caddie, given he had done so with great success for Floyd, Norman and other pros. "Earl just told me there were incredibly high expectations on Tiger, and that he was under a tremendous amount of pressure from media, fans and frankly himself," Williams recalls. "He said Tiger had lofty goals but encouraged me to keep him as grounded as I could. He also urged me to prevent Tiger from getting ahead of himself and to focus on the very next tournament, not what winning that event would mean in the big picture." Earl wrapped up the conversation by inviting Williams to call him if he ever had any questions or needed help.

Earl had become famous in his own right as the eloquent and wise father who, along with Woods's mother, Kultida, had raised a child prodigy. As a collegiate athlete in the early 1950s, Earl had become the first Black athlete to make the American Legion all-state team in Kansas and had broken the color barrier in baseball in the Big Seven Conference, when he was catcher for Kansas State University. He went on to a military career after college and became a Green Beret who completed two tours of Vietnam. In 1976, a year after Woods was born and three years after Earl had taken up golf, he introduced his son to the game. Earl had noticed Woods loved watching his dad hit golf balls into a homemade net inside the garage and so Kultida would sit his high chair near Earl during those indoor practice sessions. One day, Woods climbed out of the chair, picked up an infant-sized golf club Earl had cut down to size for him and executed a perfect golf shot. Earl was stunned. He let Woods hit balls as often as the toddler wanted and, within a year, at age two, Woods had appeared on the *Mike Douglas Show*, showcasing his precocious talent. He later played exhibitions with golf legends such as Sam Snead and Nicklaus. As his son rose meteorically through junior and amateur golf ranks, Earl had a proclivity for making grand predictions about what the teenager would eventually achieve in professional golf, many of which came true. Earl even suggested Woods's eventual superstardom would revolutionize race relations in America.

Woods, throughout his career, referred to his dad as his best friend and the pair had a unique bond. When Woods was a child, Earl said he tried to always kneel down when talking to him so that his son felt like he was equal. Once Woods began to travel extensively for junior tournaments, Earl was his chaperone. Even when Woods became a pro, he would call his father when struggling with his game and ask if Earl had noticed anything on the TV coverage of his round. Often, Earl would have a technical nugget that would solve Woods's problems the next day. Perhaps their most famous moment as father and son was at the 1997 Masters, when Earl and Kultida waited beside Augusta National's 18th green as Woods finished. CBS cameras captured the emotional moment as Woods and his father hugged and cried tears of joy. Earl could be heard saying repeatedly, "We made it!" Overall, he knew Woods's game and personal tendencies better than anyone and Williams was happy to listen to him.

Just over a week after their meeting, on Wednesday, March 17, Williams had his first day on the job at a practice round for the Bay

Hill Invitational. The famous Bay Hill Club and Lodge sat within the Butler Chain of Lakes in Windermere. The club was centered around a golf course created by legend Arnold Palmer, and it became his beloved home and office.

Bay Hill also sat on the opposite side of a lake from Woods's Isleworth home, allowing him to practice in peace at Isleworth Country Club that week. Trying to limit the hysteria of "Tigermania," Woods skipped Monday and Tuesday practice rounds and didn't show up at Bay Hill until Wednesday for his 6:50 A.M. tee time in the pro-am. Pro-ams (meaning "professional-amateur") typically happen the day before a tournament begins. A number of pros each play a round of golf at the host course with several amateurs. They were usually guests of the tournament sponsor, often business clients, but the amateurs were often celebrities brought in for publicity.

The first time Williams saw his new boss's golf bag up close was in the car park at Bay Hill, at around 5:30 A.M. It was a black-and-white Titleist leather staff bag with "TIGER WOODS" emblazoned on the front. It was heavy, filled with Titleist clubs. Williams looked through the sticks he'd be handling: a 975D driver; a 970 fairway wood; 681T Grind Prototype irons (which later sold in auction for $5 million); Vokey Design wedges; and a Scotty Cameron Newport 2 GSS putter. His ball was the Titleist Professional 90. The driver was encased in a bright orange plush toy tiger for a head cover.

Williams noticed the outside of Woods's bag was well worn. He'd later learn that the bag occasionally copped heavy treatment; Woods would hold a club by the clubhead, the part that strikes the ball, and whack the grip end of the club against his bag in anger after a bad shot. He also noticed the clubs were dirty. Because Woods had been practicing at Isleworth and then come straight to Bay Hill, he'd forgotten to clean his sticks. Williams would come to learn if Woods had been practicing intensely at home in Isleworth in the lead-up to a tournament, there'd be dirt and grass all over the clubs.

On this beautiful, sunny spring morning at Bay Hill, Michael Jordan was playing in the pro-am with seven-time major winner Palmer, who was tournament host, as well as with the governor of Pennsylvania, Palmer's home state. The group teed off at 11:39. Frustratingly for Woods, the crowds were biblical. Local newspapers encouraged fans to arrive early for Woods's tee time and hang around for Jordan, meaning Woods had enormous galleries before, during and immediately after his pro-am round.

Jordan, after drinking a Budweiser in the locker room, delighted the crowd with his trash talk, cigars and swagger. He was wearing a Bay Hill bucket hat, an argyle sweater and stylish gray slacks. The Chicago Bulls legend later eagled the par-5 16th hole after hitting driver and then 7-iron for his second shot to within 10 feet of the hole.

The entire week was stratospherically different from what Williams experienced over 21 years of carrying clubs for pro golfers. Even when the Kiwi caddied for Norman, while the Australian icon was world number one, he didn't have the PGA Tour security detail that followed Woods. Suddenly, Williams was meeting various security officers assigned to Woods, and was being fitted in Nike apparel. Caddies typically wear their boss's apparel sponsor. "It was all a bit overwhelming," Williams says.

There were other responsibilities that came with caddying for a golfer as in demand as Woods. At times, professional golf could be incredibly social; at the driving range of a tournament, it's common to see players talking and laughing with another player in between hitting balls. Other players, coaches, caddies, equipment reps and officials will also greet the golfers. Williams, though, was Woods's gatekeeper. He was intimidating, standing over six feet tall and with the muscular build of a rugby player. At tournaments, Williams was compelled to take on a serious demeanor.

One of Williams's duties was to create a bubble around Woods so he could get in quality practice on the range. Woods was rigorously disciplined, and the range was his office. His looper needed to keep people away, politely, regardless of who wanted to chitchat.

"Tiger had a signal; he would take a slight peek out of his peripherals to see who it was, and he would flick his head to indicate he wanted me to ask them to leave, but in a friendly manner," Williams says. He would tell that person Woods was working on something in his swing, and ask them to come back later or when he was finished practicing. Constantly, fans, volunteers and officials would tell Woods random stories—they'd played with him in the pro-am the previous year, or they'd watched one of his victories in person—or a tournament director would want to greet the event's draw card. "If Tiger talked to everyone, he wouldn't have time to hit a single golf ball," Williams says. "He was the ultimate professional. He was there to get work done."

Woods also had a deeply ingrained pet peeve: the click of a camera's shutter going off during his swing. Williams needed to be on constant alert for photographers attempting to take swing sequence photos for newspapers and magazines. "Sometimes guys would be hiding in the distance taking photos, and I'd have to be very quick to hear and locate where that was coming from," Williams says. Woods also became frustrated if a path he was taking at a tournament became obstructed by swaths of fans. As well, he'd often exit a car and a crowd of people would be waiting in the parking lot for pictures and signatures. "The smoother you could make the journey from A to B for him, the better it was going to be for everybody," Williams says. "It was stressful, but it was also the job I signed up for, no question." Baker-Finch thought the unrelenting attention forced Woods to put a wall up around himself, which some took as rudeness. A tough character like Williams was going to be incredibly useful while Woods's star rose meteorically. "Tiger got a bad rap, but he had to deal with the world looking in every day. Steve could help shield him and bear a lot of the brunt," Baker-Finch says.

Perhaps the nerves of Woods and Williams's new chapter contributed to a poor performance at Bay Hill, their first event as a duo. Woods failed to break par all week when he shot rounds of 74-72-72-72. He tied 56th at 2 over par. Woods's prize money was $5,625. It was only the sixth time in 55 total PGA Tour events since turning pro that he'd finished outside the top 40.

Some comic relief was needed, especially in the first round at Bay Hill. At the par-4 13th, Woods laid up with a perfect iron for his tee shot to the middle of the fairway. "Tiger then hit arguably the worst golf shot I've ever seen from a professional of his caliber," Williams says. Woods had 130 yards to the green, which should have been a smooth wedge shot he could hit with his eyes closed. But Woods hooked it so far his ball landed 30 yards left of the left greenside bunker. As Woods and Williams marched to the ball, Williams said, "Geez, mate, for a huge star you are seriously overrated." Woods erupted with laughter. It was risky, but the mood needed lightening.

That ability to laugh at himself was part of a gentler side to Woods that stood out to Williams at Bay Hill. "One thing I took away from Bay Hill was the sincerity of Tiger shaking my hand after every round and looking me in the eye and saying, 'Thanks for your help today.'" Other players Williams had caddied for, on any given day, might have been too focused or frustrated to say anything. Woods had struggled that week but found time to show gratitude. Williams called Baker-Finch soon after his debut on Woods's bag and told him how it had gone. "I wasn't surprised to hear Tiger showed gratitude to Steve; I always thought he was brought up very well by his mum and dad. Earl, being a military man, and also Kultida were tough but extremely loving," Baker-Finch says.

On the Monday after the Bay Hill Invitational, Williams stayed at Woods's house and the pair took their minds off the previous week by washing Woods's cars. Woods, prior to signing a deal with Buick in December 1999, was a fan of the Cadillac Escalade, a large SUV. He had several models along with a Porsche in his Isleworth garage.

"We really bonded because I took immense pride in washing my cars; it's therapeutic to me because you see a car dirty, then you see it clean," Williams says. That day, the two started a joke that would last for years. Because Woods had played poorly at Bay Hill, where Williams called him overrated, he joked to his caddie, "If I don't get my shit together, you'll be working for me at TW's Car Wash. I need to get my ass into gear, and you do, too." That line came after every bad round or result.

O'Meara, though, saw a little more meaning in the hobby; washing one's car indicated you were a stickler for perfection, and if you wanted something done properly, you did it yourself. One day in 1999, he drove by Woods's house and saw him and Williams soaping up Woods's vehicles. "He had this incredible, mid-engine Porsche," O'Meara recalls. "Steve was a perfectionist, so was Tiger. To be successful at anything in life, you have to be a perfectionist. They were a great match."

Williams knew, over decades looping on tours, that it was critical in the early stages of caddying with a new player to develop a rapport and banter with that person. "In the player-caddie dynamic, there are never any guarantees it's going to work out and you spend a lot of time together," Williams says.

Woods and Williams showed early signs of a special bond. His next tournament was the elite Players Championship at TPC Sawgrass near Jacksonville, Florida. Over dinner on Monday, March 22, Williams and Woods discussed what time to meet at TPC Sawgrass for a practice round the following morning. One of the most important disciplines for a caddie was punctuality. Specifically, being at the course well before their boss arrived.

"Let's meet at 'dawn thirty,'" Woods said.

Williams had never heard of the term. "I'm guessing that means thirty minutes after dawn?"

"Exactly." Woods grinned.

Woods was introduced to the benefits of teeing off at first light by O'Meara, whom he called M.O., two years earlier. In 1997 at Bay Hill, Woods wanted to play a Tuesday practice round with O'Meara, who welcomed his company—for a 6 A.M. tee time. "M.O., it's not light at 6 A.M. Why the heck would we tee off that early?" Woods responded. The two reached Bay Hill's par-5 sixth, which wraps around a lake, and not a soul, apart from O'Meara, had seen Woods hit a shot. "He thought it was absolutely unbelievable; he was hooked," says O'Meara.

Woods and O'Meara had developed a strong bond since first meeting in 1991 with Baker-Finch at Isleworth. Woods adored the family lifestyle O'Meara had built and that had played a large part in bringing him to Orlando once he'd turned pro in 1996. They were two peas in a pod; O'Meara was an adopted Southern Californian who had spent his teenage years in Mission Viejo, 30 minutes from Woods's hometown of Cypress. O'Meara and his wife, Alicia, had two children and Woods spent countless hours with the family. No one played more golf with Woods than O'Meara. And while he became something of a mentor, O'Meara said drinking from the fountain of youth was beneficial to his own game. "Tiger certainly changed my career; being around someone so talented and driven made a big impression on me and it was motivating," O'Meara recalls. "I probably wouldn't have won two majors, at 41, if he hadn't come into my life."

The Players Championship is considered golf's unofficial fifth major due to the elite caliber of its field, an overwhelming majority of the world's top 100 golfers. Its host course, TPC Sawgrass, is one of the best layouts on tour. Celebrated architect Pete Dye designed the Stadium Course there to visually intimidate the world's best players, while manufacturing drama and providing a stunning tree-lined, water-laden course for fans to marvel at in Ponte Vedra Beach. The Stadium Course at TPC is renowned for the 137-yard, par-3 17th, which is surrounded by water with only a narrow walkway. It creates heart-stopping moments every year when some players crumble at having to hit to an island green under final-round pressure.

In 1999, Woods was marketed as the headline act and many hoped he'd have a showdown with world number two David Duval, a Jacksonville native. The crowds were frothing to see Woods in action, while PGA Tour officials, whose headquarters is at the golf course, were also buzzing. Woods knew it would be important to practice at dawn thirty.

O'Meara and Woods teed off at 6 A.M. again on Tuesday and Wednesday. For Woods's five thirty warm-up, not only were he and Williams the first people on the range, it wasn't even open yet.

Woods relished practice rounds at Sawgrass without thousands of fans asking for autographs and taking photos of him walking between greens and tee boxes. He could conserve energy. Williams also got a good look at the course when nobody was around;

he and Woods could see the entirety of each hole and its landscape without crowds. Williams found it soothingly peaceful; there was often mist in the air and fog coming off ponds on golf courses early in the morning.

There was a fly in the ointment, though. Often, Woods would play practice rounds before the superintendents, who already woke at the crack of dawn, had started work. "We'd have to wait on each hole as they cut the fairways or greens," Williams says.

At TPC Sawgrass, Woods and Williams registered their first top 10 together. Woods still did not have his A game, shooting 75-75 on the weekend rounds and sharing 10th place. The closing scores didn't offer hope for the majors season, given it was Woods's last competitive start before the Masters. Once Williams arrived on the grounds in Augusta National, in Georgia, weeks later, there was a bad omen via the white overalls caddies must wear. The numbers on the overalls at the Masters are based on the order the caddie's player registers on-site. "I was caddie number 75, a nice reminder of what Tiger shot on Saturday and Sunday at the previous tournament," Williams says.

Williams felt a mixture of excitement and intense nerves. Woods was among the world's most high-profile athletes, and the Masters is golf's most famous tournament; it transcends all other sports for a week, every April. The Masters' popularity stems from the gobsmacking beauty of Augusta National. It's a sprawling and hilly property in Augusta, Georgia—two and a half hours southeast of Atlanta—which was once a plant nursery. Augusta National is littered with towering Georgia pines, azaleas, usually in full spring bloom, and the tranquil Rae's Creek running through several holes. Sports fans know of Augusta National as perhaps the world's greenest golf course; its turf conditioning is incomprehensible to the average person. With a nickname like the Cathedral in the Pines, Augusta National takes on a mystical *Field of Dreams*–type aura in the eyes of its fans, who once on-site can visualize the ghosts of golfers past in their iconic Masters moments.

The Masters is also a networking place to be seen. Some of the most powerful CEOs in the world, high-profile athletes, musicians and Hollywood actors are among the hundreds of thousands who pilgrimage annually. If golf fans are lucky enough to be a badge holder, or to win tickets in the annual lottery allocation, the tickets are about $115 a day. Despite a stipulation that ticket holders are forbidden from reselling, a secondhand market still exists and tickets can go for as much as $4,000 for one day.

Both the club and the Masters sit in somewhat of a time vacuum; certain rules and traditions are upheld. Cell phones are forbidden on the course. There are no giant TVs common in stadiums, only analog leaderboards manned by volunteers who change the scores by hand.

"To caddie for any player good enough to win the tournament was a huge honor, but looping for Tiger Woods at the Masters was really special," says Williams. After a few practice rounds, Williams could see Woods was at one with the nuances of Augusta National: the changing wind direction, the break of the greens and where to leave errant shots. He also saw that Woods was capable of overpowering the design; in 1997, Woods posted the lowest-ever winning total of 270 (18 under par). "He had a love for the mysteries of the course," Williams says.

The Masters familiarity also comes from being the only major of the four to return annually to the same course. The PGA Championship, U.S. Open and Open Championship rotate host courses each year. Both TV viewers and on-site "patrons"—as Augusta National calls its attendees—build a rapport with the course from seeing their favorite players hit shots from similar positions every year. Each champion dons a green jacket, a garment all members wear at Augusta National. Palmer's reign at the Masters, combined with the introduction of professional golf to broadcast TV in the 1950s, put golf and the Masters on the map. Palmer claimed four wins between 1958 and 1964. Nicklaus was also immortalized at Augusta with a record six victories between 1963 and 1986.

Augusta National is one of the most exclusive clubs in the world, with an estimated 300 members who are unfathomably wealthy and powerful people who must be invited to join. Peyton Manning, Bill Gates, Warren Buffett and Condoleezza Rice are known members. But the green jackets pull back the curtain on this mysterious golf club and beam it to the world every Masters.

Williams first witnessed Woods's talent when the golfer was a skinny teenager competing as an amateur at the 1995 Masters. Woods's invitation was earned by winning the 1994 U.S. Amateur, the first of three consecutive titles. On Tuesday, April 4, Raymond Floyd asked Woods to play a practice round with himself, 1992 Masters winner Fred Couples and two-time British Open winner Greg Norman. Woods was rugged up in his Stanford Cardinals sweater on a cold morning when the ball wasn't going to travel as far in dense air. On the downhill par-5 second, Woods hit a drive so powerful it carried over a fairway bunker on the right that Norman, one of golf's longest hitters, never dreamed of doing. Norman slumped his shoulders in disbelief, staring at the soaring golf ball. Woods's average driving distance that week was 311.1 yards, longer than any of the professionals. He didn't need more than 7-iron into a par 4 in all four rounds.

For Williams, Woods's prodigious driving distance wasn't the most telling sign of things to come. It was his eagerness to learn from the greats. "Tiger spent a four-and-a-half-hour practice round asking Ray absolutely *everything* on the secrets of playing

Augusta. To caddie for Tiger at the Masters four years later, in 1999, was surreal."

Williams also felt plenty of pressure. Woods was still searching for a second major to validate his 1997 Masters victory. His earth-shattering first major was watched by 43 million viewers in the U.S. and tens of millions more globally. Many predicted golf's chosen one had arrived to obliterate the Masters feats of Nicklaus. But Woods, immediately after winning in 1997, overhauled his swing with coach Harmon to produce more consistency. He felt it was "across the line," or pointing right of the target. Adjusting it required perfect timing, which is often the first thing a golfer loses under pressure. He didn't register a top 10 in the other three majors after Augusta. In 1998, Woods felt more comfortable with his new move, and posted top 10s in three of the majors including a third place at the Open Championship at Royal Birkdale, won by O'Meara. He won four PGA Tour regular events during the swing changes.

The Masters is the first major each year and hopes were high Woods would tick off major number two in 1999. He was within five shots of the lead starting the final round but plummeted to a tie for 18th with a final-round 75. That number haunted Woods. There were always enormous expectations on Woods at the Masters, but Williams knew he was hitting too many erratic shots.

Newspapers were running polls after Augusta, asking readers who would win more majors in their careers: Woods or his friend and great rival Duval. He had wrestled world-number-one status from Woods on March 28 and held it through July. He'd won 11 PGA Tour titles between October 1997 and the 1999 Masters.

Woods was frustrated; he'd been working tirelessly to groove the new swing in time for Augusta. Since Williams had joined, Woods did not shoot under par in any of the four rounds at Bay Hill, nor a round in the 60s at TPC Sawgrass, and at the Masters he had only one round (day three) under par. "I was starting to feel his urgency to win a second major," Williams says.

A breakthrough came one month later, in Germany. Woods traveled on the Orlando Magic basketball team's plane, which he chartered with Williams and others across the Atlantic to Heidelberg. Woods was going to play the Deutsche Bank-SAP Open TPC of Europe, his first European Tour event on European soil as a professional (he had previously won a co-sanctioned event in Thailand).

In this first overseas trip Williams took with Woods, the two spent more time bonding as colleagues and friends. Their first five tournaments were very businesslike—the only dialogue exchanged after a round was organizing the following day's meeting time at the course. "It takes weeks, or months, to build trust and a relationship with a golfer," Williams says. In Germany, they were staying at the same hotel, traveling to and from the course, and forged more chemistry. On the flight over, they had eight hours to get to know each other better. Woods asked exactly where in New Zealand Williams lived, where he grew up and what sports he'd played. Williams revealed to Woods he had partial Maori ancestry, the indigenous Polynesian people of mainland New Zealand. Woods enjoyed learning about the Maori culture and was interested in Williams's love of rugby and car racing. "Tiger also explained to me his favorite sporting teams, like the L.A. Dodgers in baseball and the Lakers in basketball," Williams says. "I got a sense of who his closest friends were at Isleworth, like O'Meara, which I knew, but also John Cook and others." Woods and Williams also went out to dinner several times that week, and a friendship began to grow. On the course, Williams noticed Woods was remarkably punctual. He admired that trait. Williams had seen, during decades of caddying, bagmen continuously wait for pro golfers who took far longer than they'd arranged to meet up. "If Tiger said he was grabbing lunch and would be on the range in 45 minutes, he wouldn't take a minute more," Williams says.

The Deutsche Bank-SAP event was a big stop on the European Tour and had the backing of Dietmar Hopp, the German billionaire software engineer and cofounder of the company SAP. Six of the top 10 players in the world teed up in 1999, with Woods reportedly receiving a $1 million appearance fee to play. "I never received a million," Woods said a month later. "That's a hypothetical number people like to throw out. A million's not bad, though," Woods joked. But Williams felt the number didn't matter; Woods always justified an appearance fee, given the efforts he showed not only to win but entertain. "He never, ever, mailed it in while overseas on a paid appearance; he gave 150 percent for the fans," Williams says.

For the bean counters, Woods always generated plenty of economic activity. More than 60,000 German fans came out to watch Woods defeat South African great Retief Goosen by three shots on a star-studded leaderboard. "I think the tournament got what they wanted; we all played well," Woods said.

It had taken 68 days, but Woods and Williams secured their first victory together. Williams had been feeling the pressure, if not externally, then certainly by his own lofty standards, for the win. He knew the scrutiny Woods was under, and the longer he went without a win, given the caddie change, the more questions he'd face. Germany was immensely satisfying for Williams, who felt the train had finally left the station. "I could sense from the handshake with him on the 18th green after winning that something had clicked; as if the swing changes, and using them in competition, had come together."

Back in the U.S., Woods captured his first PGA Tour victory with Williams at the Memorial Tournament, a prestigious event hosted by Nicklaus at his Muirfield Village Golf Club in Dublin, Ohio. "I felt confident after Memorial that, going forward, this would be a lasting relationship," Williams says. That confidence, however, had taken almost three months to develop—even for the most talented golfer in the world and arguably the best caddie.

The first time Woods contended in a major with Williams was the 1999 U.S. Open. Williams knew Woods's urgent need to win a second major. It had been almost 800 days since he romped to an earth-shattering, 12-shot win at the 1997 Masters. Swing changes hindered his performance in majors for the following two years, but in 1999 Woods was feeling good about his reconstructed move. Although his performance was poor at the Masters, he felt ready to win a major again when the U.S. Open arrived in June at Pinehurst No. 2 in North Carolina. With two holes to play in the final round, Woods was one shot back of the lead. But a bogey on the par-3 17th dashed his hopes. Woods tied third while his Isleworth friend Payne Stewart won his third major by defeating Phil Mickelson by one shot. At the Open Championship at Carnoustie, all Woods needed was a final-round 70 to join a playoff. He shot 74 and tied for seventh. There was only one major remaining for the year, the PGA Championship, and Woods couldn't leave the '90s stuck on one major.

"Tiger always had massive expectations, but I don't know if he ever felt more pressure at a major than leading up to the 1999 PGA," Williams says. Woods internalized a lot of that pressure, but Williams could tell when he spoke about visiting Medinah for a scouting mission, or practicing certain shots he'd need there, like a 2-iron stinger off the tee, or their game plan for the many dogleg holes, that there was a desperation to win that second major.

During his two decades in the job, Williams had observed that the second major win was the hardest for a pro golfer to obtain, and significantly more burdensome than the first. Winning a major required the best golf in the world on that particular week, and there were only four opportunities a year. Being eligible for them was an achievement in itself. Once there, a golfer needed to play his way into contention and then be gifted certain strokes of luck—to be on the side of the tee times that weren't affected by bad weather or delays, or for a few bounces and putts to go in their favor. Lining up the variables a golfer can—and can't—control was why many major winners had only won one. Indeed, at the end of 2024, there were 233 golfers who had won at least one men's major championship. Of those, only 89 had won two or more majors.

After the U.S. Open at Pinehurst, Woods suggested he felt it was a matter of *when*, not *if*. "He repeatedly kept saying after Pinehurst, 'The more times I get in contention, I'm going to win another one of these and then I'll be off,'" Williams says. "He knew it, I knew it, Steinberg knew it and Butch knew it. Tiger just needed to get that second major and the floodgates would open."

CHAPTER 2

THE FIRST

Just after 4 P.M. on August 2, 1999, a hot summer's day, Williams arrived at Sherwood Country Club, an ultra-exclusive club set in the hills of Thousand Oaks, having made the 40-mile drive west along the 101 from Los Angeles. After telling security he was Tiger Woods's caddie, and that he was here for the *Showdown at Sherwood* exhibition match, the boom gate opened dutifully. Williams drove through the visitor section of its grand entrance—a pair of giant redbrick walls that bookended a black steel archway—and through the streets of unfathomably large mansions. He pulled up near the front of the clubhouse and was startled by the sheer opulence of the building: a white Georgian clubhouse standing sentinel behind a series of perfectly manicured hedges, one of which was trimmed to spell "SCC." Williams always felt out of place at these lavish country clubs; he was a member of a modest golf course in Auckland called South Head Golf Club, and he liked it that way.

Woods was facing off against David Duval in a made-for-television first called the *Showdown at Sherwood*. IMG wanted to create a golf equivalent of *Monday Night Football* and represented both world number one Woods and his rival and friend Duval, so there was very little resistance. They were facing off in an East Coast prime-time TV slot, finishing at 11 P.M., on ABC, who hoped their $1.5 million purchase would attract a younger audience to golf on TV via an intimate battle between two big names in their twenties. The prize money for the 18-hole match was $1.5 million, with $1.1 million to the winner. Pulling back the curtain on Sherwood was also part of the appeal given the A-listers within its membership. Saxophonist and Grammy Award winner Kenny G, a talented golfer, had been the club champion at Sherwood Country Club, while Jack Nicholson, Sylvester Stallone, Sean Connery, Justin Timberlake and even NHL great Wayne Gretzky were members. Sherwood's setting beneath the Santa Monica mountains was beautiful, with a lush, green course winding its way over and around rolling hills, with stone bridges arching over tranquil creeks. Sherwood has been used to film scenes from TV shows such as *The Mentalist*, and Hollywood movies like the rom-com *Bridesmaids*.

Williams climbed out of his rental car, startled by the heat, with an index already over 94F degrees. It had been a scorching summer, especially in California. Williams had assumed that, because it was an exhibition match, and not an official PGA Tour event, he was allowed to wear shorts. The PGA Tour was in the final week of a trial in which caddies were allowed to wear shorts when the heat index reached 100F degrees. But a showdown *before* the showdown kicked off when a PGA Tour official told Duval and Woods that tournament rules applied. Williams, and Duval's caddie, Mitch Knox, had to change into long pants. Williams, sweating, knew that while the heat index was reading in the mid-90s, it was still climbing.

Woods was furious when Williams was confronted, and barked, “This isn’t an official tournament.” He thought it was cruel to force caddies to wear long pants while carrying heavy golf bags. But rules officials attempted to make it clear that if Williams failed to comply with the PGA Tour rule, he would be banned. “I guess I’ll be playing the European Tour next year,” Woods said bluntly, instructing Williams to remain in shorts. Williams says it was one of Woods’s most inspiring gestures during his 12 years working for the golfer. “I was really moved, because it was the first time he had backed me up in front of a large group of people and officials; he really had my back. Tiger stood behind you if you were on his team.” As for Duval’s looper, he made a statement of his own. Knox went into the pro shop, bought a pair of pants and then rolled them up four times. “Strictly speaking, he was still wearing pants,” says Williams.

Woods won the actual *Showdown*, claiming a 2-and-1 victory over Duval. Within a year, the pants rule was abandoned and caddies were allowed to wear shorts on the PGA Tour. “That incident got the ball rolling on the entire push for shorts,” Williams says. By 2019, that partially extended to players. Tour pros on the European Tour were permitted to wear shorts in practice rounds and pro-ams, and the PGA Tour followed. Common sense prevailed; pro golfers and caddies worked in some of the hottest climates around the world, and usually traveled year-round with the sun, by nature of competing in tournaments. “A lot of the tournaments are based right around the equator,” Woods said in 2019. “Even with my little chicken legs, I still would like to wear shorts.”

The *Showdown at Sherwood* reinforced what Williams had been learning over the spring and summer, privately, about Woods’s generosity and loyalty. The topic of how and, more important, how much caddies should be paid on professional golf tours was hot. Bagmen were fearing for their livelihoods when more than 12 top golfers changed caddies between January and May. O'Meara's two majors in 1998 had combined for over $1 million in prize money. But in 1999, he parted with caddie Jerry Higginbotham. O'Meara's new caddie was 45-year-old Robert Larson, a former tour pro on mini tours who worked for O'Meara's coach, Hank Haney.

There was also speculation that some players were moving their caddies away from being paid a percentage of prize money and into a flat fee per tournament. Williams had heard gossip about Woods being frugal when it came to tipping for various services, like locker room attendants, restaurant waiters and baggage handlers at private airports. Such comments have also been made by Haney, who would eventually coach Woods, and even fellow major winner Darren Clarke. Haney wrote in his 2012 book, *The Big Miss*, that Woods "seemed to think it was funny to be cheap." Clarke joked that Woods "didn't quite pay for too many dinners whenever we were out."

Williams, though, disagreed. "He was extremely generous to me and my family," Williams recalls. He certainly never feared any link between those rumors and if Woods would move his caddie onto the new pay structure. After all, Woods won more than $1.4 million in prize money in his first 11 events in 1999. How much of that did a caddie need? "Tiger wanted no part in that idea," says Williams. "He had this phrase, 'If I'm doing well, you should do well.'"

The motto was comforting to Williams while tensions simmered on tour between other players and caddies over working conditions. The sentiment was that golfers were the ones under pressure hitting the shots, not the caddies. A typical agreement between caddies and tour pros starts with a weekly retainer. It varies by player, but in 1999 the retainer on the PGA Tour was approximately between $500 and $1,200. (In 2024, the guarantee ranged between $1,500 and $2,000.) Caddie retainers account for travel, hotel and on-road costs at tournaments, while acting as a regular wage in weeks that a golfer doesn't play, leaving the caddie at home and not earning a percentage of prize money. In addition, a caddie typically receives a percentage of a player's prize money—about 5 percent for a top 10; 7 percent for a top five; and 10 percent for a win. Golfers also have to pay an agent a percentage and, in some cases, their coaches, too.

John Cook, an 11-time PGA Tour winner and friend of Woods, said in 1999: "I respect what caddies do, and I pay mine well. [But] people love watching the greatest players in the world, not the caddie; we're the ones hitting the shots."

Some suggested to Woods that, given his career was taking off like a rocket from Cape Canaveral, he should look at how much he was paying Williams. After all, Woods would finish 1999 with $6,616,585 in prize money. If Williams was paid 10 percent, his earnings would be $661,658. That was high enough to be 65th on the PGA Tour money list that year—for players. Williams likely outearned players like Brad Faxon ($582,691) and his former boss Greg Norman ($570,879) in 1999. Reevaluating how caddies were paid was partly due to boosts in total tournament prize money for the year, which was $131 million across all tournaments, up by $40 million from 1998. "Some players were starting to think that at 10 percent of the winnings, caddies were maybe getting too much money," Williams says. Ironically, a large reason for the increase *was* Woods. TV networks were desperate to broadcast him. Woods, though, never even raised the topic of a flat fee with his caddie. "In fact, on a couple of occasions during my time caddying for Tiger, he increased my weekly retainer because it was getting more expensive to travel to tournaments," Williams says.

Williams was steadfast in his belief that a caddie who worked for a below-average player, who was not always contending on the leaderboard, should not lose money if his boss missed the cut. While golf sold itself as a sport of meritocracy, where pros didn't get paid if they missed the cut, the reality was, at least at the PGA Tour level, tour pros had sponsors that tipped in plenty of money. If the total value of those sponsorships was broken down and averaged over 52 weeks, most tour pros were not losing money, even factoring in their expenses during missed cuts. Getting a PGA Tour card was not unlike an English soccer team getting promoted from the second-tier Championship League to the Premier League—simply making it to the highest level was attractive to brands wanting real estate on shirts, hats and bags, given a golfer's newfound exposure to sports broadcasting. "If you were a caddie for a below-average player, and they missed the cut, your expenses were far higher than your weekly retainer," Williams says. "I always felt caddies should be compensated in those weeks."

* * *

Woods's support of Williams had the caddie eager to repay the gesture. In his mind, putting in 100 percent effort to help Woods win the 1999 PGA Championship would be the perfect reciprocation. The 1999 PGA was being held only 10 days after Sherwood, on the No. 3 course at Medinah Country Club. The private club, located 27 miles northwest of downtown Chicago, near O'Hare Airport, had hosted several major championships over the years. Woods felt he had a handle on the golf course after being given a private tour on June 29 by Michael Jordan, a Medinah member who joined during his time in the city with the Chicago Bulls, where he won six NBA championships. Woods was in town in June for the Motorola Western Open, and Jordan, a keen celebrity golfer whose golf handicap was in the low single figures, was preparing for September's Chicago Open. Woods and Jordan played 36 holes at Medinah that day with Chicago amateur golfer Joel Hirsch.

Woods brought Williams out to map the golf course for his notes ahead of the PGA Championship. Woods, therefore, could play it in peace and for fun with the retired basketball icon. "Those two together on a golf course was hilarious; Michael was a very keen golfer and he had an extraordinary amount of ability," Williams says. The banter was high as the two stars trash-talked each other all day, whipping around both loops in a golf cart. Jordan hated losing and Woods hated losing to his friends. Williams, who would get to know Jordan through Woods, received some reassuring advice from him that day. "He said to me, 'Stevie, this guy's got an amazing talent and you've just got to keep him grounded. You're doing a great job so far. The sky's the limit for this guy, so keep him normal and stick with him.' It was really meaningful coming from one of the greatest athletes who has ever lived."

The scouting mission was beneficial for Woods's future attack on the PGA Championship, where he was aiming for career major number two. Jordan offered several insights for Williams and Woods. One nugget that stood out to Williams was that putts on the No. 3 course never broke as much as they appeared. The other valuable piece of advice was that, in the afternoons, the winds were stronger than players and caddies could see from simply looking at how much the trees swayed. Williams ducked into the pro shop and asked the club professional and assistant pros about the secrets of the No. 3 course. Both Jordan and the assistant pros said the same thing: the greens had less break than they showed.

Williams also recorded distances on certain holes from particular spots away from the fairway where he knew Woods might be prone to missing it. He discovered early on with Woods that he could be an erratic driver of the golf ball. He was long, but not always straight. But he knew his strengths and weaknesses, and if there was trouble on one side of a golf hole, Woods would always favor the opposite side and was willing to miss the fairway if it meant avoiding a hazard, or out of bounds. Although highlight reels made Woods look like a swashbuckling player who always went for the hero shot, he was actually a meticulous and ruthless plodder who managed risks. "I knew it was to my advantage to get a distance from random spots in the rough and trees because come the tournament, there'd be too many spectators to move," Williams says.

Woods, with an average drive of 293.1 yards in 1999, was the third longest on tour behind John Daly but was easily the most in-form. He was the favorite at Medinah, which was going to play 7,401 yards. It was the longest major championship host course in history, apart from the high-altitude Columbine Country Club at the 1967 PGA.

The PGA Championship began on a rainy Thursday morning on August 12, 1999. Woods was grouped with eight-time major winner Tom Watson, and Brian Watts, an American player on the Japan Tour. Woods scratched out a 2-under-par 70 while 19-year-old Spanish pro Sergio Garcia took the first-round lead with a 66. In doing so, the former amateur star vanquished some demons from a month earlier when he'd shot 89-83 at the Open Championship at Carnoustie. At Medinah, Garcia bristled at a reporter's question about his performance there: "I think I've proved myself today. I think the British Open is done, so I don't want to hear any more questions about the Open."

On Friday, Woods rolled into Medinah just after 11 A.M. for a 1:16 tee time, laughing and cracking jokes as fans chased and screamed after him for autographs. He signed several as he marched onto the range with a swagger noticeable to reporters. Williams observed that Woods's body language before a round could be very telling. When Woods laughed and engaged with fans, Williams knew he felt confident in himself and wasn't coming to the course wondering if he had his A game. "If he was uptight, and had limited interaction with the fans, he usually had some concerns about how he was going to play," Williams says.

On the 388-yard, par-4 first hole, Woods hit a pitching wedge to within a foot and tapped in for birdie. On No. 2, a 188-yard par 3, Woods hit a 7-iron to three feet. Another birdie. At the 415-yard, par-4 third hole, he hit a 2-iron from the tee and a 7-iron to 15 feet. Yet another birdie. Woods picked up two other two strokes en route to a 65. He was only two back of 36-hole leader, Jay Haas. "I got myself right back in it . . . that's right where you want to be," Woods said.

The size of the galleries Lee Westwood experienced in Saturday's third round, when he was paired with Woods, were epic. Woods had become immune to the crowds, despite being only three years into his pro career. He had dealt with hysteria since childhood, which ramped up as he went to college at Stanford University. In late February 1992, Woods made his PGA Tour debut at the L.A. Open at Riviera Country Club. Thousands of fans lined each hole Woods played, trying to get a glimpse of the skinny amateur who became the youngest-ever player to debut on tour at 16 years, one month and 27 days. Woods had won four straight Junior World Championships and the 1991 U.S. Junior Amateur. At Riviera, it would prove career-defining that he loved having the crowds' attention and pressure, despite missing the cut. "You hit good shots, you get rewarded by the crowd applauding," Woods said that week.

Truth was, there wasn't much a gallery could do to rattle Woods. Not after years of military-style training his father, Earl, put him through as a teenager. Woods wanted to learn to completely block out noise and allowed Earl to administer techniques inspired by his days in the Special Forces. Over several years, whenever the two played golf, Earl would shout insults and expletives, or rattle car keys during Woods's swing. Anything to try and put his son off. The result was a golfer with a mental fortress.

Westwood wasn't exposed to such training, nor was any tour pro. The Chicago crowds at Medinah hung off Woods's every move and went wild when he nearly holed a bunker shot for eagle at the par-5 14th. On the 15th, Westwood was distracted by fans running after Woods, who had crafted a delicate recovery shot from the trees, and subsequently caught a sand wedge thin and it sailed over the green. Westwood eventually shot 74. Afterward, he blasted security officials for doing a "pathetic" job.

"Tiger's focus was unlike anything I'd seen, and he could compartmentalize so well," Williams says. "But some guys found it tough to play with him due to the size and noisiness of the crowds, and the fact Tiger attracted new fans who didn't necessarily understand golf etiquette and when to be quiet."

Woods, meanwhile, took control of the 81st PGA Championship with a 68 that launched him into a share of the 54-hole lead with left-handed Canadian Mike Weir at 11 under. The last time he'd failed to convert a 54-hole lead was the 1996 Quad Cities Classic (now the John Deere Classic), before he'd even won his first PGA Tour title. Woods had held at least a share of the 54-hole lead on seven occasions and won each time. A month earlier, at the Western Open at Cog Hill, only 26 miles from Medinah, Woods led going into Sunday. Coincidentally, he beat Weir that day.

The final group of Woods and Weir teed off at 1:20 on Sunday, August 15. Woods picked up two birdies in his first six holes while Weir struggled. At the par-5 seventh, Woods hit a shot that dumbfounded Williams. From the fairway, he had 237 yards to the green, but his line was blocked by thick trees on the right side of the hole. Woods wanted to go for the green in two, but there was plenty of danger and his ball was on a downhill slope, which makes it harder to execute *any* shot. If Woods didn't slice the ball left to right enough, it would fly straight, and he risked losing the ball. "He hit one of the biggest slices I'd seen a golfer hit in a major," Williams says. It skirted around the trees and rolled onto the green, about 20 feet from the hole. He two-putted for birdie. Executing the risky shot under pressure made Woods walk a little freer and his facial expressions became a little less anxious, Williams noticed. The birdie was followed by another at No. 11, which put Woods at 15 under and helped build the cushion he would desperately need on the back nine. Woods had a five-shot lead over Garcia with seven holes to play. "If there was one shot that entire week that calmed him down, it was that fairway metal on No. 7," Williams says.

It appeared Woods's back nine was going to be a formality, but the golf gods had other ideas. Everything fell apart for Woods in one of the most dramatic two-hour windows in modern major championship history. On the par-4 12th, Woods three-putted from 60 feet for bogey. "There probably wasn't anything on this earth Tiger disliked more than three-putts; they were wasted strokes," Williams says. As Woods walked to the tee at No. 13, Garcia rammed in a birdie putt with authority, then looked up at the tee toward Woods and, with a smirk, sent an aggressive fist pump. It was a brash move for a youngster. "I wanted him to know that I was still there and to show him that he had to finish well to win," Garcia said later. Williams thought it was an unusual move and was immediately asked by Woods, "Can you believe that?" Williams smirked, knowing it had added fuel to the fire. Woods was not going to lose.

At least that's what Williams believed, but his theory was tested moments later when Woods hit a 6-iron tee shot so aggressively it flew over the green and into deep rough. His ensuing chip shot rolled into rough on the other side of the green and he eventually took a double-bogey 5. In a matter of 15 minutes, his four-shot lead had crumbled to one.

Garcia made bogey at No. 15 and was in further trouble at No. 16 when his 3-wood tee shot flared to the right and settled behind the trunk of a large tree. But he went for a hero shot, lashing at the ball with a 6-iron while closing his eyes in case the ball ricocheted back. The ball exploded with wicked slice spin, turning hard right toward the green. Garcia sprinted up a hill to see the ball, pounding his heart with his hand once it settled 60 feet from the hole. He two-putted for par. Minutes later, Woods made bogey on that hole and his cushion was again reduced to one shot.

Smelling blood in the water, or at least hoping for a tight finish, the Chicago crowds turned on Woods. "I knew the crowd was changing when I heard, 'Hope you don't slice it in the water,' on [the par 3] No. 17," Woods said. "I didn't think that was fair." They wanted to see Garcia, the underdog, stick it to the world number one. They felt Garcia was Woods's most talented rival. He was also a showman in full flight.

Woods certainly struggled to execute on No. 17, hitting his tee shot into juicy rough and leaving his pitch shot well short of the hole. Over a six-foot par putt, Woods faced a defining moment in his career: Save par and take a one-shot lead into the last hole. Or miss it and endure the incredible stress of being forced to birdie the 18th in regulation to win his long-awaited second major title. Failing to make birdie in that scenario would mean a sudden-death playoff with Garcia, who had all the momentum and almost all of the crowd's support. Woods stood over the putt and felt it was going to break about a cup (4.25 inches), from left to right. Williams, though, during a practice round, had poked several wooden tees into the 17th green for Woods to rehearse putting, including the likely Sunday hole location. As Woods practiced putting to the prospective Sunday hole, Williams noticed it didn't break as severely as Woods thought. Williams had been watching for such detail after Jordan pointed it out. In the final round, Woods called in Williams and said he was aiming about a cup outside the hole but wasn't certain.

"No way, aim inside of the left lip," Williams said.

"Are you sure?" Woods asked.

"F——ng absolutely, it only breaks a bit. Aim inside the hole," Williams responded.

The ball rolled gently right and entered in the middle. Par was saved. It was a pivotal moment for Woods, and for his partnership with Williams. If the putt broke more severely, Woods's original read would have been correct, and Williams would have been wrong in overriding him. Had Williams not spoken up, Woods would have missed the putt on what golfers call the "high side"—or allowing too much break. Williams risked everything, placing the importance of the putt and its role in helping Woods win above his own future with Woods.

"It would have been very easy for me in that situation to say, 'Yep, I think you're correct.' He would not have blamed me because he read it the same way. But you have to tell the truth in what you see as a caddie." Had Williams been wrong, Woods would have had significantly less trust in Williams's judgment the next time he faced a crucial decision in a major and, ultimately, that would have eroded their belief in each other.

Moments later, Woods, buoyed by saving par in a pressure moment, hit his 3-wood from the 18th tee and found the fairway. Up ahead, chants of "SER-GI-O! SER-GI-O!" bellowed from the grandstands. They were enamored with Garcia. "I said when I turned pro, I wanted to be the number one golfer in the world," he said that day. "I knew I would be a rival for Tiger."

Woods hit a brilliant approach shot to close range, before his birdie putt came up inches short. He was renowned for animated fist pumps after tournament-winning putts, but this one was different. He marked his ball, collected himself and tapped in for par. A final-round 72 secured victory at 11 under par. Woods slumped his shoulders and closed his eyes in a sigh of relief. He hugged Williams, then shook hands with Weir, who shot 80—the worst final-round score by a playing partner in any of Woods's 15 major championship wins.

After signing his scorecard, Woods walked out with a big grin. He hugged Williams and said, "Stevie, don't ever change. Never doubt your gut. You made the right call and we're going to need your instincts." That pep talk resonated with Williams.

Woods was particularly relieved because it was a dreaded three-putt bogey on No. 12 that triggered his unraveling on the back nine. Woods's disdain for three-putts was so strong that Williams included it as a metric in a variety of statistics and notes he kept from every single round Woods played. He wrote them down in an exercise book every night. To encourage Woods, Williams would tell him when he was on a long stretch of holes, across multiple rounds and tournaments, without three-putting. "If it was over 100 holes without a three-putt, I would tell Tiger," Williams says. In 1999, according to Williams's notes, Woods avoided three-putting from the fifth hole in round three at the Byron Nelson Classic in mid-May to the sixth hole in the second round of the U.S. Open in mid-June. That included the remaining holes of the Byron Nelson, the entire TPC of Europe event in Germany, the Memorial Tournament, and the beginning of the U.S. Open. It was 198 holes without three-putting. The second run Woods enjoyed went for 182 holes. It started at the 14th hole in the final round at the National Car Rental (Golf) Classic Disney in Orlando, in late October, to the 16th hole on the second round of the Johnnie Walker Classic in Taiwan in mid-November. That run included the last four holes of the Disney event, 72 holes at both the Tour Championship and the World Golf Championships-American Express Championship at Valderrama in Spain, and 34 holes at the Johnnie Walker Classic. "A lot of great players had likely never gone 100 holes in their entire career without a three-putt and Tiger had two such stretches in 1999 alone," Williams says.

Woods and Williams would have bets during these streaks, too. If Woods ticked over 100 holes without a three-putt, Williams would offer up $1,000 if he could get to 150 holes. "If he went 150 holes without three-putting, he was likely to win a tournament in there anyway," Williams says.

At Medinah, Woods had averaged more than 308 yards off the tee for the week, which was the most ever by a PGA Championship winner. Among the 73 players who made the cut that week, Woods was at least 10 yards longer than every other player. Williams, though, says the putt on No. 17 was the championship shot. To this day, he maintains that par save, and the ensuing victory over Garcia, was a sliding-doors moment in the trajectory of Woods's career.

Woods was showing cracks on the back nine and was in danger of letting victory slip through his fingers. "Had he lost, who's to say he would've gone on to claim 15 major wins?" Williams asks. "Blowing a five-shot lead, you don't want to picture the consequences. I'm not suggesting Tiger wouldn't have recovered; he was far too talented and hardworking and mentally strong. But you wouldn't want to find out, would you?"

For some players, choking would have been catastrophic to their confidence. Williams felt if Woods had stumbled and Garcia won, the Spaniard may have gone on to win a handful of majors when in the hunt with Woods. Instead, Garcia's only major came at the 2017 Masters.

Had Woods not won the last major of 1999, he would have faced questions about it for eight months until the 2000 Masters. He would have arrived at Augusta knowing it was exactly three years since he'd won his first major. "The '99 PGA allowed Tiger to break loose and he suddenly seemed far less burdened," Williams says. For his caddie, Medinah had released the pressure valve from the anxiety of helping a superstar end a drought. He didn't want to be the caddie who failed to help get his boss over the line in any of three good chances he had in 1999. "I didn't want to be nicknamed Owen, as in 0-and-3."

Weeks after Woods's Medinah win, he sent his caddie a framed photograph of himself holding the Wanamaker Trophy, a piece of silverware awarded each year to the PGA champion. Woods scribbled a message:

Hey Stevie, Nice read.

But Woods also sent Williams a second picture that wasn't framed. It was an action shot from the final round, where Woods was crouched down on the 17th green, with two hands on his putter, reading the break. He was wearing a scarlet Nike shirt with white stripes, a black Nike cap—and an intense stare. Williams stood behind, also looking at the hole, with the yellow flag in his right hand and his left pointing at the hole. It was the moment Woods trusted Williams's read on that pivotal par save.

Woods, though, had made a creative alteration to the image. "Tiger had glued a sheep in front of me, where Tiger was crouching, making it look like I was mounting it, as if to say, 'Great read on that putt, you sheep shagger!'" Williams laughs. It referred to a joke used by acid-tongued Australians to playfully insult New Zealanders on a rugby pitch. "I don't know where he found out about that joke," Williams says. "But I knew it was going to be a funny partnership going forward."

CHAPTER 3

THE GREATEST GOLF EVER PLAYED

The Plantation course at Kapalua, on the far western shores of the Hawaiian island of Maui, is among the most stunning properties in the world of golf. Here, dramatic hills run down toward the ocean, blanketed by green fairways and punctuated by the occasional bunker. The contrast of manicured turf meandering through unkempt and cavernous tropical ravines is striking. In the distance, clouds hover over the neighboring Molokai mountains, forming ancient and soothing views.

Kapalua's hills are also the most severe of any course on any professional golf tour. The Plantation layout measures 7,596 yards, but the actual walking distance is over 9,600. It's so hilly that tour pros and caddies walking the tournament need to be driven between a few of the holes by volunteers in courtesy cars. At the downhill, par-5 18th, the elevation drops 150 feet from the tee box atop the hill to the lowest point of the fairway below.

Course architect Bill Coore and two-time major winner Ben Crenshaw designed Plantation for resort guests, in golf carts, on vacation. Not for an impromptu Maui marathon Williams ran during a practice round with Woods during the early 2000s. Woods was preparing to play the Mercedes Championships at Kapalua and, because it was a practice round, he and Williams were allowed to ride in a golf cart. On the front nine, Woods joked about wishing players could continue using motorized carts during the tournament. “Kapalua would be a hell of a course to run,” he said. Somehow—and these conversations always took a funny tangent—Woods wondered how long it would take for Williams, a fitness fanatic, to run the much hillier back nine once they reached it. Williams guessed he could do it in 30 minutes. Woods nearly fell out of his cart, laughing at the suggestion. Williams was adamant, and so the pair made a bet.

“He stitched me up with the terms, because I had to start at the clubhouse, which is half a mile from the 10th tee, and touch every tee and every green along the way,” Williams says.

Woods threw down $500 dollars. His coach, Butch Harmon, also laughed at the ridiculousness. He threw in $1,000. Woods’s agent, Mark Steinberg, wanted in, saying he was good for $500. Running down the 18th, with $2,000 on the line, Williams was red-faced, breathless and sweating profusely, but he was making good progress. Naturally, Woods, Harmon and Steinberg, who were riding in carts, heckled the caddie the entire way down the final hole.

“But I did it . . . in 28 minutes,” Williams says.

Fitness had become increasingly important to Woods. During his teens and early twenties, he had been a lover of regular fast food—something Williams observed in his first year with the golfer. “I’d never seen anybody eat at McDonald’s that often, especially an athlete,” Williams says. Toward the end of 1999, though, Woods drastically changed his approach to nutrition. There was more maturity and discipline. Woods stacked muscle onto his naturally slender frame, moving serious weights in the gym. Williams, meanwhile, had grown up playing rugby. He'd represented New Zealand in an under-15 schoolboys' rugby match against Australia in 1977. He was big, muscular and had marathon endurance. But Williams was 12 years older, and Woods wanted to put his caddie to the test, to see if he'd be a suitable workout buddy going forward.

Woods found Williams's 28-minute accomplishment at Kapalua hilarious, but not surprising, given an experience in late 1999. The pair were at The Mines Resort in Malaysia, a tropical oasis from the congestion and smog of busy downtown Kuala Lumpur. Woods was representing the United States with O'Meara in the World Cup of Golf, an event with two-man teams. For Woods's final pretournament workout inside the resort, he invited Williams to a gym session—their first workout together as colleagues—on Wednesday, November 17.

Woods paced Williams through his regular routine, a grueling upper body workout: bench press, lateral rows and other exercises. The following morning, Williams awoke in his hotel room to get ready for the first round. "I couldn't lift up the toothbrush to my mouth; I was in agony," Williams says.

Exacerbating his pain was Kuala Lumpur's hot and humid weather that week. During the first round, Woods chuckled each time Williams slung the golf bag over his shoulder or raked sand in a bunker. He could hardly move, but toughed it out. Woods even had Williams tend the flag—holding it inside the hole, so a golfer can see it from long putts—just so Williams had to hold his arms out. "I thought it was hilarious, but there was no way I was letting him know I was in pain," Williams says. Woods and O'Meara went on to win that World Cup of Golf by five shots.

Now, in January 2000, Woods kicked off one of the greatest seasons in golf's history on that exceptionally hilly terrain at Kapalua. He had played his own charity event in Scottsdale, Arizona, the week prior, over New Year's, before kicking off his official season at the Mercedes event in Hawaii. At the end of the Maui tournament, Woods faced a pulsating duel with Ernie Els. Woods had to pull out his most sorcerous golf—matching Els's eagle to end regulation before birdies on two extra holes—to defeat the smooth-swinging South African in a playoff. Having won nine times worldwide in 1999, including consecutive victories in his last four official starts, Woods kept alive what was the longest winning streak in golf in 46 years. His fifth straight win was the most since Ben Hogan's four consecutive in 1953. "He's 24 [but] probably going to be bigger than Elvis when he gets into his 40s; he's a legend in the making," Els predicted.

* * *

Woods was playing sensational golf in 1999, but he was about to enter a league of his own in 2000 after making changes and improvements during a short offseason. Some were minor; others were significant tweaks aimed at a more well-rounded game.

A minor change was made to Woods's golf bag following his inking of a reported $25 million, five-year sponsorship deal with car manufacturer Buick. The bag is one of the most valuable pieces of advertising a professional golfer can offer as it is always visible on TV broadcasts, and Woods was one of the world's most marketable athletes. Buick had been the first-ever corporate sponsor of the PGA Tour, joining in 1958. With Woods, Buick was hoping to reach a younger audience for its vehicles. In exchange for its investment, Buick could also negotiate with Woods to play in PGA Tour events it sponsored, such as the Buick Invitational at Woods's beloved Torrey Pines course in La Jolla, California. To celebrate the partnership, Woods and a Buick executive stood on a dais in a ballroom at the Torrey Pines Hilton on a cold Wednesday afternoon, December 15, and unveiled his new golf bag. It had been hiding under a silver cloth like a newly commissioned statue.

"I hope you can fit all your clubs in there," the executive said.

"Don't worry," Woods replied. "Stevie will be carrying it."

Carrying it reluctantly, though. Williams disliked Buick with a burning passion, given its parent company was General Motors. Williams was a lifelong fan of Ford, a great rival of GM's, and that was reflected heavily in his car racing. He raced Fords and even had Ford model cars around his house as decorations. "I said, 'Come on, Tiger, seriously? Buick?'" Williams's tolerance eventually paid off in 2005, when Woods stunned him with a surprise gift.

All black with a red and white panel, the bag was slightly smaller than the Titleist bag he'd used previously. "Buick had [U.S. bag maker] Belding create it; it was beautiful," Williams says. Woods gifted Williams the decommissioned Titleist bag, knowing his caddie collected them, and eventually the Buick bag, too, once Woods needed a new one.

The contents of Woods's bag were standard for a pro golfer: clubs, balls, tees, gloves, rain gear, ball markers, sunscreen and water. Plus, one quirky item Williams was known for. He made peanut butter and banana sandwiches for every player he'd ever worked for. In tournament rounds, golfers would get their peculiar sandwiches at one-third of the way through a round, on the seventh tee, and two-thirds of the way, on the 13th tee. Woods had never eaten a peanut butter and banana sandwich in his life, nor had Ray Floyd or Greg Norman. Williams's reasoning was the energy in the peanut butter and the nutrients in the banana helped stamina and concentration. He'd grown up watching his father eat them during golf rounds. "Tiger, at first, thought the combination sounded unusual but, as soon as he took a few bites, he said, 'Not bad!' He became very fond of the sandwiches and he knew exactly when he'd get them," Williams says.

Woods also made technical changes in his 1999 offseason, one suggested by Williams that laid the platform for Woods's historical 2000 season. Williams kept handwritten statistics from every single round, monitoring trends with certain shots, clubs or distances. Some years, there'd be a glaring weakness with Woods's 8-iron, and other years it might be putts from a certain length. In 17 events together in 1999, or 68 rounds of golf, Williams noticed an Achilles' heel.

Woods's wedge shots between 90 and 120 yards out from the green weren't elite. He noticed Woods was not hitting it close enough and thus wasn't making enough birdies from that distance, which he faced often because he was overpowering par 4s with his driver. He often had a pitching wedge or less when other players were sometimes 140 yards out, or more. Williams observed that, specifically, Woods would pull shots to the left, due to a closed clubface (pointing left of the target). That would de-loft the club, which added unwanted distance. Woods was regularly overshooting his target on the greens. It had to improve if he wanted to go to another level. "To Tiger's credit, whenever I suggested an improvement based on my stats, he would work furiously at the weakness," Williams says. "His work ethic was astonishing. Great players don't reach that level without serious dedication. But the way Tiger *approached* practice was better than anyone I'd seen."

What most impressed Williams was Woods's sense of purpose. He'd seen plenty of players hit a high volume of balls to feel as though quantity would improve their swing. But Woods's sessions were about *quality*. Williams rarely saw Woods hit a single ball in practice that didn't have an intentional trajectory, shape and target. He was always working on a particular movement or pattern, and he didn't leave the range until it was grooved in.

Woods's Mercedes win at Kapalua with the new bag was followed by a win at the Pebble Beach Pro-Am. His next five starts included a tie for second at the Buick Invitational at Torrey Pines, a win at the Bay Hill Invitational and two additional second-place finishes. Woods's validating second major win at the 1999 PGA Championship, after two years stuck on major number one, vanquished immense pressure and built confidence. "A weight was lifted from his shoulders," Williams says. "Our team—me, Mark and Butch—could sense special results were coming."

That's one way of putting it. The brand of golf Woods was about to start playing bordered on supernatural.

* * *

On a foggy Monday, February 7, 2000, Woods was seven shots behind the lead with seven holes remaining in the final round at the Pebble Beach Pro-Am. PGA Tour rookie Matt Gogel was leading, and also wearing black slacks and a red sweater-vest, not unlike Woods's signature colors on Sundays (a tradition Woods's mother started for him in final rounds due to a belief that red was a power color for Capricorns, and he was born December 30).

When Woods birdied the par-3 12th, he was six back with six remaining. He'd picked up four shots; impressive but nothing spectacular for a tour pro. He did not even birdie the par-5 14th. But then Woods conjured the magic the golf world was about to see regularly: on the next hole, the par-4 15th, Woods finessed a pitching wedge from 97 yards that bounced into the hole for an eagle 2. "Right back in it," Woods said. He nearly holed out again for his second shot into the 16th, and almost chipped in for birdie at the par-3 17th. He made another birdie at the iconic par-5 18th at Pebble Beach to earn an improbable two-shot win. It was Woods's sixth straight victory on the PGA Tour, at the famous Monterey Peninsula course that was hosting the 100th U.S. Open four months later in June. Previously, Woods's largest comeback victory on the PGA Tour was four shots. On the European Tour in 1998, he overcame an eight-shot deficit to beat Ernie Els at the Johnnie Walker Classic.

Woods was also playing the mind games he was about to become renowned for. Gogel, relegated to a share of second with Vijay Singh, walked off the dais having just spoken to reporters about losing. Woods was up next, and Gogel graciously shook his hand.

"Nice eagle on No. 14! What did you hit?" Gogel asked.

"It was No. 15," Woods said, winking.

"Oh . . . 15 . . . oh, geez," Gogel said.

Woods and Gogel were both capable of eagle at the 573-yard, par-5 14th, given that powerful tour pros can reach a lot of par 5s in two shots and make eagle putts. Gogel had seen an eagle on Woods's scorecard on the leaderboard and assumed it was No. 14. Woods could have said "Thanks," and not corrected Gogel. But he relished crushing competitors' spirits by letting them know exactly *how badly* he'd beaten them. Sometimes, Woods would walk up to an opponent's ball in the fairway, pretend to think it was his and walk to his own ball farther down the hole as a reminder he was longer off the tee.

Two months later, at the Masters, Woods faced his first big test of 2000. Augusta was where Woods always faced the most pressure, given it had been three years since his '97 breakthrough. His

Masters hopes were almost extinguished on day one, as he made a double-bogey 6 on the par-4 10th and a rare triple-bogey 6 on the famed par-3 12th. Still, Woods clawed his way back into contention by the final round and finished fifth behind Singh. "I don't think he ever got within three [shots] of me," Singh said when asked about Woods, who'd become his fierce rival. Woods had a different opinion; he started poorly but on Sunday, he had a mathematical shot at winning. "I was very close," Woods said. "I still gave myself a chance. I'm proud of that."

* * *

Early on the morning of Tuesday, May 16, 2000, two men walked through rain and whipping, cold wind as they approached the first tee at the Gut Kaden golf course in Germany. The Hamburg area was hosting the European Tour's Deutsche Bank-SAP Open TPC of Europe. Williams stood waiting for Woods to arrive for a practice round. Kel Devlin, the global director of sports marketing at Nike, and a golf ball engineer from Bridgestone, Hideyuki "Rock" Ishii, caught Williams's eye.

"What the f——k are you two idiots doing here?" Williams asked.

Devlin explained Woods had phoned that Sunday night and asked him to deliver the Nike Tour Accuracy golf ball to Germany. He was going to put it in play for the first time, after Nike had spent almost two years testing it with their star ambassador.

"Bullshit!" Williams said, in disbelief the ball was ready that quickly.

Woods had previously used the Titleist Professional golf ball, which essentially had a liquid core—a layer of tightly wound rubber bands and then soft covers. But the Nike Tour Accuracy—the shoe giant's foray into the golf ball market—was different. It had a solid core comprised of molded rubber and was covered by several layers of urethane.

On the first tee at Gut Kaden, Woods teed up the Titleist ball and smashed a drive. It drifted on the wind and into the right rough. Williams tossed him the Nike Tour Accuracy. Woods struck the exact same shot, only it landed in the middle of the fairway. "It was better in the wind," Williams says. "The Nike ball made it very easy for Tiger to keep the trajectory where he needed it to be; it didn't balloon into the air vertically and it didn't drift sideways on a crosswind as much."

Woods was the best player in the world and Williams felt this monumental technological breakthrough was an added advantage. Many of Woods's PGA Tour peers were using a wound ball, but he was among the first big names to adopt the solid-core ball. At the 2000 Masters, 59 of the 95 golfers invited to Augusta National used wound balls. By the 2001 Masters, four players had wound balls. Of the top 25 on the leaderboard, 24 players teed up with a solid-core ball. Kirk Triplett was the outlier. Woods's peers spent 2000 watching him blow away fields using the solid core.

Woods outclassed his peers in every facet in 2000. His adjusted scoring average of 67.79 remains the lowest in PGA Tour history. He did not need an advantage, and to suggest his success was due to the ball is to discount perhaps the greatest year of golf that has ever been played. But it certainly helped, each and every round, Williams believes.

"You would have to say it was worth one or two shots per round," Williams says when asked to quantify the advantage. The Tour Accuracy was so rigorously tested and calibrated for Woods's needs—his typical spin, height and deviation—that the ball reacted precisely how he wanted on every shot. If he needed to hit a long iron off the tee, using a stinger shot, where he kept the ball low and with very little spin, it would shoot out low and flat. If he tried to hit it high, or left to right, the ball obeyed. It was an enormous confidence booster for a tour pro to have 100 percent trust in the ball. It was unlikely an equipment manufacturer had ever spent as much time and money developing a ball for a player as Nike did for Woods.

The ball also went a little farther—Williams estimated five yards each club—but that wasn't why Woods used it. It was the control. His ball flight was deliberately lower than other players' because if a ball reached its maximum height, it could be more affected by the wind.

Woods shared third place in Germany while he adjusted to the new ball in a tournament setting. His next start came at the Memorial Tournament in Ohio, which he won by five shots. Everything was in place to use the Nike ball in a major for the first time, at the U.S. Open at Pebble Beach Golf Links.

* * *

There was an aura about Woods early in the week at the 2000 U.S. Open at Pebble Beach, from June 15 to 18. It was one of the most hyped majors in decades. Pebble Beach, on the rugged Northern California coastline, is among the world's most beautiful courses. It's also publicly accessible (though in 2024 the green fee was $730). From holes three to 10, as well as 17 and 18, Pebble Beach plays alongside the Pacific Ocean. Here, the renowned par-5 sixth features a picturesque downhill tee shot, with Stillwater Cove to the right, then a steep uphill climb around a cliff to the green. The following hole, the 102-yard, par-3 seventh, is one of the most photographed holes in golf.

Fans were eager to see the stars, like Woods, Els, Duval and Singh, play Pebble Beach in brutal U.S. Open conditions: fairways narrowed, rough thickened and the tiny greens at Pebble Beach (the smallest on the PGA Tour) cut and rolled to lightning-fast speeds. Pebble Beach has poa annua grass on its greens, a low-growing grass with short, canoe-shaped leaves that thrives in temperate climates. The greens also flower and get bumpy in the afternoon. It was going to be a torture chamber, like watching your favorite golfers go to the dentist for four days.

As Williams walked the course during practice rounds early in the week, gazing over Stillwater Cove and the Pacific Ocean, a song became stuck in his head. Among the golfers he'd worked for, Williams was notorious for choosing one song and singing it over and over at every major. He liked to create a soundtrack for the week, based on the course, host city and circumstances surrounding his boss at the time. For some caddies, it was a tool they used to reinforce positive messages to their boss. Baker-Finch recalls his former caddie, Phil Wright, would regularly pick a song with uplifting lyrics and sing it repeatedly after Baker-Finch had a good opening round. "There was one tournament where Phil kept singing 'Hit Me with Your Best Shot' [by ADONA], and it was funny and repetitive, but I played well," Baker-Finch says. Williams's long mix tape was full of classic rock songs from the 1970s, '80s and '90s. Every night before bed, he'd play his chosen song for that tournament repeatedly. Williams wasn't sure why, but it calmed the stress of caddying and focused him. For Pebble Beach, he picked "Waterfront" by Scottish rock band Simple Minds, a song which describes metaphorically moving up to a waterfront in a million years. *Get in, get out of the rain. So far, so good, so close, yet still so far*. The song played in his head when he picked up Woods's clubs from his room at The Lodge suites at Pebble Beach. "That song inspired me; I pictured walking up the 18th on Sunday along the waterfront," he says. "As his caddie, I was going to get Tiger out of the rain and fog. Tiger was going to walk up and be standing higher than anybody else on that 18th green holding the U.S. Open trophy."

Feeling the significance of the 100th U.S. Open, Woods was determined to win a major at one of pro golf's most iconic venues. Pebble Beach had hosted three U.S. Opens, with Nicklaus (1972), Tom Watson (1982) and Tom Kite (1992) the winners. Among Woods's entourage at Pebble Beach, besides Williams, Harmon and Steinberg, was a man named Sam Reeves, a Monterey-area resident and accomplished amateur golfer. Reeves was introduced to Woods by Harmon and quickly became a friend to the team. He had qualified for the 1972 U.S. Amateur at the age of 38, with four children and working full-time. He knew what good golf looked like.

"Something special is happening with Tiger," Williams recalls Reeves saying. Reeves walked most practice rounds at majors with Woods for several years but had never seen the same aura about him. He was hitting every single shot, whether he was trying to fade it (left to right) or draw it (right to left), straight, low or high, exactly to plan. The control he had was astonishing. Harmon said to Williams, "It's perfect; we just have to make sure Tiger doesn't over-practice and fatigue."

On Tuesday of the U.S. Open week, Woods played the neighboring Spyglass Hill course for fun. Williams had arranged for several members from his childhood golf course, Paraparaumu Beach, who had traveled from New Zealand, to meet the golf star. Allan James was the first golfer Williams ever caddied for, as a child earning $5 per 18 holes. James also gave Williams a job working in his butcher shop for extra money. Kevin Corkill was the other Paraparaumu member. Woods had his team arrange U.S.

Open tickets for Williams's two mates and encouraged Williams to bring them out to Spyglass. "Tiger was so gracious with them, allowed them to walk with him at Spyglass and was asking them questions," Williams says. "He gave them memories they'll never forget." Over the years, Williams observed this was common for Woods. When Williams occasionally brought friends to a golf tournament and introduced them to Woods, he would have a brief, but genuine, conversation with them. "Some pros you can tell can't wait for it to be over," Williams says. Woods took time to make Williams's friends feel included, with a joke or a quip about what country they were from.

* * *

The California sun rose over Pebble Beach on Wednesday, June 14, burning off the eerie fog as a memorial service began for golf great Payne Stewart. While the buildup to the 100th U.S. Open had been electric, it also had an air of sadness. The defending champion, popular and charismatic American golfer Stewart, had tragically died October 25, 1999, when a private plane he was traveling to a tournament in lost cabin pressure and eventually crashed. He was the first defending champion in more than 50 years not to compete the year after winning, since Ben Hogan was in a car accident in 1949.

On Wednesday morning, 40 of the U.S. Open competitors hit balls into the ocean from the famous par-5 18th, like a 21-gun salute at a military funeral. Stewart's wife, Tracey, an Australian and the sister of golf pro Mike Ferguson, had long been friends with Williams. She gave a touching speech. "If [Stewart] were here in person today he would say, 'Don't ever give up. Don't ever lose hope. Your future is not measured by your past. Keep trusting.

Keep believing. Keep hoping for the best. With God's help, you can live and die victoriously.'"

Major winner Paul Azinger fought back tears as he said, "If golf was art, then Payne was the color." Woods, though, faced some criticism when he did not attend the memorial. Instead, he played a practice round despite being a close friend, and Isleworth neighbor, of Stewart's. He reasoned that he had attended a previously held memorial service. "I felt by going it would be more of a deterrent for me during the tournament, because I don't want to be thinking about what transpired," Woods said at Pebble Beach.

Woods would have also become the focus of the TV cameras had he attended. The spotlight could have been unfairly taken away from Stewart and the service. "It surprised people, but that's how Tiger operated," says Williams. "Tiger would not do anything outside of tournament duties and practice. His focus was solely on the major."

Later that morning, Woods's practice round group, which featured O'Meara, Cook and Paul Goydos, stood on the 16th tee as Woods gripped a 3-iron he was laying up with. O'Meara felt a tug on his shirt from golf great turned TV analyst Johnny Miller.

"How's the kid hitting it?" Miller asked.

"That kid right there is going to be the greatest player who has ever lived," O'Meara declared.

Woods then blasted a 3-iron farther, higher and straighter than any pro O'Meara had ever seen. It had a distinct sound O'Meara could assign to Woods if blindfolded.

"Well, he can't control the distances on his wedges, can he?" Miller asked.

"Oh, yes, he can," O'Meara quipped, referencing Woods's work in the offseason. "I'll get him to hit a wedge 90 yards to the inch right now, if you want."

Later that day, Williams's phone rang in his hotel room in downtown Monterey. He thought work was done for the day, but Woods had been practicing putting in his room and didn't like his stroke. He wanted Williams back at Pebble Beach at seven to watch a session on the practice green with Harmon.

Woods worked on his stroke as the sun went down while Williams provided confirmation of what Woods was trying to tweak in his technique. "He felt his hands were too low standing over the ball," Williams says. That caused Woods to pull his putts left. The session was fortuitous considering what the sporting world was about to witness from him on Pebble Beach's greens.

The first tee time of the 2000 U.S. Open, on Thursday, June 15, was 6:30 A.M., while Woods teed at 8:40 A.M., grouped for the first two rounds with quirky Swedish golfer Jesper Parnevik and Jim Furyk. Only 30 minutes earlier, Hal Sutton, who had beaten Woods to win the Players Championship months earlier, holed an 8-iron on No. 1. It was the first opening hole eagle in U.S. Open history. The U.S. Open was off to a wild start, and it only got more dramatic.

Nicklaus, who in addition to the 1972 U.S. Open had won the 1961 U.S. Amateur at Pebble Beach, was given the 12:40 P.M. tee time saved for the defending champion, Stewart. On the first tee, Nicklaus called for a moment of silence from the crowd for Stewart. As he addressed the ball, Nicklaus started to cry, and backed away to collect himself.

Woods, meanwhile, shot 65 to take the first-round lead at 6 under par. Severe fog rolled in that afternoon, forcing 75 golfers to finish their first rounds Friday morning.

Tee times for the opening rounds for Woods and Nicklaus were serendipitous, with Nicklaus due to finish on Friday afternoon exactly as Woods would be teeing off at 4:40 P.M. with a delayed tee time.

It was the last U.S. Open Nicklaus ever played. In 1998, "the Golden Bear" announced that the four majors in 2000 would be his swan song on the PGA Tour. Nicklaus wanted to use Pebble Beach to retire after his 44th appearance.

On his last-ever hole, Nicklaus, 60 years of age, went for the green in two with a 3-wood from 260 yards and reached it. The crowd went wild. Tom Watson, back in the fairway on 18, stood clapping. Nicklaus three-putted for par, shot 82 and missed the cut. At about four thirty that afternoon, the winner of 18 majors—among them four U.S. Opens—waved goodbye with tears streaming down his face.

From a couple hundred yards away on the practice putting green, Woods heard it all. "Tiger took a deep breath and listened to the roar," Williams says. "He was taken aback. It was like a changing of the guard." Williams often heard Woods refer to Nicklaus as the "benchmark," and thought it was fascinating he knew every single statistic and milestone, from the age Nicklaus was (26) when he won the career grand slam, to his podium finishes at the majors: 18 wins, 19 second-place finishes and nine third-place results.

Moments later, Woods teed off in his second round. He was almost in a trance as he executed a perfect swing and Williams could sense Woods wanted to pay tribute to Nicklaus by playing like him, or even better. "Jack's last U.S. Open definitely gave Tiger more motivation," Williams says. Woods wanted to show the golf world he was good enough to be a U.S. Open champion despite criticism of his inaccuracy with the driver or wedges.

Within six holes, Woods would hit one of his most famous shots in the majors. At the par-5 sixth, Woods blocked his drive into the right rough. Whenever Woods put himself in trouble, Williams would watch intently. It's one of the reasons why he marched furiously ahead of Woods after every shot: to get a 20-second head start on devising a strategy. On No. 6, Woods had 204 yards to the green but needed the height of a 7-iron for the ball to rise quickly over the enormous cliff, which was covered in rough and separated the first portion of the fairway from the second atop the cliff.

The ball was sitting deep down in rough, and Williams thought it would be tough just to get the ball to the top of the hill, let alone the green. It could also shoot right and into the water. Williams watched Woods's stare. "Tiger, quite often, looked straight at his intended target and I could instantly tell his intent," he says. Williams would adjust his caddie advice accordingly. Sometimes, Williams protested. Sometimes, the risk was too great. Either way, Williams's advice had to be well thought out, delivered quickly, precisely and persuasively. Woods was a fast player and decisions had to be made instantly. On this occasion, Woods's body language was resolute. He was clearly going for the green in two, so Williams didn't bother suggesting Woods should lay up.

Woods took an almighty lash at the ball with a 7-iron, and it rocketed off the face as a clump of rough flew into the air. The ball soared over the hill, bounced on the fairway short of the green and rolled onto the right edge. He'd hit his 7-iron, which normally carried 185 yards, just shy of 200, from thick rough. "*It's just not a fair fight!*" commentators shouted on the broadcast. Woods narrowly missed the eagle putt and tapped in for a birdie to lead by two. The U.S. Open seemed all but over, only 24 holes into the tournament.

"That shot was superhuman," Williams recalls. "A bad shot could have severely affected his U.S. Open chances but Tiger's strength and speed out of the rough was his most underrated quality."

Woods played only 12 holes on Friday due to a weather delay and returned to finish his second round on Saturday morning. That Friday night, he was still unhappy with his putting stroke, so he took three golf balls out from his golf bag to putt in his hotel room but forgot to return them. Woods now only had four balls left. Williams didn't discover the faux pas until they were on the course and it was his job to avoid freaking Woods out. Then came the most nervous 90 minutes of Williams's 40-year caddying career.

It was an early morning restart, so there weren't many spectators on the course. On the 13th hole, Woods drove it into rough from the tee and had to take a big swing to hack it out onto the green. In doing so, he put a scuff mark on the ball which would affect its performance. Woods gave the ball to a starstruck young fan near the 13th green. "I was thinking, 'F——k, I need to go and get that ball back,'" Williams says. Now, Woods had only two balls in the bag. He got through holes 14, 15, 16 and 17 unscathed, but he also gave *another* ball to a fan. Williams, though, still hadn't told Woods about the missing balls.

At the 18th tee, Woods hit a shot that would make a weekend hacker blush. He hooked it 30 yards left of the fairway and into the ocean. "Just an ugly golf shot," Woods said. Williams could almost see steam billowing out of Woods's ears.

Woods was down to the last ball. Without giving away why, Williams was trying to tell his boss that maybe he should just hit a 2-iron, while strategically placing his hand on the driver. "Tiger said, 'Get your f——g hand off that driver head cover!' I didn't want to tell him it's our last golf ball, because he probably would have told me to get my ass onto 17-Mile Drive [the main road within Pebble Beach Resort] and onto a Greyhound bus out of there."

The stress of the ball dilemma had Williams shaking. He was also wildly planning out his options if Woods were to hit that last ball in the water. He even looked in the distance, past the 18th green, to Woods's Lodge suite. *Can I get from where his ball crossed the water to his hotel room, up the stairs, grab more balls and sprint back? How quickly can I sprint 500-plus yards?* The rules, in 2000, allowed Woods five minutes to look for the original ball. Given he was using a Nike ball, borrowing from a playing partner wasn't an option. Plus, that would have required Williams to tell Woods about the situation.

Woods found dry land with his second tee ball, which was his third shot. He managed a bogey on 18 and shot 69. He moved to 8 under par and two shots ahead of Spain's Miguel Ángel Jiménez and Denmark's Thomas Bjørn. Williams breathed a huge sigh of relief.

Weather and turf conditions for Saturday's third round were diabolical. The greens were dry, crusty and quick after days of foot traffic. The rough was juicy. Winds were blowing over 30 miles per hour around the Monterey Peninsula. But Woods was cruising, making birdie on No. 2 to lead by eight.

Then, disaster struck.

On the par-4 third, Woods racked up a triple-bogey 7. His second shot from the fairway found deep rough, and he couldn't escape it for his third. It took five shots to get on the green and he missed the putt for a 6. Woods, though, laughed.

"That's what impressed me most and signified Tiger was in complete control," Williams says. "When did you ever see Tiger Woods laugh when he made a double- or triple-bogey? Never." Woods reminded himself how unlucky he'd been with two treacherous lies in the rough. Remarkably, he calmed himself and shot 71 to lead after three rounds at 8 under. For perspective, Woods's playing partner, Bjørn, shot 82, while Kirk Triplett and Miguel Ángel Jiménez, in the group behind, shot 84 and 76, respectively. The scoring average on day three was 77.2, 6.2 shots over par. Two players who did enjoy that Saturday were Els, whose sublime 3-under 68 put him in second, 10 shots behind Woods. The other was mini-tour player Todd Fischer. He resumed his second round Saturday morning with the tee shot at the iconic par-3 seventh. Fischer's pitching wedge went in for a hole in one.

Woods's 10-shot lead was the largest 54-hole lead in U.S. Open history. He had slept on a nine-shot lead at the 1997 Masters, and won that by 12. "In the lead, or neck and neck coming down the stretch, that's where I want to be," Woods said.

At 2:40 P.M. on Sunday, June 18, Woods teed off the first hole at Pebble Beach with Els in his march toward history. Weather delays, fog, thick rough, lost golf balls and the pressure of chasing Nicklaus's majors record were not going to stop him. Woods's ball-striking remained sublime even under the microscope of a U.S. Open final round. On the front nine, he found six of seven fairways and hit eight of nine greens in regulation. Still, he made nine straight pars and no birdies. "It was the utmost display of patience; he was absolutely obsessed with not making a single bogey and he was saying it over and over Sunday morning before teeing off," Williams says. In most rounds he played, Woods would have a mini goal separate from winning a tournament. It might be not making a bogey, avoiding three-putts or hitting a certain number of fairways. He always bet that goal with Williams, usually a $100 gamble.

The birdie drought ended for Woods on the par-4 10th. He added birdies at the difficult par-3 12th, the par-4 13th and the par-5 14th. He was 12 under, and 15 shots clear. The final four holes were just a formality.

At the par-4 16th, Woods faced a 15-foot par putt to keep his bogey-free round alive and poured it right in the center. The emotional fist pump immediately after looked like it was to win the tournament, a gesture that was noticed by NHL coach Scotty Bowman, who was walking inside the ropes with Woods's group.

As a head coach, Bowman had won the Stanley Cup eight times, including in 1997 with the Detroit Red Wings. Williams could see Bowman looked confused as to why Woods celebrated a par putt on the third-last hole when leading by 15. "No one in the world but Tiger and I knew about the no-bogey goal, but I could see Bowman to the left of the green and he figured it out," Williams says.

Afterward, Bowman noted the intensity of Woods and Williams's dynamic to a reporter. "[Woods's] eye contact is directly with his caddie and nowhere else when he's preparing to hit a shot. He's oblivious to everyone else."

If Williams didn't know it after 15 months in the job, caddying for Woods was intense regardless of the circumstances. Most players, if they led a U.S. Open by 15 shots with two holes remaining, would have soaked up the historical significance of winning what was Nicklaus's final U.S. Open. "But Tiger would have had some disappointment if he made bogey even with winning," Williams says. Woods wanted to send a message to his peers: he was not going to stumble when leading.

At No. 17, Woods nearly holed a bunker shot from beside the green and easily saved par, making the par-5 18th a 543-yard victory lap. He hit 4-iron from the tee for safety, and about 15 minutes later, tapped in for par. His 4-under 67 was the day's low score. Most important, it was bogey free. In fact, his final 26 holes at Pebble Beach were bogey free. Woods finished at 12 under (272), 15 shots ahead of Els and Jiménez, who shared second at 3 over. Woods was alone in finishing under par and was the first player in 100 editions of the U.S. Open to finish 72 holes at double digits under par.

Within minutes, an urgent call came for Woods in the scoring area. It was from Bill Clinton. Woods's performance was presidential.

Woods's obliteration of the 2000 U.S. Open field is considered by many the greatest 72-hole performance in golf history, when factoring in the conditions. His 15-shot win remains the record margin in majors. "It was an awesome display of golf; he's the Michael Jordan of our sport," Els said. Added Watson: "Everyone else is playing for second place and I think they know it."

Woods averaged 299.3 yards on his tee shots and had hit 71 percent (51 of 72) of greens in regulation. That yielded 21 birdies. His total of 51 greens in regulation was seven more than any other player's. From Williams's handwritten statistics, several numbers stood out. He recorded 111 putts for 72 holes, one more than the official number of 110, considering Williams counted all putts from the fringe or just off the green. Still, 111 remains the lowest total putts in all the majors Williams worked for Woods. Woods had 25 putts in the first round, the fewest in a major round Williams had caddied. Woods also didn't have a three-putt for the entire tournament, one of only two majors with Williams he avoided them (the 2003 PGA Championship was the other). At no point was Woods over par. Of the 437 rounds completed by the field, only three were bogey free. Two of those were Woods's: his opening 65 and closing 67. He also played the par 3s, par 4s and par 5s in 4 under each (adding up to 12 under). In U.S. Open conditions, Woods's statistics remain unfathomable.

In the hours after his victory, Woods finally found out about Williams's stressful ball situation. Signing his scorecard, Woods asked, "Stevie, what was up on Saturday morning on the 18th tee?" Williams then revealed the chaos. Woods laughed. "You're f——g kidding?" He quizzed Williams about why he had not mentioned the incident all weekend. "Well, you never asked me!" Williams responded.

Later, in Woods's room at The Lodge after the trophy presentation and champion's commitments, Woods surprised Williams with an unexpected mission.

"Stevie, best you get your ass to St. Andrews and learn every blade of grass at the Old Course. I'm going to play even better at the British Open." After his next event, which was a month later at the Western Open in Chicago, Woods wanted Williams to fly to Scotland to scout St. Andrews an entire week before the Open Championship. Williams was gobsmacked; they weren't 90 minutes removed from lifting the U.S. Open trophy and he was planning the next major. "It's funny now, but looking back, that put a lot of pressure on me," Williams says. "Tiger knew he was in great form, and I felt the only thing that could stop him winning was poor caddying."

Later that night, flanked by his two mates from New Zealand, Williams boarded a flight at the Monterey airport to connect through San Francisco and back to Auckland for two weeks off. Nursing a celebratory beer, Williams spent most of the 13-hour flight to Auckland going through the holes at St. Andrews in his mind.

CHAPTER 4

DRINKING FROM THE JUG

The sun had just risen over the east coast of Fife in Scotland, on a balmy Tuesday, July 11, 2000, when Williams left his modest dorm room at the University of St. Andrews for an early morning stroll around town before heading over to the famous Old Course. The 129th Open Championship was 10 days away, but Williams was already in Scotland, alone, while Woods enjoyed a social golf trip in a remote pocket of Ireland. Even when separated, Williams began workdays at dawn thirty. After all, he wasn't in St. Andrews on vacation; he had flown into nearby Edinburgh on Sunday night, directly from Chicago after the PGA Tour's Western Open. The challenge was simple, if hefty: map the 500-year-old links in rigorous detail for Woods's shot at history.

Williams seldom traveled across the Atlantic Ocean to the U.K. major without Woods. One year, Williams was at his U.S. residence in Sunriver, Oregon, with his father-in-law, Ian Miller. The two were waiting for a flight out of Bend Municipal Airport to Orlando, to meet Woods and travel on his private jet to the Open. When

Williams's commercial flight to Orlando was canceled, Woods immediately sent his jet to retrieve the pair from across the country.

In St. Andrews, Williams walked with his usual haste but stopped when he saw the pale brown and gray Holy Trinity Church, the oldest in the town. He was in awe of the church's northwestern tower, with its cone-shaped spire and arcade arches—the only parts of the church retained from multiple rebuilds and restorations since its construction in 1144. There was a striking contrast between its cold, gray stone exterior and the beautifully manicured green lawn and gardens out front.

The history of St. Andrews resonated with Williams, conjuring memories of one of his favorite songs, "Belfast Child," by Simple Minds. Its lyrics provided a soundtrack to what Williams was seeing, and what he was envisioning for Woods as he attempted to complete the career grand slam:

Someday soon, they're gonna pull the old town down.
One day, we'll return here.

"I thought to myself, one day they might pull the old town of St. Andrews down," Williams says. "If they do, you'd want to leave a mark. I sang that song to myself the entire week. Tiger knew the lyrics by the end of it."

Williams approached the Old Course's first tee, which sits on one side of a rectangular field, 129 yards wide, that houses the adjoining first and 18th holes. It's a majestic amphitheater where, during the Open, cheers of the enormous crowds ricochet off the 400-year-old buildings, hotels and St. Andrews clubhouse to create a noise unlike any event in sport.

Williams flipped open his yardage book, almost like a topography map for caddies that was different at each tournament. Most professional caddies on the PGA Tour used "The Book" at each tournament, a bespoke yardage book designed and published by George Lucas. Not to be confused with the *Star Wars* creator, Lucas was a former caddie who became a "yardologist" and traveled around the U.S. mapping courses and selling the books to caddies at every event. Players were addicted to the information.

Williams, though, was used to drawing his own yardage books. It's what he'd always done on other tours around the world, and he had a particular style for laying out each hole with notes. His Old Course book was worn and dated. He'd hand-drawn every tee, bunker, mound and green at the Old Course. He'd paced off every approach shot to every green. The book worked just fine looping for Mike Clayton at the 1984 Open at St. Andrews, and Raymond Floyd at the 1990 and 1995 editions there. Why change now? Woods was looking to become the fifth golfer in history to capture the career grand slam—winning all four major championships—and Williams's illustrations were as relevant as ever.

Almost nothing had changed about the Old Course since Williams had started caddying at the Open. There were 112 bunkers, each of them devilishly narrow pots that were hardly big enough to stand in, let alone swing a golf club. Often, golfers had to come out sideways, or backward. For the 129th Open, the championship's organizer, the Royal and Ancient Golf Club of St. Andrews, had deepened every bunker and rendered their walls more upright, making it even harder to escape. Tour pro Darren Clarke remarked that course officials had "gone a little bit silly" renovating them. Only one bunker was not already in Williams's book, and it was down the left side of the par-5 14th. Frankly, he didn't know it existed.

Caddies faced more examinations of their attention to detail at Open Championships than at any other tournament because links courses, particularly St. Andrews, threw up so many variables.

Woods might need to play down a different hole from the one he was standing on because a change in the wind forced such a decision. It was rare, but Williams could predict the holes where that was likeliest to happen, and he wanted to have notes in case it did. Woods also might find himself in a weird spot on the course, given the unpredictable way a ball could bounce on the firm, rippled turf. Williams spent that whole week focusing on Woods's targets, or "lines," from each tee. He had to have multiple options, one for each wind direction. It was arguably the most important aspect of Williams's job at St. Andrews, given some of the tee shots were rendered blind by mounds, bushes or changes in depth that blocked the golfer's view to the fairway. During the tournament, Woods was likely to ask, "Stevie, what's the line off the tee here?" Williams couldn't afford to hesitate or have a "maybe" option if he wanted to be successful. That would indicate he lacked conviction and Woods wouldn't swing with the same assurance. "It had to be accurate and be delivered like, 'Tiger, you've GOT to hit it right *here* and *this* is where you want the ball to finish,'" Williams says.

Woods, meanwhile, was 500 miles away in Ireland. He had grown fond of visiting the Emerald Isle en route to the Open since his Isleworth neighbors first sold him on the benefits of such a boondoggle in 1998. That year, O'Meara and Payne Stewart were invited by two Irish businessmen and philanthropists, J. P. McManus and Dermot Desmond, to spend a few days in Waterville playing links golf, fly-fishing and drinking the occasional pint of Guinness. O'Meara suggested Woods come along, given he had never played golf in Ireland.

Waterville is an ancient town in County Kerry that sits on an isthmus between Lough Currane to the east and Ballinskelligs Bay to the west. The town is revered in the golf world for having a seaside links frequently voted the best in Ireland. The week after

Waterville, O'Meara won the 1998 Open Championship at Royal Birkdale in England. Naturally, Waterville became an annual tradition.

In 1999, a month after Stewart had won the U.S. Open at Pinehurst, the trip grew in numbers to include fellow pros Lee Janzen, David Duval and Stuart Appleby. One night, O'Meara, McManus and Desmond sat near the window of their Waterville house as the sun was about to set late in the evening when they saw, in the distance, the distinct figures of Woods, world number one, and Duval, number two, in a field nearby. The pair were hitting golf balls from their own practice bags and, after the session, they walked out into the field to pick up the balls by hand. "JP and I looked at each other and he said, 'There isn't any place in the world but Waterville where you can see Tiger and Duval doing this,' and he was right," O'Meara says.

O'Meara and Woods maintained a reasonable bedtime during that trip. But Stewart immersed himself into the local culture. He drank with the locals and poured Guinness at the Butler Arms Hotel. He played his harmonica and sang with pub guests until 3 A.M. He was so adored by the locals that, in 1999, they made Stewart the honorary captain of the Waterville Golf Club for the year 2000. After the trip, Stewart had large framed maps of Ireland created, featuring a series of fly-fishing flies stuck at all the spots they fished, and gave them to Appleby and the group.

Stewart's presence was certainly missed on the 2000 Ireland trip, especially on a windy afternoon on Wednesday, July 12, when Waterville Golf Club held a memorial ceremony for him. It was attended by his widow, Tracey, as well as Woods and Appleby. Several fellow PGA Tour pros also joined, including Robert Allenby, who had played the JP McManus Pro-Am at Limerick Golf Club two days earlier. Woods won that charity event, which Manchester United coach

Sir Alex Ferguson and other celebrities had played in. Waterville GC unveiled a bronze statue of Stewart that McManus and Desmond commissioned for talented Irish sculptor Jim Connolly to create. "Everybody who watched and participated knows how much he enjoyed being here," Woods said. "Now, we know he's looking down and taking care of us."

Appleby says those trips to Ireland helped settle Woods before the Open Championship each year. He had seen, during Woods's first three years on tour, the chaotic energy that came with Tigermania. Ireland was a quietening of the mind. "I can't imagine living in his boots for a day; he couldn't go and order a burger in a restaurant without being stared at and it's hard to believe how energy-sapping that would've been," Appleby says. The Aussie, who had won three times on the PGA Tour before 2000, also noticed in Ireland the calming influence O'Meara had on Woods. "He was Tiger's greatest emotional influence, as a competitor, and a friend who could pull him aside and give him advice," Appleby adds. In terms of golf technique, it also helped Woods, Appleby and others develop their ground game, practicing low, running shots on Irish links courses. For most tour players, the Open was the only week each year they weren't playing "target golf" in the U.S., lofting the ball high in the air on every shot.

Allenby, meanwhile, loved his first Irish trip with the Isleworth gang. He had just won the Western Open in Chicago and in the hours afterward had flown straight from Chicago to Shannon and then drove to Limerick Golf Club for the McManus Pro-Am. "JP is probably the most generous man on the planet, so I was happy to come," Allenby says.

The pro-am featured a charity auction and Woods's donation was a round of golf at Isleworth with himself and O'Meara. In a large tent, as guests sat around their tables, Allenby remembers the bids started at €200,000 but quickly climbed over €1 million. The winning bid was reportedly €1.78 million, coming from British billionaire financier Joe Lewis, who had developed Isleworth. "Tiger knew how important it was and he loved JP," O'Meara recalls. "I don't know if anyone's ever raised more money for charity in two days than JP."

Allenby, like Appleby, observed how the anonymity of Ireland contributed to Woods's Open victory. He felt in order for a tour pro to contend in a major, they had to enter a mental state of nirvana and shut off from the world. "I think Ireland was great for Tiger; whatever golf course in Ireland he wanted to play, he just jumped on a helicopter straight there, landed on its practice fairway and teed off," he says. Allenby watched in awe as Woods familiarized himself with Irish turf, which was similar to Scotland's, and how he used Waterville's 20-to-40-mile-per-hour winds to practice his low stinger shot. Woods would punch the ball with a 2-iron and an abbreviated follow-through. He'd send the ball spinning right to left with a low, flat trajectory, just underneath the breeze.

Woods and O'Meara helicoptered out of Waterville to the K Club in County Kildare, outside Dublin, for more fishing and golf. O'Meara caught a six-pound Atlantic salmon one morning while Woods, who was relatively new to fishing, was at breakfast. "When he was starting out, I don't know if he had the patience for stringing flies to catch salmon in the river," O'Meara says. O'Meara, 43, and the world number six at the time, would go into a Zen state while fishing, but Woods's concentration would wane. He would ask when they were going to catch something, and O'Meara would remind Woods there was a chance they might not catch anything at all. Such was the nature of fishing. "This is ridiculous," Woods would say. After 45 minutes, he'd bail to go grab a coffee. "I'd step in where he got out, and 10 casts later I'd get jacked up on a salmon," O'Meara says.

Woods had no trouble focusing once he set foot on the grounds of St. Andrews. He morphed into a different person. He was friendly, and played practice rounds with his peers, but Woods's concentration levels surged so much that it was almost jarring for the friends who were with him in Ireland the week prior. "Once he put his shoes on in the locker room, he was tactically trying to outrun everyone," Appleby says.

The hype surrounding Woods as he arrived in Scotland had reached fever pitch. He was the heaviest favorite in the history of betting on the Open with 2-to-1 odds; crazy figures considering there were 156 golfers in the field. Woods could complete the career grand slam at St. Andrews and sports fans knew how big the stage was. In fact, media reports claimed a £10,000 prize was being offered by an anonymous source to streakers if they ran nude during the championship. Security officials were on high alert after a string of streakers interrupted various sporting events in the U.K. across the summer, from Wimbledon to Test cricket matches.

For Woods, it was all a part of Tigermania and his security were already working overtime to ensure his preparation went uninterrupted. Woods had little tricks of his own to avoid the crowds; he knew the first and 18th holes were especially busy because fans were guaranteed to see a majority of players begin, or end, their rounds. But both were straightforward par 4s with no bunkers, so Woods chose to begin his practice round with O'Meara at the par-4 second on Monday, July 17, given its proximity to the players' hotel. "We were staying at the Old Course Hotel, and Tiger's room was next to mine. We'd get up at 4 A.M. and walk out to the second tee," O'Meara says. "It was 7:20 A.M. when we'd finished."

The sleight of hand did not go unnoticed by British tabloids, with London's *Daily Telegraph* writing, tongue in cheek, that Woods "left his fans back at the clubhouse and his fellow professionals for dead." For the latter, the *Telegraph* was describing the advantage Woods had over his competitors in overpowering the links. At the 397-yard third hole, during that practice round, Woods blasted a drive that settled just short of the green. The fans who happened to be at No. 3 went wild. They knew it was a monster drive, even if pros got 60 to 70 yards of rollout on the hard turf.

Nick Faldo, a winner of three Opens, including a record score of 18 under par in 1990 at St. Andrews, calculated Woods could "drive six of the [par-4] greens and hit the par-5 fifth [568 yards] with a driver and a wedge." The Englishman anointed Woods the man to beat.

Woods's sleight of hand on the second tee wasn't the only move he pulled that week. The following day, Woods played a practice round with a group including rookie Adam Scott. The 20-year-old Australian had advanced through local and final qualifying to earn one of the last spots in the Open field. It was Scott's major debut, and he shared a swing coach with Woods in Harmon, who organized for his two pupils to play the practice round.

Scott was giddy, or "a deer in the headlights" as he described himself, with bigger crowds than he'd ever seen. He was relieved that at St. Andrews, the galleries were at least a good distance back from the players. In practice rounds, Scott discovered, Woods liked to play a "$1,000, no bogeys" game. If any player went bogey free, the other players in the group each had to pay him $1,000. Scott's professional career was four weeks old, and he didn't really have $1,000 cash just sitting in his pocket. Thankfully, after 10 holes, the Aussie was the last man standing—the only player in Woods's group without a bogey. On the par-3 11th, which was 174 yards and into the wind, Scott took a 5-iron out of his bag. But he wanted to know what Woods, who stood waiting for another player to hit, was using. Scott walked over to Williams and the bag, and casually peeked inside. Seeing this out of his peripherals, Woods waited, faked being uncomfortable with his own 5-iron and returned to grab the 4-iron. He made a smooth swing and found the middle of the green. "I went back, grabbed my 4-iron, made a normal, powerful swing and flew it straight over the green and made bogey," Scott says. He hadn't realized Woods had deliberately taken some juice out of his 4-iron to mess with the youngster. Woods walked over to Scott, flashed a grin, and said, "You shouldn't ever check my bag" and laughed. No $1,000 payday for the rookie.

St. Andrews wasn't the only time Woods pulled a trick on Scott. He knew the tall, athletically gifted youngster had the potential to win majors, become world number one and be a serious threat. After all, he was a phenomenal ball-striker who was already in good hands with Woods's own swing coach. At the Open the next year, at Royal Lytham, Scott and Danish stalwart Thomas Bjørn asked Woods one afternoon to play a practice round with him the following morning. "Tiger was always quite welcoming of other golfers wanting to play practice rounds with him," Williams says. Woods told Scott and Bjørn to be on the first tee at 5:30 A.M. sharp. "Thomas and I felt we were nice and early getting to the locker room around 5 A.M., to grab our golf shoes, but it didn't open until 6 A.M.," Scott says, laughing. Woods didn't wait a minute after 5:30 A.M. and had played four holes by the time Scott and Bjørn finally joined. The message was clear: they were in his world.

Scott was fresh-faced and unburdened by playing in Woods's shadow. His rivals, on the other hand, were beginning to show fatigue. His 15-shot victory at the U.S. Open, when he was the only player under par in brutal conditions, put an exclamation point on the narrative that he was now peerless. As revered Associated Press golf writer Doug Ferguson wrote at St. Andrews, "His only real rivals now are the records established by Jack Nicklaus." At the Open, Vijay Singh balked at suggestions Woods could bring St. Andrews to its knees like he did Pebble Beach. "Tiger played great golf but everyone else was average; if they played half decent, they wouldn't have been that bad." He did acknowledge, though, that the mere presence of Woods was intimidating for his fellow pros. Singh's tactic was to avoid thinking about him. "Once you start worrying about him, you're already in trouble," he said.

* * *

The 129th Open began at 7 A.M. on Thursday, July 20, in what was the 26th time it was played at St. Andrews. With warm weather and one of the world's most recognizable athletes trying to make history, a record 47,000 spectators filed into the Old Course. Senior officers from the Fife police force even considered sealing off St. Andrews, as an unlikely last resort, if crowds continued to rise for the remainder of the event. "There has to be a shutoff [number]," a police spokesman said.

Woods began his quest for golf's Holy Grail at 9:30 A.M., and Williams marveled at his total avoidance of bunkers and piercing, low ball flight as he compiled a 5-under-par 67. That left Woods one shot behind first-round leader Ernie Els, who bristled at reporters' questions about his 24-year-old rival. "Guys, that's a little unfair; I just shot 66," he said. "Talk about *my* round or get on the phone and call Tiger."

In round two, Woods seized control of the Open with 66 and led by three shots over David Toms. Play on Friday moved at a glacial pace; the many bottlenecks between greens and tee boxes at the Old Course combined with record crowds to see Woods's group take five hours to play 18 holes. The group of Stephen Leaney, Ian Poulter and Roger Chapman clocked 5 hours, 58 minutes. They finished at 9:58 P.M. Play was so slow that Gary Player—the only golfer to have won the Open in the 1950s, '60s and '70s—caught up to Woods's group on the seventh tee, despite being in the three-ball behind him. Williams turned around and saw the South African wearing strikingly loud pants, with one leg black and the other white. "It was a good laugh that distracted us from how slow play was," Williams says.

In round three, Woods and Toms teed off at 3 P.M. in the final group. Woods's first hole went smoothly, but he stumbled at the par-4 second, three-putting from off the green for bogey. It was Woods's first bogey at the majors since the 10th hole of the third round of the U.S. Open at Pebble Beach. According to Williams's handwritten statistics, that second-hole bogey also ended one of the most remarkable stretches of putting he ever witnessed from Woods. It was his first three-putt in 248 holes, since the fifth hole of the first round of the Memorial Tournament seven weeks earlier. That stretch included the remainder of the Memorial, the U.S. Open, the Western Open and 37 holes at St. Andrews.

It was a small hiccup during a 67 that doubled Woods's lead from three shots to six, by Saturday's end, over Duval and Bjørn. No player had ever squandered a six-shot advantage after three rounds at the Open. But Woods wasn't thinking about that; he was hell-bent on breaking Faldo's Open scoring record for 72 holes, which was 270 (18 under).

At 2:40, Woods began the final round paired with Duval, their first final-round grouping in a major. It was fitting, considering only a year earlier they'd hit golf balls together into darkness on an Irish field the week prior to the Open. As in 1999, they were number one and two in the world rankings, and even though Duval was six strokes back, he believed there was a chance at reeling Woods in. "You get to look him in the eye," Duval said of the benefits of being in the final twosome, which he predicted would be a "circus" and "exciting." Williams knew the pairing was beneficial to Woods, who admired Duval's game more than any other player's. He thought Duval would push him to the limit, narrowing Woods's focus and elevating his game.

Woods only birdied the fourth hole on the front nine to make the turn in 1 under (35), while Duval shot a 32 that brought him within three shots. At the 379-yard, par-4 10th, Woods drove the green, while Duval's tee shot was off the putting surface. After each hit their second shots, Duval was slightly farther away and was putting first for birdie. He had an opportunity to make it and put pressure on Woods to sink his birdie, or have his lead cut to just two. But Duval missed, and Woods added another two birdies in the next four holes. "The whole tournament could have gone the other way," Williams says.

Duval never recovered and eventually found the treacherous Road Hole bunker on No. 17. He took four shots to escape, made a quadruple-bogey 8 and plummeted to a tie for 11th at 7 under. His final-round 75 included a spirit-crushing back nine score of 7-over 43. The drop to T11 also cost Duval around $300,000 in prize money.

Late in the round, Woods reached an unprecedented 20 under, which had never been done in majors. But a bogey at the Road Hole brought him back to 19 under, and put his goal of Faldo's scoring record in jeopardy. He needed to make par on No. 18 to earn the record outright. Woods blasted a drive down the left side of the 18th fairway holding an eight-shot lead. With the victory beyond doubt, Williams fought back tears. His boss was about to complete the career grand slam at the cradle of the game. Thousands of fans walked in the fairway behind Woods and Williams, creating a rock concert atmosphere. Williams's mind flashed back to 1990, when his great friend Fanny Sunesson caddied for Faldo as he enjoyed a victory march up the 18th at St. Andrews. Williams was working for Raymond Floyd at the time, who had tied 39th and was already finished with his round. Williams waited around and walked up the 18th hole inside the ropes to support his friend. "It was just the most amazing scene I'd ever witnessed," he says. "It lit a fire inside of me; I wanted to walk up the 18th at St. Andrews with a player assured of winning the Open." When Williams saw the Open's enormous golden scoreboard and Woods's name, he felt the hairs stand on his neck. The stroll only lasted two or three minutes, but Woods and Williams were trying to take it all in. "You don't know if you're ever going to get that moment again," Williams says.

On the green, Woods carefully two-putted after overpowering his wedge shot, signing for a 69 and an eight-shot victory over Els and Bjørn, the largest margin of victory in the Open since 1913. Woods had completed the career grand slam, while securing the scoring record of 19 under (269) and becoming just the second champion to shoot all four rounds in the 60s. Woods had also avoided all 112 bunkers for the entire tournament, leaving no doubt in Williams's mind that it was the most complete performance he ever saw from Woods. "Avoiding every bunker made it a strategic dissection of the Old Course," Williams says.

After signing his scorecard, Woods walked onto the 18th green to accept the claret jug awarded to the Open champion, who is formally announced by the R&A as "the winner of the gold medal, and the Champion Golfer of the Year." Completing the career grand slam was so momentous in golf history that tour pros like Scott stayed around on the weekend, despite missing the cut. "It was such an incredible experience, for a landmark Tiger victory to be my first major right in the middle of Tigermania; it was indescribable," Scott says.

Although he had become the fifth player to complete the career slam—after Gene Sarazen, Ben Hogan, Player and Nicklaus—Woods remains the only golfer to complete the milestone at an Open at St. Andrews. Sarazen, the first to accomplish it, took the slam at the 1935 Masters, winning the second edition of the Augusta major. Hogan hit the mark at the 1953 Open at Carnoustie. Player wrapped up all four majors with his 1965 U.S. Open triumph at Bellerive in St. Louis. Nicklaus, at 26, was the youngest to bag the career slam at the 1966 Open at Muirfield. Winning the career slam was so elusive that some of history's best players—such as seven-time major winner Arnold Palmer and eight-time winner Tom Watson—never pulled it off. "I find it difficult to see the stars ever aligning again to allow another golfer to win the career slam at St. Andrews," Williams says.

Williams began to wonder whether there was an element of divine intervention in Woods's victories. He'd won the U.S. Open at Pebble Beach, in Nicklaus's final appearance in the event, a month before capturing the slam at the Home of Golf in Nicklaus's last British Open. "There was a lot of fascination in Tiger's red shirt on Sundays, but I didn't think it was a red shirt. It was almost like a red cape. So many of his wins you couldn't script how rare they were."

* * *

Late in the evening on Sunday, July 23, hours after the Open had ended, the bright lights of the R&A clubhouse beamed over the first and 18th holes, producing a magical shade of gold against the night sky. Woods stepped out of the Old Course Hotel, one hand clutching a small bag with Cartman, the satirical *South Park* cartoon character, stitched on its front, and the claret jug in the other. He ducked into a building to make a toast to the town of

St. Andrews and to pose for photos with R&A staff. After that, he met up with his entourage to board a private plane to Orlando chartered by IMG, the agency for both Woods and Duval. Woods was flanked by his girlfriend, Joanna Jagoda, as well as Williams, Duval and Isleworth neighbor Appleby, who made their way to Lucas Royal Air Force base, five minutes from the Old Course.

On board, champagne was popped and Williams held the claret jug for the first time. He thought the trophy was mesmerizing; its sterling-silver spout resembled a swan's beak while its handle was shaped like a bass clef. The jug was 21 inches tall, about 5.5 inches in diameter and weighed 5.5 pounds. The first claret jug was awarded to winner Tom Kidd at the 1873 Open, 13 years into the Open's timeline. A replica was introduced in 1928, and the original was placed in a museum. Still, this jug was 72 years old. Williams noticed two of his former bosses' names on there: Norman (1986, 1993) and Ian Baker-Finch (1991). The jug was originally designed to fit a bottle of claret, a British term for a Bordeaux red. Williams poured two Heinekens in there and smiled as the condensation chilled the jug into a misty shade of silver. He was the winning caddie, drinking out of the claret jug, a dream he had manifested 10 years earlier. "Even if your boss is Tiger Woods, you don't know if you're going to get the chance again. You have to drink from the jug," Williams says.

Williams handed it back to Woods, who ran his fingers over the letters of his own name. Williams was expecting his boss to be ecstatic about winning the career grand slam. After all, Woods had joined an illustrious group. "Tiger was far more focused on his record score of 19 under par; he didn't mention the career grand slam more than once or twice on that flight," Williams says. "He spoke about how thrilled he was to not only have joined the list of winners at St. Andrews—Nicklaus, Faldo, Seve Ballesteros and others—but also how chuffed he was with shooting the lowest score at St. Andrews out of all of them. It was a real badge of honor for him."

There was a slight air of awkwardness on the flight, though. Duval had a chance to reel in Woods but unraveled. Woods, meanwhile, was celebrating his first Open triumph. If only Woods could have told Duval it would be him winning the Open in 12 months' time, at Royal Lytham. "David was somewhat reserved, and I felt for him," Williams says.

Appleby, who shared 11th with Duval, 12 shots behind Woods, sat up in the front and soaked up being on a flight home with Duval and Woods, the kings of the sport. "It was a pretty small plane [relative to other private jets] and I was the rookie, you could say. I was the guy who didn't have a bed to sleep on," Appleby says. He felt there was a business-as-usual atmosphere to the celebrations, as though Woods had expected to win. It was still a party, but not a rager.

Williams walked off Woods's private plane at the Orlando airport after 2 A.M. on Monday, July 24. Not even the stinking hot humidity of central Florida in late July could dampen his spirits after what had unfolded in Scotland. All Williams could think about was the spectacular giant golden leaderboard reading "Well done, Tiger . . . See you at Lytham . . . 2001." After a quick nap at Woods's house, Williams returned to the airport for a connecting flight to Bend, Oregon, and was back in his Sunriver house for the sleep of a lifetime.

* * *

Sunriver is a pocket of Pacific Northwest paradise set among high desert country in central Oregon, along the Deschutes River, 175 miles southeast of Portland. It reminded Williams of the mountainous regions of New Zealand, like Queenstown on the South Island, so he purchased a property there during his years caddying for Floyd. If Woods had one week off, Williams would stay in Sunriver. If he had two weeks between tournaments, Williams would usually fly home to New Zealand. But with New Zealand in the middle of winter, Williams stayed in Oregon. Once the significance of the Open settled in, Williams started remembering random details. The first was a memento Woods kept as a good luck charm—a wooden tee supplied by the tournament—that Williams would be responsible for keeping safely in the golf bag.

For his drive on the second hole in round one, Woods used a white tee given to competitors with "Open Championship 2000" printed on it. That wooden tee didn't break, and Woods had hit a great drive, so he used it again on the third hole. Despite the firm Scottish turf, the tee still didn't snap at impact. Woods considered it a good omen and used that tee for the entire tournament—except on par 3s, when he would pick up a discarded tee on the ground. Woods immediately retired the tee to a Stanford University Cardinals pouch within his bag, where his wallet, phone and watch lived during tournament rounds. Williams learned Woods was somewhat superstitious, at least a healthy amount, and wanted to use that to his advantage. Occasionally, if things weren't going well at a tournament, Williams would urge Woods to reach in and grab the 2000 Open tee; holding it might summon good luck. Eight years later, in the first nine holes of the 2008 U.S. Open at Torrey Pines, Woods was in agony, playing with a broken leg that would later require surgery. "I said to Tiger, 'Get the 2000 Open tee out. But don't just hold it; put it in your f——g pocket,'" Williams recalls.

Three weeks in Oregon allowed Williams to repay a moving gesture from the staff at SunRiver Golf Club, whom he'd befriended. In 1999, they were ecstatic when Williams secured his first major win as a caddie with Woods. To celebrate, Bob Garza got together with the greenkeeping staff and threw a surprise party for Williams. They sent him out for a game of golf, so that dozens of guests could file in without him seeing. Coming up to the 18th hole, Williams noticed more cars in the parking lot than usual. When he walked into the clubhouse, they gave him a standing ovation. "I was really moved by that," Williams says. He then promised that every time Woods won a major, there'd be pizza and beer on him upon his next visit to SunRiver. When Woods won the 2000 U.S. Open at Pebble Beach, Williams flew straight home to New Zealand, but organized pizzas anyway. Now, Williams was able to organize lunch for SunRiver staff in the greenkeepers' shed, on Thursday, July 27 at 11 A.M. "I had come to know the guy at the local pizza shop and he knew the drill; if I called, I was buying 12 large pizzas and several cases of beer," Williams says.

The following day, Williams, a keen outdoorsman, volunteered to help the greenkeepers on the golf course on a beautiful Oregon summer's day. They could hardly believe it; the man who was on TV carrying Woods's clubs only days earlier at St. Andrews was now raking bunkers and cutting grass. But that was Williams's outlet, his reality check from the circus of Tigermania. "I tried not to get too caught up in all the hype," Williams says. "When I'd come back to New Zealand, or Oregon, I loved mowing lawns or washing cars."

It was going to be impossible to ignore the significance of the Open when, three weeks later, Williams was back at Isleworth to meet Woods and head off to the Buick Open. Woods had arranged for a photo of himself holding up the claret jug on the 18th green at St. Andrews to give to Williams. Woods was flashing a pearly-white smile and wearing a deep scarlet Nike sweater as he delicately supported the base of the old trophy with his left hand. Underneath the jug, Woods wrote a thoughtful tribute to Williams for the week he'd spent mapping the Old Course:

To Stevie,
No bunkers, good navigating by the caddie!
Tiger Woods.

CHAPTER 5

YOU'RE TIGER F—G WOODS

Rock and roll legend Bob Seger walked out onto the first tee at Warwick Hills golf course in Grand Blanc, Michigan, on a steaming-hot Wednesday morning, July 29, for a six fifty pro-am tee time with Woods. It was the 2009 Buick Open, and the car manufacturer had paid Woods handsomely to be an ambassador for 10 years. Part of his deal included playing in the Michigan event it had bankrolled for over 60 years, when it became the first corporate sponsor of the PGA Tour in 1958. The beloved tournament was not far from the company's headquarters in Buick City, 70 miles north of Detroit, and with Seger and Woods, Buick was going to make a splash.

Seger, with his trademark white beard, was almost as recognizable as Woods, at least in Michigan. He'd grown up in nearby Ann Arbor and was the singer of "Night Moves" and "Old Time Rock & Roll," among other hits. Sweat was already soaking through

Seger's sky-blue golf polo, perhaps a bad color choice for a round of golf in the late July humidity. But perspiration wasn't going to stop Seger, an avid golfer, from playing with Woods. And money wasn't going to stop Seger's fellow amateur playing partners in the pro-am group, either. At least one other member of the group reportedly paid more than $100,000 to play 18 holes with Woods and Seger.

Williams noticed Seger was wearing a golf glove on each hand, which wasn't common. His manager was caddying for him and, walking down the first hole, Williams broke the ice by saying, "Your man is really sweating here." The manager responded, "Bob's not used to being out of bed this early in the morning." Williams laughed, intrigued to say the least. It turned out Seger—who had found out the previous summer he was going to play with Woods in the Buick pro-am—was just incredibly nervous. He had even practiced six days a week in preparation. "Yeah, nerves," he said after his round. "Oh my gosh, through the first six holes I was a wreck. To stand that close . . . to someone that great . . . is such a privilege."

Seger was much calmer when an opportunity appeared to do something closer to his line of work. The group arrived at the 16th at Warwick Hills, a par 5, which was surrounded by new houses under construction. Each house had a boom box set up in the backyard. Contractors must've known Seger and Woods were coming through, as the moment the group reached the fairway, the boom boxes started blasting "Night Moves" in unison. The classic rock song's lyrics and piano riff reverberated across the 16th: *Workin' on our night moves. Tryin' to lose the awkward teenage blues*. Seger started belting out the vocals to his own tune and danced his way up the fairway, while thousands of fans who'd come out to watch Woods started singing along. "Bob certainly put on quite the show walking and singing," Williams says.

Woods went on to win the event, which was the final edition before Buick pulled its sponsorship. The Seger pro-am was the highlight for Woods and Williams in a tournament that sat in a tricky window of the golf schedule. Woods's calendar was a balancing act; he had to play enough tournaments to be sharp for the majors, but not so many that fatigue was a risk. Woods preferred brutally difficult courses, where his talents would shine brighter. He avoided events like the Bob Hope Classic in the California desert or the Phoenix Open, whose host courses were considered easy for tour pros. That had the effect of allowing more pros to make more birdies, thus deepening the competition. In 2000, Warwick Hills, while narrow from the tees, measured 7,101 yards, which wasn't considered long. Woods had a theory for courses like Warwick Hills and other easier courses on the PGA Tour. Those events had fields of 144 players, of which Woods felt 100 were capable of shooting 62, 63 or 64. But a challenging course like Muirfield Village, host of the Memorial Tournament, had a field of 120, of which Woods fancied 30 players were capable of shooting 64 or better.

Woods also wanted his schedule to include events hosted by golf's greatest champions, like Arnold Palmer, Jack Nicklaus and Byron Nelson. Then there were sponsor commitments like the Buick Open.

As Buick's $25 million man, Woods was obligated to play in the 2000 Buick Open from August 10 to 13, the week prior to the PGA Championship at Valhalla Golf Club in Louisville, Kentucky. Woods rarely played the week before a major, opting to finalize his preparations at home at Isleworth. The event was eventually brought forward a week, in 2003, to sit two weeks before the PGA. "Typically, Tiger wouldn't have played a course like Warwick Hills outside of signing with Buick," Williams says.

In 2000, though, the Buick was Woods's 15th official event of the year. He'd won six times, two of which were majors, in stunning fashion. Woods chose the Monday and Tuesday, August 7 and 8, to fly on his private jet to Louisville for a reconnaissance mission to Valhalla. Woods found it useful to play a major championship host before the tournament chaos became an obstacle. Louisville hadn't hosted a major in four years, and didn't have an annual PGA Tour event. There was going to be a lot of noise and distractions come tournament week. Williams tagged along to Valhalla, and used the scouting trip as an opportunity to glean information from the professional golf staff about nuances of the course.

The newspapers in Michigan noticed Woods's absence from the typical Tuesday practice round. An article in the *Detroit Free Press* the following day titled "Tuesdays Without Tiger" read: "Tiger Woods, Buick's prize pitchman since December, must report to work for the auto company early this morning. Woods was nowhere in sight [Tuesday]." He finally arrived in Michigan on Tuesday night and teed off at 7 A.M. at the Buick Wednesday pro-am with three Buick car dealers and a brand manager.

Pennsylvania native Rocco Mediate, a gregarious personality, eventually won the tournament while Woods tied 11th, seven strokes back. There were 27 golfers who finished at 10 under par or better. The newspapers sensed Woods's restlessness, writing on August 10, "Woods would rather not play this week, with the PGA a week [later], but Buick is one of his sponsors." Woods conceded that while he wanted to win, he had one eye on the PGA.

Woods's body and golf swing were readjusting to competition from a break after the Open at St. Andrews. He had altered his swing slightly for the windy conditions and firm turf in Scotland in July. The Buick Open presented a chance to dial his swing back to U.S. conditions: hitting the ball higher with his irons and shaping the ball in different directions with the driver.

Whenever he returned from a break, Woods worked furiously on the fundamentals: grip on the club, posture, alignment (aiming) and the position of the club on the backswing. He'd go through a checklist. When Harmon wasn't at a tournament, Woods would often ask his caddie to look at certain positions while standing behind him.

Woods and Williams flew back to Orlando on the Sunday night after the Buick Open to spend Monday practicing at Isleworth. "Every time it got closer to a major, his practice would become more intense and he'd rehearse a lot of specific shots for that upcoming major," Williams says. The course might require a lot of drives shaped from left to right, or, in Valhalla's case, a lot of high approach shots with less spin due to the soft greens. When he arrived at a major venue, Woods didn't need to practice or change anything. On Tuesday morning, August 15, Woods and Williams left Orlando for Louisville, hoping to defend Woods's 1999 PGA Championship title.

Valhalla Golf Club was designed by Nicklaus and opened in 1986, not long after the Golden Bear had won the Masters for his 18th major. Some 20 miles east of Louisville, Valhalla sits on a 486-acre property with Floyd's Fork, a 60-mile tributary of the Salt River, snaking through the golf course. Valhalla was awarded the 1996 PGA Championship and again in 2000. The crowds at Valhalla were expected to push over 35,000 for each of the four tournament rounds, some spectators hoping to see Woods for the first time, given he hadn't turned pro until after the 1996 PGA. More than 115 Jefferson County police officers worked the 2000 PGA, in addition to contracted security guards. The same two police officers detailed Woods the entire week.

More than 25,000 fans turned out to watch Woods play a practice round with O'Meara at 11:30 A.M. on Tuesday. "It was just bedlam," Williams says. The hysteria had been ramped up days before Woods even arrived in Louisville, when PGA of America officials announced on the weekend prior that Woods would be grouped for the opening rounds with Nicklaus, who was playing his final PGA Championship, and Vijay Singh. Singh had won a second career major months earlier at the 2000 Masters.

There was no love lost between Woods and Singh, a towering Fijian who had scrapped his way through golf tours in Asia and Europe en route to the PGA Tour in 1993. Tigermania had reached unfathomable levels, and Singh appeared to be among a group of tour pros fatigued at the hype. They constantly fielded questions from reporters about Woods, and watched, or read, as pundits picked him as the favorite for every tournament he teed up in.

Williams knew his boss received a lion's share of the attention, and it was obvious that some great players were feeling overlooked. But Williams felt the hype was nothing Woods tried to encourage; he just wanted to win. "There were certain players who gave Tiger the respect he had earned, and it seemed Vijay was one of the guys who paid Tiger very little of that," Williams says. Typically, at tour events, the winner from the previous tournament was congratulated by all their peers. But Williams noticed Singh was usually silent. He was intensely competitive and didn't want to pump up his rivals.

Nicklaus and Woods were also rivals, in some ways, but from different eras. Their grouping at Valhalla—the only time they were paired together at the majors—was seen as a symbolic passing of the baton from the greatest golfer ever to his successor. Woods was attempting to win a fifth career major, nearly a third of the way into Nicklaus's record 18.

The grouping was nearly over before it began. Nicklaus was on the fourth hole on Wednesday playing a practice round when he was informed his mother, Helen, age 90, had passed away. Tempted to withdraw from the tournament and rush home to Columbus, Ohio, a tearful Nicklaus said, "I think I should stay [and play] for her."

Nicklaus, Singh and Woods walked onto the first tee at Valhalla for the first round on a sweltering hot Thursday morning, August 17. The trio posed for a picture, then struck their first tee shots just after 9:13 A.M. Crowds for day one reached almost 40,000, with a large percentage following Woods's group. The gallery, at times, was 20 people deep on either side, craning their necks to get a glimpse of Woods.

Woods was normally a quick player with a deliberate stride, but Williams noticed a slower gait during those first two rounds with Nicklaus. He was more focused than usual. "He was really into it; he wanted to impress Jack," Williams says.

Australian pro Greg Chalmers teed off at 9:40 A.M. Thursday, three groups behind Woods. He compared the atmosphere to a rock concert; the excitement was palpable but there was also an expectation for Woods to perform. "I thought that was a big advantage because the crowds gave Tiger energy," he says. Chalmers, playing a major for only the third time, was so nervous he nearly shot his way out of the tournament in the first 30 minutes. He opened with a double-bogey, and at the par-5 second, left-handed Chalmers cold-topped his second shot. He almost missed the golf ball, striking it above the equator—an embarrassing shot for a pro. "I thought it was going to be a long week," Chalmers says.

Woods was in cruise control as he shot a 66 to share the first-round lead with Scott Dunlap at 6 under par. His ball-striking was sublime, but he only used a driver five times. A 328-yard bomb off the 10th tee showed he was mixing power with strategy. Woods hit 11 of 14 fairways, 16 greens in regulation and needed only 29 putts on day one. Nicklaus noted Woods still missed a half dozen more birdie putts and that he could have shot 60. "Phenomenal control, phenomenal concentration," Nicklaus said. "I wouldn't want to spend the next 20 years trying to beat him. I take that back; of course I would." Dunlap nearly raised a white flag when he said Woods winning the previous two majors by a combined 23 shots made his presence at Valhalla "nothing more than discouraging to the rest of the field."

Play was suspended at 8:27 P.M. while 18 golfers were still on the course. Nicklaus, who finished just after lunch, had enough time to fly to Ohio for the evening to be with his family and return to Kentucky for his 1:25 tee time Friday with Woods and Singh.

Friday at Valhalla was slated to be Nicklaus's last-ever round in the majors. He had shot 77 on Thursday but birdied the first two holes Friday to get to 3 over. He was sitting on the cut line, but the 60-year-old rolled his sleeves up and fought until the very end. On the par-5 18th, Nicklaus needed an eagle 3 to make the halfway cut on the number. Only problem was, he was 72 yards from the green and would have to hole out a sand wedge for his third shot. Nicklaus struck the ball perfectly, sending it hurtling toward the flag as it pitched past and spun backward, nearly going in for eagle. Williams overheard the discussion between Nicklaus and his caddie, who was his son, Steve Nicklaus, and was stunned that the legend truly believed he could hole it for eagle. "It was like watching an artist at his best; he never gave up," Williams says. Nicklaus signed for a 1-under 71 but missed the cut by one shot.

Williams could feel the emotion of Nicklaus signing off from the majors and fought back tears himself. He flashed back to a compliment Nicklaus gave him years earlier when Williams worked for Ray Floyd. Floyd was playing the Skins Game tournament in Hawaii on the PGA Tour seniors and beat Nicklaus at Mauna Lani on the Big Island to win the 1997 edition. Nicklaus put his arm around Williams, 33 at the time, and told him he had the utmost respect for his ability as a caddie; how scrupulous he was on every shot, of every round. "He said he could see that I was improving Ray's performance and I held that compliment close to my heart," Williams says.

Woods shot 67 and took the 36-hole lead for the third straight major. Nicklaus had never played with Woods in a tournament and said, "He is so much better than I thought; it actually amazes me." Nicklaus took Williams aside, like he had in 1997, and said, "Just make sure you stick with this guy, Steve."

In round three, Woods teed off in the final group with Dunlap just after two thirty and cruised through the front nine. But on the back nine, a three-putt double-bogey on No. 12, and a bogey on 15, forced him to dig deep. Woods needed to birdie the 18th just to book a spot in Sunday's final pairing. He did, signing for a 70 and holding on to a one-shot lead.

Woods's playing partner for the final day was Bob May, an unheralded pro from Los Angeles to most people. But Woods knew exactly who he was. May was once a junior golf star in Southern California, hailing from Hacienda, in the eastern suburbs of L.A. He was the son of a gas station owner and had won several American Junior Golf Association (AJGA) events in his home state and around the country. He went on to play college golf at the elite Oklahoma State University. At the 1991 Walker Cup, an amateur version of the Ryder Cup, May helped the U.S. team to an away victory against Europe at Portmarnock, in Ireland. Woods, seven years younger than May, had grown up in nearby Cypress, closely following May's junior golf records, determined to beat them.

As a tour pro, May had less success, although he had won the British Masters on the European Tour in 1999. In 2000, he had also finished T-23 at the U.S. Open and T-11 at the Open Championship. Based in Las Vegas, May would spend weeks at a time playing in Europe during a five-year span, before getting his PGA Tour card in the U.S. through qualifying school. Earlier in his career, he had been funded for a year by Hollywood actor Joe Pesci, who loved golf and had a mutual friend with May in L.A. May stood five-foot-seven but, as one U.K. newspaper described him, he had thick, muscular arms that "would serve as decent legs for a sprinter." A fellow European Tour pro had described May's prodigious talent for competing as "having a season ticket for the leaderboard." After a good 1999 season in Europe, May arrived at Valhalla ranked 48th in the world.

May's regular caddie, a New Zealander named Max Cunningham, had grown up at Paraparaumu Beach and knew Williams well. Cunningham was based in England, but didn't make the trip over to the U.S. for Valhalla. He had health issues that required him to avoid the extreme heat and humidity in Kentucky. "I can't imagine what he was thinking, sitting on the couch watching what unfolded on the final day," Williams says.

The contrast in appearance between Woods and May was striking as both teed off at 2:30 P.M. on Sunday, August 20, at Valhalla. Woods's athletic frame was draped head to toe in Nike apparel: a loose-fitting scarlet shirt and black slacks. May had a shorter, stockier frame and had chosen a khaki and olive outfit, looking like a military officer as he prepared for battle with the superstar. The stoic expression visible from underneath his PING hat was a sign of things to come.

May struck his opening tee shot, the first time millions of sports fans around the world had ever seen him play. His swing was smooth yet had a noticeable hitch on the downswing. But that didn't give Woods any extra confidence; he knew May was relentless. Woods was trying to become the first player since Ben Hogan in 1953 to win three majors in a calendar year. May was looking to spoil the party.

Through four holes, it looked like May just might. He had grabbed two early birdies while Woods had bogeyed No. 2. Suddenly, May led Woods by two shots. May bogeyed No. 6, but so did Woods. Williams wasn't worried, though. After a year in the job, he noticed it was almost a relief when Woods made an early bogey or two, because he knew that would light a fire for the rest of the day. From the seventh, Woods began to stir, making four birdies in the next six holes. May, though, peeled off three consecutive birdies of his own from the 10th.

"Walking off the 12th tee, Tiger called me over and said, 'Hey, Stevie, this guy will not back down. Trust me, I know him. We need to go hard,'" Williams says. He thought it was unusual for Woods to acknowledge his opponent mid-battle, but his observation was accurate.

At the par-3 14th, both hit good tee shots. Woods drained a downhill birdie putt from 15 feet, but May matched it. At the par-4 15th, May hit a 7-iron to six feet while Woods hit a poor approach. Woods was on the ropes until a dramatic twist moments later.

May, who was looking to earn a two-shot swing on the hole, missed his short birdie putt while Woods managed to sink a difficult 15-footer for par. At the par-4 17th, Williams sized up Woods's second shot when he decided to change his entire approach to caddying. Williams had occasionally experimented with altering the real distance to the green on approach shots to steer his boss into hitting a certain club that Williams instinctively felt was the right choice. It was easier to fudge the numbers than to get into a debate with Woods. Williams tried it only in regular tournaments, but he felt it was the right time to try it in a major. "I'd figured out that when Tiger got a perfect yardage, he'd hit a perfect shot," Williams says. The second shot into the 17th was 104 yards, but Williams told him it was 98. It was a ballsy call to make, given the shot was over a bunker. Handing Woods one club less could see the ball not carry far enough and drop into the sand, and coming in with height, it likely would have buried into the face. "I wanted Tiger to hit a 60-degree wedge because I knew he had adrenaline and a 56-degree wedge was going to fly over the green," Williams says. That was too much to convey in the moment, so he lied about the yardage being 98 yards. "I was sweating on that shot," Williams says. Woods struck it close, made birdie and drew level with May. One hole remained.

May and Woods reached the par-5 18th in two shots. May, though, was heavy-handed and putted his eagle attempt off the green. His birdie putt coming back took an eternity to reach the hole, wiggling in two different directions before sneaking in the side of the hole. Bizarrely, it threw the pressure back on Woods to make his downhill birdie to force a playoff. Miss it, and Woods, the world number one, would have lost a significant battle to a player who had not previously recorded a top 10 at a major. Woods told himself, "You're Tiger f——ng Woods. Bury this putt," before draining it. He had shot 67, and roared to the crowd with two huge fist pumps.

Woods had hit at least 11 fairways every day, and at least 15 greens in regulation in three of four rounds. But a three-putt each round from Friday to Sunday held him back. May, meanwhile, posted three consecutive 66s from round two. He had beaten Woods by six shots across those 54 holes. It was Woods's opening 66 that, in the end, kept him hanging in there with May.

"I really believe Tiger being paired with Jack was one of the reasons he had shot 66 in the first round of his first major playing with Jack," Williams says.

Woods and May, who finished at 18 under (270) in regulation, had both broken the PGA Championship scoring record. The PGA of America had also changed its format for extra holes, from sudden death—where golfers play as many holes as required until someone records the lowest score—to a three-hole aggregate. On the first playoff hole, the 16th, May nearly holed his chip shot for birdie and tapped in for par. Woods had 25 feet for birdie and it inspired one of his most famous celebrations. Woods ran after his rolling ball, hanging his right shoulder low. As the ball tracked toward the hole, Woods pointed at it with his finger, almost willing it into the hole. It dropped, and Woods took a one-stroke lead. Both players missed the green and saved par on the second playoff hole. At the 18th, the third extra hole, a strange incident unfolded that was never truly explained and was labeled by some fans as the Phantom Bounce Theory. Woods hooked his 3-wood tee shot left into the trees, but after several seconds of the ball disappearing, it shot backward along a cart path and out into the rough. Fans ran after the ball. "At the following tournament, there was a lot of talk that somehow the ball might've got help from someone in the gallery, but I don't think that was the case," Williams says. The Associated Press spoke to the 18th-hole marshal, Tim Gilpin, who said the ball struck a sycamore tree and dropped straight down onto a cart path, bouncing high enough to hit the tree again. The ball then shot down the cart path and onto trampled dirt and rough. "That was all gravity and Mother Nature. Everybody was around it, but nobody touched it," Gilpin said.

Woods took advantage of his good break by making par to win the aggregate playoff by one shot. He was officially the PGA champion. Only he and Hogan had won three majors in a calendar year. Woods had won three majors in 2000, each with a scoring record. At the U.S. Open (15) and British Open (8), he had set records for margin of victory. Valhalla was also Woods's first title defense at a major, having hoisted the enormous silver Wanamaker Trophy in Chicago in 1999. "This was probably the most exciting [of the three in 2000]," Woods said afterward.

Both he and May made five birdies and two impressive par saves on the closing nine holes in regulation. "That's as good as it gets; we played one of the greatest duels in major championship history," Woods said. At the Wanamaker Trophy presentation, Woods put his arm around May and told him it was a great match and that he'd played incredible golf. "He was very nice to me, very complimentary," May said.

As for May's regular caddie, Cunningham, he was devastated to miss the tournament but saw the silver lining. "I felt gutted watching it on the [TV] but I'm pleased for Bob; it'll do his world ranking a lot of good and it'll benefit me, too," he said. May pocketed $540,000 and jumped 18 places in the world rankings to 30th. The following morning, May walked onto a flight out of Louisville when CBS golf announcer Jim Nantz, who was sitting in first class, noticed May walk past him and into coach without any passengers recognizing him. Meanwhile, travelers *had* noticed Nantz, remarking what a tournament it was and congratulating him on a great broadcast. "And there was the costar of this epic movie," Nantz said of May sitting behind him.

After the carousel of mini functions for the PGA champion, Woods limped into a limousine in Valhalla's parking lot. "My calf is killing me," Woods said. Two consecutive tournament weeks, the second of which was 75 holes of major championship golf, had exhausted Woods.

A year earlier, Woods had arrived at the 1999 PGA Championship nervously searching for a second career major. Now he was leaving Valhalla having won four of the past five. "We are witnessing a phenomenon here that the game may never see again," eight-time major winner Tom Watson said. Williams didn't see another duel like it for the remaining 41 majors he caddied for Woods. "That was Tiger's biggest-ever battle in the majors, no doubt," Williams says. "Tiger respected Bob and enjoyed that day more than other battles because he was forced to elevate his game to win."

After Woods and May, Thomas Bjørn finished in third at 13 under. Aussie duo Chalmers and Stuart Appleby tied fourth at 12 under alongside Spaniard José Maria Olazábal. Chalmers had birdied the 12th on Sunday to get to within two shots of May, who was leading.

Only two months earlier, at the Memorial Tournament in Dublin, Ohio, Chalmers had a light bulb moment when he realized Woods was going to dominate golf for decades. He had first seen Woods's gifts while playing with him at the 1994 Eisenhower Trophy, also called the World Amateur Teams Championship, in the final round at Le Golf National southwest of Paris. The U.S.A. won, and Chalmers recalls Woods being erratic off the tee. "But his good shots were better than any player I'd ever seen," Chalmers says. Six years later, he played with Woods again when he scraped into the elite Memorial Tournament as the first alternate for Craig Stadler, who withdrew. Chalmers was grouped with Woods for the first two rounds. "He hit four shots in the second round that made me want to clap; I had to remember I was playing, too," Chalmers says. As a tour pro, Chalmers could move the ball aggressively left to right, and right to left, but Woods and Greg Norman were the only two players Chalmers saw who could deliberately make the ball turn one or two yards, gently, toward the target. "Subtle movement is the hardest," Chalmers says. Being an Aussie, Chalmers had known Williams for years on the Australian tour. He saw Williams as an alpha male and ultracompetitive, bringing an energy Woods thrived on. "Tiger was the most talented player, ever. Stevie and Tiger were a recipe for success," Chalmers says.

* * *

As exhausted as Woods seemed after the showdown with May, he had to fly immediately to Akron, Ohio, for the World Golf Championships-NEC Invitational. It was an elite event that debuted on the schedule a year earlier, and which Woods had won, at the challenging South Course at Firestone Country Club.

Late on Sunday, August 27, 2000, Woods stood on the right side of the 18th fairway at Firestone with an inconceivable 10-shot lead. It was the final hole of the $5 million tournament, and thousands of fans had surrounded the par 4 hoping to get a glimpse of Woods as he romped to yet another dominant PGA Tour win. The fans, though, could hardly make out the superstar's figure. Total darkness had engulfed the course because a storm delay had forced Woods and his playing partner, Hal Sutton, to complete the final round at about eight thirty. The northeastern Ohio crowds weren't deterred by the late finish, nor the weather. Woods was fresh off his captivating PGA Championship victory and Akron was enjoying watching the new champion in person. He dazzled them all week, shooting a 61 in the second round, the equal-lowest score of his PGA Tour career.

On the Sunday, Woods had 168 yards to the 18th green and chose to hit a smooth 8-iron. His ball pitched just past the flag and spun back, settling two feet from the cup, sending the crowd wild. Fans held up burning lighters, making Firestone look more like a rock concert than a golf tournament. The 8-iron shot would eventually be dubbed the Shot in the Dark, one of Woods's most famous swings in a non-major.

Woods had put an exclamation mark on his eighth title for the year 2000, securing a second straight year with at least eight victories. Moving to the green, the TV cameras cut through the darkness and illuminated Woods and Williams exchanging a double high five before Woods ripped his glove off excitedly.

Since Woods had brought Williams on to the team 17 months earlier, they had frequently discussed his career goal for major wins. Nicklaus had won 18, between the 1962 U.S. Open and the 1986 Masters. Woods had always rounded up to 20 from the necessary 19 in those chats with Williams, but the caddie's favorite number was 21. It was even emblazoned on the saloon car he raced in New Zealand. Woods would humor Williams by jokingly agreeing to the number, at least verbally. Williams turned around to Woods and joked that, after a fantastic year, it might be time to retire from caddying. "No way; we've got to win 20 majors before your lazy ass can retire," Woods said. The pair frequently joked about the idea of walking off into the sunset if Woods ever surpassed Nicklaus. "He wouldn't hit another golf shot in a tournament and I'd hang the bag up," Williams says. Williams piped back, "Well, I'm only sticking around if you make the goal of 21 majors." So, Woods took out a Sharpie and scribbled *21* on the Nike glove's palm and threw it to Williams, whose eyes lit up. It's why they had so gleefully exchanged high fives. Woods wasn't referring to the 21-under-par score he was about to finish the tournament on with a certain birdie to win by 11; that had only reminded him of the bigger picture. The goal of 21 majors was now in writing.

Williams considered the glove so monumental that he kept it permanently in his backpack. "I put it in a Ziploc bag to make sure it didn't get stained or aerate too quickly," Williams says. The glove looked like every other that Woods wore in 2000: white synthetic leather with a black strap on the front, emblazoned with a Nike swoosh. But with its extra meaning, Williams would often look at it during tough times, which, while rare, did happen. "Sometimes, the job could be a bit overwhelming with the pressure of Tiger's expectations to win every single event," Williams says. There was also the continuous travel and the exhaustion of being around a global superstar, day in and day out. That feeling of being consumed by the topic of Woods and his majors quest was why Williams never moved to the U.S.; he flew home to New Zealand frequently during the season to escape the professional golf scene. That was despite the impracticality of a caddie on the PGA Tour living 9,000 miles from the U.S. "I just had to get away from golf and the spotlight on Tiger; at home, my friends would rarely ask me about work," Williams says. It was also part of the reason why Williams and Woods drew a line between their burgeoning friendship on the course and many aspects of their personal lives. Apart from topics they frequently discussed, like sports, Williams's car racing hobby and Woods's fascination with video games and cartoons, the pair kept plenty to themselves. Not that it took much effort; Woods could compartmentalize better than anyone Williams knew. And Williams cherished the ability to switch off from Woods and golf when he was back in New Zealand.

After Akron, Woods still had five more tournaments to close out 2000, and two unofficial events. He had a measly eight days off before flying north to Toronto with Williams. The Canadian Open, which was among the 10 oldest golf tournaments in the world, was being held at the Glen Abbey course in Oakville on the western outskirts of Toronto. Glen Abbey was Nicklaus's first-ever solo course design in 1976.

On the Wednesday night before the tournament, in downtown Toronto, Williams, Woods and O'Meara were having dinner at a Boston Pizza when O'Meara decided to needle Woods, whom he called The Kid.

"I just realized, I have something you don't, Kid," O'Meara smirked.

"Oh, yeah? What might that be?" Woods asked.

"A Canadian Open," O'Meara, the 1995 champion at Glen Abbey, said.

"For now." Woods smiled.

Once the tournament kicked off, Woods wasn't feeling good about his swing but had managed to stay high on the leaderboard. On Saturday night, Woods and Williams were driving back into Toronto along the Queen Elizabeth freeway when Woods asked his caddie to stop the car. "I've got to do something," Woods said. Woods climbed out of the car, took out a 7-iron from the trunk and began rehearsing swings for several minutes on the side of the highway. He hopped back in the car, looked at a bewildered Williams and said, "I've got it. We'll be good tomorrow."

Coming down the last hole on Sunday, the par-5 18th, Woods had a one-shot lead over New Zealand pro Grant Waite. Playing with Waite was a dream scenario for Williams. "A Kiwi pro in the final group with Tiger, playing well, was sentimental for me," Williams says. Waite had found the 18th fairway with his drive, while Woods had pushed his into a fairway bunker on the right. For his second shot, Woods needed to strike the ball cleanly with a 6-iron and fly it over water to a narrow green. "It was pouring rain and the bunker was wet, so when the ball rolled through the bunker, it had made a little track and sat down in its tracks," Williams says. If Woods didn't pick the ball cleanly with his strike, it would grab too much sand for the ball to fly at 100 percent velocity and it would likely drop into the water. Woods almost had to deliberately strike the equator of the ball, hitting it thin, to avoid the sand but still generate enough force to reach the green.

Waite, meanwhile, had reached the green in two and had a putt for eagle. Woods hoisted his fairway bunker shot way into the air, the ball soaring over the water and past the hole. He two-putted for birdie and a one-shot victory. Similarly to the Shot in the Dark, the 2000 Canadian Open fairway bunker became one of Woods's most famous swings. For Williams, he learned an important competitive trait in that fairway: Woods had mentally conceded Waite was going to make his eagle putt, so he aggressively tried to make a birdie to force a playoff. Waite only managed birdie, but that didn't matter. "Whenever one of Tiger's opponents made an incredible putt, or chipped in, or hit a shot close to the hole, Tiger was always mentally prepared because he'd played out the scenario in his mind," Williams says.

Woods walked out of the winner's press conference clutching the Canadian Open trophy, reached into his pocket and called O'Meara. "Hey, M.O., now I have something you don't have," Woods said. "My name is way further down the trophy than yours."

The remainder of Woods's 2000 season was incomprehensible. He had three consecutive top fives on the PGA Tour before playing several "silly season" events, a nickname given to unofficial tournaments held at the end of the year. At the Grand Slam of Golf exhibition in Hawaii, Woods made eagle on the last hole to force a playoff with Singh, and then another eagle to beat him. He won the WGC-World Cup of Golf in Argentina, teaming up with Duval and defeating home heroes Angel Cabrera and Eduardo Romero.

In all, Woods played eight consecutive weeks, flew 27,000 miles and passed through every time zone on the planet. Among those weeks was the 2000 Presidents Cup in Virginia, where the U.S.

team grabbed a home victory over the International side. But one incident soured an otherwise spirited event. On the final day, Woods was drawn to play Singh, a star member of the International team, in singles play. Singh's caddie, Paul Tesori, arrived on the driving range wearing a hat with "Tiger who?" stitched on the back. Woods was furious. Williams agreed; it went beyond a prank and wasn't good-spirited, especially considering Woods's success in 2000. With three majors and a career grand slam, Woods was generating global interest in golf. "When Tiger was physically upset, he'd walk quicker, he'd be completely silent and there'd be a look of anger on his face. When he arrived at the range, he said to me, 'Can you f——g believe that hat? At a *Presidents Cup*?' It was up there with probably the top three most disappointed I've ever seen Tiger on a golf course," Williams says. "I don't think anybody else thought that was funny, either."

The match became heated, with Woods not conceding a putt of Singh's longer than 12 inches all day. In match play, a golfer is allowed to tell their opponent that a short putt is "good," meaning they can pick it up and count it as successfully holed. Conceding opponents' short putts is considered good etiquette. But there was almost no etiquette that day while Woods went on to win the match, 2 and 1 (two holes up with one hole to play). "Tiger was not someone you wanted to piss off and he put 120 percent into the match," Williams says. Tesori and Woods, years later, shook hands and forgave each other.

Toward the end of 2000, Williams was at home in New Zealand, preparing for the debut event of his new charitable organization, the Steve Williams Foundation. Williams created the organization, at the age of 37, at the encouragement of Woods's father, Earl. Earl was integral to Williams's philanthropic efforts in New Zealand. In 1999 and 2000, Earl had noticed Williams's soaring popularity in

New Zealand and urged him to give back. "He told me how to start a foundation, exactly what to look out for, the best ways it could be run and how to have the most charitable impact," Williams says. Years later, Williams was made a member of the New Zealand Order of Merit for services to youth sport and recreation and, in 2008, he and his wife, Kirsty, donated NZ$1 million to a cancer ward at the Starship Children's Hospital in Auckland. "That is my proudest moment and finest achievement in anything," Williams says.

Williams married Kirsty Miller in 2006, six years after he met her. Their introduction came in late 2000, at the foundation's first charity golf day at Waikanae Golf Club, only five miles from his childhood course of Paraparaumu Beach. Kirsty's father, Ian Miller, was Waikanae's club president at the time and his daughter played in the charity day. At one of the par 3s, Williams stood on the tee all day and greeted golfers as they played through. He noticed Kirsty and made a mental note to talk to her later that night in the clubhouse. Kirsty was helping her father clean up after the function when Williams began chatting to her at the bar. They hit it off, and Williams invited Kirsty to come and watch him race cars in the coastal town of Napier, on New Zealand's North Island, the following week. A romance blossomed, despite the fact Kirsty was weeks away from moving to London to work for a bank. Williams, though, knew he'd met someone special and looked at their long-distance beginnings as an opportunity: he spent a lot of time in Orlando, which was a six-hour flight from London, and the couple could see each other frequently while growing their own careers. He felt he'd found a life partner in Kirsty and admired her for understanding and accepting the nature of being a professional caddie. Kirsty knew Williams was as determined as Woods to overtake Nicklaus's majors record, and respected his drive. Williams felt the elements of his life coming together, working with Woods and dating Kirsty.

Woods still had one last official tournament of 2000—the Johnnie Walker Classic, a European Tour event held in Thailand and co-sanctioned with the Asian Tour. Woods and Williams were staying in Bangkok but the golf course, Alpine Golf and Sports Club, was a considerable distance away. The traffic was ugly, so tournament officials organized for Woods to take a helicopter to the course each day, given the hotel had a helipad on the roof.

Williams noticed the pilot was an elderly man who'd served in the Thai air force. "We also thought the pilot didn't speak any English because he said nothing all week except smiling at us when we said hello," Williams says. The chopper's path coming into the hotel, among tall buildings, was nerve-racking for the passengers all week. On the last trip back to the hotel, on Sunday afternoon after Woods had just won the tournament, Williams felt the helicopter plummet briefly. "We thought we were all gone and we probably screamed some choice words in fright when it dropped," Williams says. After landing, the pilot turned around to the group, and in perfect English, said, "Thank you, guys. It's been an honor to fly Tiger Woods and his caddie around all week." Flabbergasted, Williams and Woods burst into laughter.

Once he'd returned to the U.S., Woods took a rest. It was needed. Although he had 10 wins from 22 tournaments, the countdown to the 2001 Masters had already begun. The world was waiting with bated breath to see if he could become the first golfer in history to win four majors in a row.

CHAPTER 6

THE TIGER SLAM

Around the fireplace in the main living room at his Isleworth home Woods kept the five major championship trophies he'd accumulated through the end of 2000. Woods's neighbor Australian golf pro Robert Allenby was struck by the beauty of the presentation whenever he'd walk into Woods's house. The world number one had a series of squares cut out of the wall, like pigeonholes, perfectly sized for each major trophy. "It was one of the most spectacular things I'd ever seen," Allenby says.

There was a sterling-silver replica of Augusta National's clubhouse, the official trophy for Masters champions. Woods got that from his 1997 victory. There were two replicas of the Wanamaker Trophy, given to Woods for his PGA Championship titles in 1999 and 2000. He had the champion's replica for the U.S. Open and the claret jug, from his triumphs at Pebble Beach and St. Andrews, respectively. Williams liked what he'd done with the place. "Tiger grouped trophies together by major. For example, the claret jugs sat together, the Masters trophies sat together. He kept it that way as he accumulated more majors," Williams says.

Masters champions receive a famous green jacket to take home for the year following their win. Although Williams occasionally saw the green jacket in Woods's house in the years he was reigning champion, he never tried it on for fun. "Tiger and I used to have this joke; I'd say, 'Tiger, you're ugly and you can get away with wearing a green jacket. I'm good-looking and need to keep it that way.' He'd say, 'Well, you should try it on, because you don't look any good in the white overalls [that caddies have to wear at Augusta].'"

For the first time in history, Woods was trying to hold all four major trophies at once, which he had an unprecedented chance to do if he could win the 2001 Masters.

Williams was two years into the job and their working friendship was thriving. Communication on the golf course was built on mutual respect and banter. But outside of tournaments, Williams had become a trusted member of Woods's inner sanctum. "We were becoming great mates," Williams says.

Still, Williams, or Stevie, as Woods called him, tried to maintain some distance from his boss. He had learned a harsh lesson after caddying for Norman in the 1980s. During their seven years working together, Williams had become too close with the Australian star, nicknamed The Shark. Their comfort with one another subconsciously gave Williams an unfounded license to speak his mind, particularly about Norman's performances and shot choices. Eventually, Norman fired Williams in 1989. More than a decade later, Williams was not going to make the same mistake with Woods. "With Tiger, I used to visualize when I was putting my hat on for the day as the moment when I could no longer speak to Tiger as a friend, but only as an employee," he says. Williams was still honest but respected the chain of command. As soon as he took the proverbial hat off at the end of the day, they were back to being friends.

It wasn't easy, though, to keep Woods at arm's length, given their growing friendship. "At each tournament, Tiger would say 'C'mon, let's go out to dinner,' but often I'd decline because I tried not to get too close to the guy," Williams says. But he had a perfect, and very real, excuse. His favorite escape from golf while in the U.S. was to look up the National Speedway Directory. It was one of the first things he did in each tournament city. The directory listed every track in the U.S., and Williams would write down which speedways were hosting car races on a Friday or Saturday night in that town. If Woods's weekend tee times allowed it, Williams would head out to the speedway. Woods was in contention, or leading, frequently, so most weekends he'd have an afternoon tee time, and Williams wouldn't have to worry about what time he'd get back to the hotel after a night at the races. He loved dirt-track speedways, the surface used for sprint cars and late-model racing. The Williams Grove and Lincoln speedways became favorites of Williams, and he visited them whenever Woods played a tournament in the Philadelphia area, which was two hours east of both tracks. "If Tiger was making weekend dinner plans, he'd say, 'I guess you'll be off to the racing, Stevie?'"

Williams was what Australians and New Zealanders described as a "petrolhead," or a car racing fanatic. Woods thought it looked fun and often asked Williams if he could try it someday.

Racing cars on dirt-track speedways and caddying on the PGA Tour couldn't be more contrasting activities. Williams's peers, and even some players, were fascinated at the Kiwi's polarizing passions. Racing was blue-collar, and golf was inherently white-collar. "There was one similarity, though, and it was huge," Williams says. A fundamental of dirt-track racing was the ability to read a track for an upcoming race and make an educated guess on what the track was going to do. "Was it going to be 'drive-y'? Was it going to be slippery? Was it going to be slick? Was it going to turn black? Was it going to have rubber laid down on it? Was it going to go 'marble-y'?" Williams says he'd ask himself. Drivers needed to set their car up according to their prediction. If it was a longer race, the question was whether a driver should set their car up for the first half of the race to try to get into the lead, or whether to set it up for the second half, when the track would change. Dirt tracks always changed, and drivers needed to keep up. Humidity, wind, sun, rain could drastically alter how a track performed. In Williams's opinion, that wasn't any different from being a caddie and having to watch and react to the golf course and the weather conditions.

On the golf course, Woods and Williams had an understanding that bordered on telepathy—and it yielded great results. Woods was rusty in the beginning of 2001, having taken an extended break following 2000's grueling schedule. Woods's swing would fatigue late in a round while he clawed back his "match fitness" on the course. Williams had a way of steering the ship, though. "We'd always have these little mini bets when a round wasn't going good, and they were usually for $100," he says. Williams would engage Woods to play $100 fairways and $100 greens. If he missed a fairway or a green, he'd have to pay Williams per miss. But if he made them, the caddie would have to cough up. He found the bets ignited an extra gear of concentration for three, six or sometimes nine holes. Woods hated losing and it didn't matter what game it was, who it was to and what the stakes were. Still, paying up was never an issue between the two. "We had this mantra, 'Fast pay makes fast friends,'" Williams says, laughing.

There were also bets off the course. On one occasion, Woods and Williams bet who could go the longest without a haircut. "Tiger won because his hair didn't grow as quickly as mine," Williams says. They'd have other challenges, such as who could go the longest without eating fast food, or in Williams's case, without his favorite soft drink, Sprite.

Williams had also become an expert in the secret language of Woods. It began with "dawn thirty" as their regular meeting time on the practice fairway to a wide-ranging series of quirky phrases. From describing the flight, direction or spin of a golf shot, to his performance on the greens, Woods had a lexicon unto himself:

Duck hook: "When Tiger hooked the ball left and it ducked low into the ground," Williams says.

Quack: "Another word for a duck hook."

Dying quail: "A violent duck hook; like a dead bird falling out of the sky."

Necked it: "When Tiger hit a shot out of the heel, also called the neck, of the club."

Yipped it: "If Tiger felt he almost has a muscle spasm during a putt. 'Yipping it' was rare."

Sniped it: "A shot pulled left of his target."

Smoked it: "Hitting both the sweet spot and his target. It only applied to the driver."

Skanked shot: "Not hit solid. Often, a skanked shot was hit low on the clubface."

Fatball: "Hitting the ground before the ball."

Williams's favorite two phrases were "Nolan Ryan" and "The Raymondo": Ryan was an accomplished baseball pitcher in the 1960s, '70s and '80s for the New York Mets, California Angels,

Houston Astros and Texas Rangers. He was in the top 10 on the all-time MLB record for shutouts, when a pitcher throws a complete game and stops the opposing team from scoring a run. Woods would say "I did a Nolan Ryan today" if he didn't make a putt the entire round. He was shut out from the hole.

The Raymondo was born out of Woods's admiration for Raymond Floyd's short game. Woods considered him one of the greatest-ever chippers of the golf ball. Floyd often chipped with the heel of the club up off the ground and the toe pressing down into the turf, which imparted right-to-left spin on the ball. That helped it roll once it landed. "Tiger called that chipping technique 'The Raymondo' and used it frequently," Williams says. Woods became a believer in Floyd's theory, which had been relayed to him by Williams, that if the ball was off the green, putting was not an option. Floyd argued that the fringe or fairway could throw the ball offline if a player putted. But if a golfer chipped a ball over that grass and onto the green, they eliminated that variable. Floyd was so crafty he would use everything from a 3-iron to a lob wedge depending on how much roll, or "release," a chip shot needed. "Tiger found that absolutely fascinating and it was common for him to ask me what club he should use for a chip-and-run shot because I had seen Ray do it so often," Williams says.

The number of Tiger-isms Woods had to describe hooking the ball left illuminated his disdain for that mishit. It was almost as strong as his disgust for three-putting. Hooks are caused by a clubface that is closed, or pointing left, at impact. A closed clubface also points to the ground, decreasing loft and shooting the ball on a lower trajectory than intended. A hook struggles to get airborne or near the target.

Frequent duck hooks and quails plagued Woods during a mediocre start to 2001, when he failed to win a tournament in January and February. His first six starts included four top 10s, but two uncharacteristically poor T13 finishes. "How could [I] not be frustrated?" Woods asked a reporter. "I hit snap hook after snap hook. I hit some skanks, some quacks, some quails. It was just not fun hitting shots like that."

Snap hooks almost prevented Woods from grabbing his first victory of 2001, in his adopted hometown event, the Arnold Palmer Invitational at Bay Hill. On the last hole during the final round, galleries were jam-packed down the left-hand side of the par-4 18th. Woods snap hooked his tee shot, which hurtled into the gallery and hit a spectator on the shoulder. Had it not struck the gallery, the ball could have easily bounced out of bounds. After getting a free drop because another fan picked the ball up, Woods hit a 5-iron from 195 yards to the green. It settled 15 feet from the hole and he drained the birdie to defeat his great rival Phil Mickelson by one shot. It was Woods's 25th PGA Tour victory.

The following week, Woods and a stellar field teed up at the elite Players Championship at TPC Sawgrass. Because the 17th is a par 3, players were expected to find the green with their tee shots. The green, however, is surrounded by water with only a narrow, grassed walkway entrance to its left. Woods had made a dramatic birdie putt from the fringe on No. 17 during his 1994 U.S. Amateur Championship win at TPC Sawgrass. But that didn't soften his dislike of the 140-yard hole once he turned pro and contested the Players Championship. He despised the hole's lack of options on the tee shot and publicly criticized it, which he rarely did about golf courses. "I think it is wonderful for the fans to watch, but I think any player who actually understands the game . . . aren't really going to say they like it," Woods said.

Overall, Woods had never fared well at Sawgrass until he became a runner-up in 2000. That laid the foundation for the 2001

Players, when Woods was at least beginning to appreciate the examination of a tour pro's game Sawgrass provided. Ironically, the 2001 Players was remembered for a birdie putt Woods holed on No. 17 during the third round en route to winning the tournament in a weather-delayed Monday finish. Woods's tee shot on No. 17 on day three barely stayed on the back of the green. He faced a 60-foot, triple-breaking, downhill putt for birdie. The putt was so difficult Williams was called in for advice on how the putt would break. Williams acted as a human target, standing to the left of the hole while tending the flag.

"On long putts, Tiger would sometimes ask me to stand on one side of the hole and place my feet where he needed to aim the ball," Williams says. Woods's putt on No. 17 began to drift left and, as it caught a slope, it slid back to the right before shooting toward the hole like it was fired from a pinball machine. The ball slammed into the right edge of the hole and dropped. Video highlights became famous for NBC commentator Gary Koch muttering the phrase "Better than most" twice on the broadcast as the putt was tracking. As it jammed into the hole for an unlikely birdie, Koch screamed "BETTER THAN MOST!" a third time. Woods produced an animated double fist pump before uppercutting the air with his right hand. The birdie sent roars from the crowd reverberating around the course.

In Woods's mind, his Players Championship win combined with the Palmer victory in Orlando as a one-two punch at critics within golf media whom he felt were fallacious in using the word "slump" in newspapers and on TV to describe his lackluster start to 2001. In fairness to reporters, for the standards Woods set himself, it at least qualified as a rough patch. Veteran TV presenter Jimmy Roberts asked a harmless question on the 18th green at Sawgrass about Woods's win, to which he answered, "Some slump," before responding to another question, "It means the slump is over." Reporters asked Woods about that awkward exchange in his winning press conference. "Some of the writers, I know who they are, had suggested [I was in a slump] and said it," Woods said. "They don't really understand the game that well . . . it wasn't like I was missing cuts every week. Now I've won two tournaments in a row, I'm sure they will write about something else."

The outburst was likely Woods feeling the suffocating pressure of the countdown to the 2001 Masters in April. That pressure had leaked outside the golf world and into mainstream media—it was a topic of frequent discussion on ESPN. Woods consumed ESPN frequently as a fan of the L.A. Lakers, Oakland Raiders and L.A. Dodgers, and also to escape the fishbowl that was golf. Because he had won the U.S. Open, Open Championship and PGA Championship, the last three majors of 2000, he could win the first major of 2001 to hold four different major trophies at once. It had never been done before. Woods and Ben Hogan were the only golfers to ever win three professional majors in a calendar year. Woods and his team were frustrated at the constant media debate about whether it would be considered a grand slam if he didn't win all four majors in the same calendar year.

There were 228 days between Woods's winning putt at the 2000 PGA Championship on August 20, 2000, and the first day of the Masters, on April 5, 2001. It was a period of Williams's caddying career he'll never forget; the speculation was relentless. "Tiger's a massive sports fan, but about a month out from the Masters, he stopped reading newspapers and didn't watch any sports on TV. In the car, he'd just have music on," Williams says. "When Tiger came home, he'd only have regular TV on, no sports." Woods didn't want to turn on ESPN and hear opinions on why he couldn't win four, or why he could do it and what it would mean. Remarkably, he managed to block out the noise and find form when he absolutely needed to, winning twice in Florida one month out from Augusta National.

Williams chose the song "As Good as It Gets" by the New Zealand band The Feelers, which was released a year earlier, to help him stay focused at the 2001 Masters. *This is real. This is as good as it gets*. "Tiger was playing as good as any golfer in history, and I felt it was my job to keep him grounded in the reality that winning the Masters was the goal, not winning four majors in a row," Williams says.

Woods began his Masters quest on a dark and stormy Monday morning on April 2, 2001, although he'd flown up to Augusta the previous Wednesday for a scouting mission. Woods walked out from the clubhouse on Monday morning, headed for the first tee for a practice round with O'Meara and Appleby, when a cameraman walked backward to get the shot of Woods beginning his Masters preparations. "Duck!" Woods shouted at the cameraman. But it was too late; he crashed into a branch of Augusta National's treasured clubhouse oak and fell over. "Tiger's security guard, a gentleman named Tyrone, had to help the poor bloke up," Williams says.

On the Tuesday practice round, Williams was nearly struck by a golf ball that landed on Augusta's famous par-3 12th green while Woods and his playing partners were practicing different putts. Augusta Country Club is a golf course that sits on the other side of a forest from Augusta National. It's a popular place for Masters ticket holders to play during Masters week. Augusta Country Club's ninth hole sits behind Augusta National's 12th green. It would have to be an extremely wayward shot from the club's ninth to clear Yorkshire Drive and the forest, and land on the 12th at Augusta National. But Williams remembers the one giveaway. "It was a yellow TopFlite golf ball, not exactly the type of golf ball that anyone in the field at the Masters was using," Williams says. "To me, it almost appeared someone had tried to hit it over on purpose. I'd never seen anything like it in my years caddying at the Masters."

When Augusta National released the tee times for the first two rounds, Woods was grouped with the left-handed Mike Weir and Finland's Mikko Ilonen. The trio teed off Thursday at 12:57. Hours beforehand, in the 8:55 group, Australia's Greg Chalmers was so nervous for his Masters debut he hit a spectator with each of his first two swings of the tournament. "I clocked some guy on the forehead," says Chalmers. "Then I clocked another guy on the shoulder with my second shot. I was really unsettled, but I made what I like to call a settling bogey."

Woods posted a first-round 70 before climbing into contention on day two with a 66. He sat at 8 under par. Chris DiMarco, a New York–born, Florida-raised tour pro, led after the first and second rounds. He had a homemade golf swing but an otherworldly short game and was fearless among players like Woods. "I wouldn't say DiMarco was one of the most naturally gifted players, but he worked hard and played well against Tiger," Williams says.

On day three at Augusta, Woods was paired with DiMarco and trailed by two shots. Woods flexed his muscles to DiMarco early in what would be a yearslong rivalry, cruising to a 68. DiMarco was stunned and after the third round declared Augusta National a par 68 for Woods. His theory was, the four par 5s were simply long par 4s and that meant his score began at 4 under. That was a lot of ground for his competitors to make up. DiMarco, while shook, showed his credentials to the golf world, proving that he wasn't afraid of throwing down with Woods. "That was the first time DiMarco had been in contention in a major with Tiger," Williams says. "Tiger thought it was important to stamp his authority on opponents because it struck a bit of fear for the next time he'd play them."

By the end of day three, Woods led at 12 under par, with Phil Mickelson a shot behind. For Sunday's final round, Woods was paired with the wildly popular left-hander in the final group. The two were archrivals and did not get along. Woods came from a working-class background in Cypress, and Mickelson had a more middle-class upbringing in San Diego. Mickelson seemed to be able to talk underwater with a mouthful of marbles; Woods had an economy of words. "Tiger and Phil weren't friends," Williams says. The two biggest stars in American golf, in the final pairing at golf's most famous tournament: it was a made-for-television showdown.

Woods was so focused for the final round, he ignored his own associates as he walked from the clubhouse to the practice putting green, steamrolling past Nike founder and chairman, Phil Knight. On the practice green, Woods and Mickelson were only a few feet apart but didn't so much as look at each other. That iciness continued out on the course; Woods didn't glance at Mickelson for the first 12 holes—until Mickelson spoke up on the 13th. "There was no talk and no banter," Williams says.

Mickelson and Woods shared the lead twice early in the round, but Mickelson made bogey on No. 4 and missed a two-foot par putt on the par-3 sixth. He then drove it into the trees on No. 11 and made another bogey. Yet Mickelson hung in there, and was two shots back as he and Woods teed off on the famous par-5 13th. The physically stunning golf hole has a sweeping right-to-left dogleg framed by towering Georgia pines and Rae's Creek running along its left side. It was on that 13th tee Woods got inside Mickelson's head.

Mickelson hit a nice, high fade down the middle of the fairway, but Woods wanted to flex his muscles. He pulled his 3-wood out of the bag, because he found the more lofted club easier to shape the ball right to left than with the driver. Woods addressed the ball and perfectly executed a sweeping hook that flew 20 yards past Mickelson's ball. Mickelson had hit driver. Walking off the tee, Mickelson said to Woods, "Hey, do you normally hit your 3-wood that far?" Woods responded, instantly, "No. Sometimes I hit it farther."

Williams thought the look on Mickelson's face was pure defeat. "Tiger had practiced that 3-wood for the 13th tee shot for two years leading up to the 2001 Masters, thousands and thousands of times," Williams says. Woods would stand on the range at Isleworth and visualize aiming at the trees on the right-hand side of No. 13 at Augusta and hit a towering shot that would orbit the right side of the practice fairway and turn aggressively back into the middle of the paddock. He would hit that shot in PGA Tour events, too. "We'd be competing at tournaments like Bay Hill, at the dogleg left, par-4 third, or the Players Championship, at the par-5 16th, where Tiger could practice the hooking 3-wood during competition. And he'd nail it." On No. 13 with Mickelson, Williams urged Woods to let it rip. He reminded Woods to trust the shot, having hit it hundreds of times before.

DiMarco, who faded on Sunday with a 74 to tie for 10th, observed how Woods's commitment to the individual demands of each shot was what set him apart. "When he's being pushed, Tiger never backed down from what the shot was asking him; he did what was needed to hit the fairway, or hit it close," says DiMarco.

Despite the verbal burn, Mickelson managed to match Woods's birdie on No. 13. When Mickelson birdied the par-5 15th and Woods didn't, Mickelson was one shot back with three holes to play. But a bogey on No. 16 ended his hopes of winning a first career major.

Woods stood on the par-4 18th with a one-shot lead over David Duval and two ahead of Mickelson. Woods obliterated his drive 330 yards up the fairway. Rubbing salt into Mickelson's wound, Woods hit his approach shot close and made the birdie putt. He signed for 68 and a 16-under-par (272) total.

On Augusta National's 18th green, Woods was overcome with emotion. He pulled his black Nike hat over his face to wipe away tears. Since winning the 1997 Masters, he had appeared to be an emotionless, winning robot—golf's equivalent of the Terminator. For the eight months between the 2000 PGA and the 2001 Masters, his focus on winning four majors in a row had consumed his life. Once the tournament started, Woods seemed to have played in a trance for four days. The roars on No. 18 were cathartic, but they'd also woken Woods from his mission. "I was so attuned to each and every shot . . . and I finally realized I had no more to play."

Woods had won his sixth major, his second Masters title and, more important, he'd become the only golfer in history to win four majors in a row. Fellow PGA Tour winner Rocco Mediate, who finished T15, summed up the four consecutive major wins best: "No one else is going to do it for the next 100 years."

To Woods's immense satisfaction, a Masters tradition that sees the previous champion place the green jacket on his successor meant Vijay Singh had to slip the coat on Woods. After the ceremony on the 18th green, Woods took a call from President George Bush.

While the presentation was unfolding, Williams walked with Woods's bag over to the clubhouse. On the opposite side of the building from where the oak tree stood, there was a door to a kitchen. It was close to an area where Masters competitors were dropped off by volunteers after they'd visited the driving range. Having been shuttled there regularly over the years, Williams came to know the chefs, who could see through the open door that he was carrying Woods's Buick bag. "It was funny because they could barely understand a word I was saying," Williams says. "They had no idea where New Zealand was, and thought my accent might have been an off-key South Carolina accent." But they understood enough of Williams to have bantered with him since his first Masters with Woods in 1999. Now, Williams wanted to celebrate his first Augusta victory on Woods's team with his chef mates. They were chuffed when he gave each of them a ball out of Woods's bag. "Not the ball he'd used that Sunday, but one in the bag from the week. It meant a lot to them," Williams says.

Debate over what to call Woods's unprecedented achievement continued to rage among media and fans. Many deferred to the definition of a grand slam in sport as one that happens in a calendar year. Asked about the name, Woods smiled and said, "I won four." Either way, no golfer had ever held golf's four big trophies at once. Not even 18-time major winner Nicklaus, who was unsuccessful in his bid to win all four in 1972. Arnold Palmer was the legendary golfer who'd conceived golf's modern grand slam in 1960 on his way to the British Open at St. Andrews. Before that, men's majors had included amateur tournaments. Palmer won halfway to the slam in 1960 before he lost the Open Championship to Australia's Kel Nagle. Ironically, the Masters Tournament creator, celebrated amateur golfer Bobby Jones, won the U.S. Open, U.S. Amateur, British Open and British Amateur in 1930 for a grand slam nicknamed the Impregnable Quadrilateral. As for Woods, one phrase was eventually universally accepted: the Tiger Slam. Winning four majors in a row was inconceivable and Williams doubted any player would ever have the chance to match it. "I went back to the caddie shed, sat down on a chair and asked myself, *Did that actually just happen?*" he says.

Weeks after Woods completed the Tiger Slam, Williams arranged for a photographer friend on tour to create an A3-sized collage of the best moments from the four major wins. Over a large image of Williams and Woods shaking hands on Augusta National's 18th green during his 2001 victory, the collage was peppered with nine smaller images of various scenes from Pebble Beach, St. Andrews, Valhalla and even Woods and his mother, Kultida, holding the U.S. Open trophy. Williams completed the piece by having Woods write, in black ink in the middle of the frame, a message:

To Stevie,
Thank you for helping me make my dreams come true.

Your friend,
Tiger Woods

Woods's peers began to believe he was capable of reeling in Nicklaus's record 18 majors. Davis Love III had initially scoffed at the idea of Woods winning 19 majors when it became a part of the tour's narrative. "But when you win four in a row like that, it makes that goal seem a little more real," Love said.

The national interest in seeing Woods was through the roof. The Sunday telecast was estimated to have had 40.1 million viewers and a 13.3 national TV rating on CBS. It was the second-highest total viewership ever for the final round, second only to the 43 million who tuned in for Woods's maiden victory at Augusta in 1997. Joyce Julius & Associates analyzed TV exposure and calculated that Nike ambassadors Woods and Duval, as winner and runner-up, generated 15 minutes of global attention, the equivalent of $4.6 million in value to an advertiser. Woods's Nike hat alone garnered 9 minutes and 6 seconds of screen time.

Woods had won 27 titles on the PGA Tour in 98 starts as a professional. Of the 17 major championships he'd played as a professional, he'd won six.

Woods's statistics from the Tiger Slam, though, were mind-blowing. He had posted 13 consecutive rounds under par, from the final round of the U.S. Open at Pebble Beach to the final round of the 2001 Masters. That remains the record for most consecutive under-par rounds in major championship history. "I don't think that will ever be broken," Williams says. "Majors are played under the most pressure, and often they are played in the toughest course conditions possible."

Woods led or co-led the field in both greens in regulation and driving distance in all 16 rounds of the Tiger Slam. He also recorded just 23 holes over par (21 bogeys, one double-bogey, one triple-bogey). Of the golfers who also played all 16 rounds, Justin Leonard was the next best with 41 bogeys. Woods made 91 birdies at an average of 5.7 per round. Bob May, second to Woods at Valhalla, was next best with 69 birdies.

Now that Woods had won majors at three of the game's most revered venues, Augusta National, Pebble Beach and St. Andrews, Williams had begun to develop a ranking of the most enjoyable, and most stressful, venues and shots.

"The Old Course at St. Andrews was my favorite tournament to caddie," Williams says. "That's because of the vibe of the town, the history, its connection to the Open and what it means to golf." St. Andrews tested a caddie's preparation more than any other major venue but it also prepared them for success. Because the R&A allowed caddies to walk the course on each tournament day before the first group was off, Williams could get to St. Andrews at 5 A.M. and check the hole positions, firmness of the turf and greens, whether any spots had been watered, and give Woods the most accurate information. It's where Williams felt most valuable.

The Masters, on the other hand, was tough on a caddie because there was no course that put a player and caddie's relationship under more stress on each and every shot. Williams often heard rumors that more caddies were fired after Augusta than any other tournament. "You couldn't wait to get to the Masters, but you also couldn't wait to leave," he says.

After the Tiger Slam, Williams also determined the most difficult shot for a caddie out of the four majors. While every shot at Augusta National seemed to be on a knife edge of risk and reward, Williams found the second shot into the par-5 15th was the most stressful in major championship golf—even for a ball-striker as capable as Woods. The green was so shallow front to back that if Woods hit his second shot even a half yard shorter than intended, the breeze would swirl and knock it down into water. But Williams couldn't suggest one extra club for safety because the ball could bounce over the back of the green and into another water hazard. It was a tightrope for caddies. "My heart was always in my mouth on the second shot at No. 15," he says.

Following the Tiger Slam, Woods tied third in his next start at the Byron Nelson event. He then won the following two tournaments, the TPC of Europe and Nicklaus's Memorial Tournament in Ohio. But the summer of 2001 presented a sharp hangover from what was a monumental achievement in April. Woods didn't finish in the top 10 in five consecutive tournaments from early June to late August, which included the remaining three majors. He finally broke the drought by winning the WGC-NEC Invitational at Firestone Country Club in Akron, where he defeated Jim Furyk in a seven-hole playoff. It was Woods's third straight victory at Firestone and his 29th PGA Tour win. Woods, who celebrated his five-year anniversary as a pro golfer the day after Firestone, pushed past $25 million in total career prize money. It was also Woods's last official victory of 2001.

Two days after Woods finished tied for 23rd at the Canadian Open, where he was defending champion, the world was upended by the September 11 attacks on the World Trade Center in New York and the Pentagon in Washington, D.C. That tragic Tuesday morning, Woods and Williams were at the WGC-American Express Championship at Bellerive Country Club in the outer suburbs of St. Louis, Missouri. Williams walked along as Woods and fellow pro Mark Calcavecchia played an early morning practice round. About six holes in, just before 8 A.M. Missouri time, Joe Corless, a retired FBI agent turned head of security for the PGA Tour, approached the group and delivered horrific news: a plane had crashed into the North Tower of the World Trade Center in Lower Manhattan. Woods's group rushed back to the locker room at Bellerive. Pros, caddies and officials huddled around a large TV in silence. Woods and Williams walked in early enough to witness the second plane hit. The tournament was canceled the next day, and Woods supported PGA Tour commissioner Tim Finchem's decision, not least because one of the Twin Towers fell on the American Express Building, and Amex was a corporate sponsor of Woods's. He learned firsthand how much the employees were struggling.

The nation was grieving, and it was not time to think about a PGA Tour event. Still, a tiny part of Williams sympathized with the people of Missouri and the efforts involved in staging a WGC event. Historically, Bellerive had not seen a lot of top-level golf. It had hosted the 1992 PGA, and outside of that, the only noteworthy men's tournaments were the 1965 U.S. Open and the 1953 Western Open. "I felt sorry for the good people of St. Louis who were starved of watching golf," says Williams. "But obviously, there were far more important things than golf."

With all flights grounded in the U.S. in the days after September 11, golfers made hasty arrangements to drive long distances to their respective home states. Woods was given a courtesy car and drove 17 hours from Missouri to Florida.

Williams, who had Kirsty visiting from London, rented a car and drove 2,000 miles back to Sunriver, Oregon. The couple completed the 31-hour drive by sharing the driving and only stopping for food and bathroom breaks. Throughout the journey, they listened to constant radio updates about the tragedy, the death toll and the rescue efforts. "It was just a terrible chapter and I feel for all the victims and their families," Williams says. Golf went out the window; there were far more important things.

After the season-ending Tour Championship in Atlanta, Woods's team had their usual end-of-year assessment. Williams wasn't surprised when not too much emphasis was placed on Woods's poor results in the majors after his historic Masters victory—he was T12 at the U.S. Open at Southern Hills in Tulsa, T25 at the Open Championship at Royal Lytham and T29 at the PGA Championship at the Atlanta Athletic Club. "Tiger struggled to get up again for the rest of 2001; it was the first time in his career he simply didn't have the gas in the tank," Williams says. Williams's handwritten statistics highlighted Woods's struggles in the 2001 majors. At the U.S. Open, he made three bogeys in each round as well as a double-bogey. At the Open Championship, he was in contention through two rounds but made a double-bogey on Saturday and a triple-bogey on Sunday. "It was uncharacteristic for Tiger to make errors like that," Williams says.

From mid-1999 through the 2001 Masters, Woods was playing

at a level golf had never seen before. But at some point, the bubble had to burst. Woods's team knew it was only human to be exhausted. Williams felt winning four majors in a row was such a monumental achievement that it would likely never be done again. But it also took a toll on Woods. The remainder of 2001 was the collateral damage. "There was so much emphasis placed on the 2001 Masters and the practice was relentless leading up," Williams says. "He needed time to rest and completely reset. If you didn't, you could risk a physical or mental breakdown of his game."

While Woods was recharging his batteries, his rivals were closing the gap. The other three majors in 2001 saw first-time winners. Retief Goosen, a sublimely talented South African, triumphed in a playoff at the U.S. Open. A month later, Woods's close friend David Duval broke through the major barrier by winning the Open Championship—a year after stumbling on the back nine at St. Andrews in pursuit of Woods. David Toms closed out the majors season by winning his first title at the PGA. Mickelson was also heating up at the majors, coming third to Woods at Augusta, then tied seventh at the U.S. Open before nearly winning the PGA, losing to Toms by a shot.

Outside the majors, arguably Woods's greatest threat, 21-year-old Sergio Garcia, won his first PGA Tour event and weeks later grabbed his second.

Woods's next challenge was clear. While he had rewritten golf's record books, his four consecutive major wins were not considered, by legends of the game, including Arnold Palmer, to be a grand slam in its purest form. "Tiger wanted to win all four majors in 2002, and he really believed he could do it," Williams says.

CHAPTER 7

DEFENDING THE MASTERS

There was dew on the ground and fog in the air on Tuesday, April 9, as Woods marched out of the clubhouse at Augusta National at precisely 7:25 A.M. His stride had the usual speed and purpose, as if he had only rented the euphoria from winning the previous Masters, for four major wins in a row, on a 12-month lease. Debate around the Tiger Slam—*was it really a grand slam?*—had made Woods determined to win four in a calendar year.

Woods paced toward the first hole for a practice round with O'Meara, eager to study recent course changes to Augusta *before* the crowds arrived. Williams, always ahead of Woods, was already at the first tee. On arrival, Williams noticed a wooden clock—one that didn't actually tell the time—set to 8 o'clock. That indicated when practice rounds were allowed to begin, according to Augusta National. But Woods had told his caddie the night before he wanted to play at seven thirty. Williams was torn. "So, when I arrived, I just grabbed the hands on the clockface and moved the time backwards 30 minutes, to 7:30 A.M.," Williams says. Woods was on the tee at 7:27, so Williams had to move the clock an additional three minutes. The group had played three holes when a Masters official approached, curious about what had happened. "I was told, in no uncertain terms, not to do that again," Williams says. The following day, the clock's hands were reinforced with screws.

The first three months of 2002, for Woods, were purposefully not as intense as that mischievous episode on Augusta National's first tee. Woods did not register a victory worldwide in January or February as he conserved energy for a shot at an unprecedented calendar grand slam.

Woods started 2002 by traveling 4,000 miles from Maui, where he kicked off the season at the Mercedes Championships, to Wellington for the New Zealand Open, scheduled for Williams's childhood course, Paraparaumu Beach Golf Club.

Unlike Hawaii, New Zealand was in the middle of its summer. On a warm, sunny Wednesday, January 9, Woods and Williams jogged across State Highway 1 in Paraparaumu Beach, a charming coastal town in New Zealand some 30 miles north of the nation's capital of Wellington, to decompress after the long flight. Williams was sporting his usual singlet and rugby shorts, while Woods ran shirtless, taking advantage of the perfect temperature.

The two made their way from State Highway 1 down a pedestrian running track surrounded by a beautiful hillside garden and onto a single-lane country road, Otaihanga Road. As Woods rounded the concrete track and onto Otaihanga Road, which travels out to the stunning Kāpiti Coast, cars began to recognize the superstar. He was teeing up in New Zealand for the first time. "There was quite a bit of mayhem; a lot of people were stopping their cars and getting out to take photos of Tiger," Williams says.

Locals had discovered where Woods and Williams were staying, in a rental house just off the state highway. Although it had a long driveway and private entry, motorists were slowing down while going past the house, hoping to catch a Woods sighting.

Williams and Woods found the locals' fascination with a sporting celebrity visiting their country innocent and, if anything, reassuring after a security concern that implicated both Woods and the New Zealand Open at the end of 2001. Fears of further terrorist attacks remained high around the world in the aftermath of September 11 and Woods was plunged into those concerns only a month before he was scheduled to fly to New Zealand.

On December 18, 2001, a letter containing a packet of cyanide and written threats to carry out suicide attacks at the New Zealand Open was sent to the U.S. embassy in Wellington, through the postal service. The letter threatened firebombing, train derailments and poisoning tournament spectators. Woods, who said in 2001 he'd received various threats since turning pro in 1996, was made aware of the NZ letter. "Things like this do happen [but] you have to go on living your life," Woods said. "It's unfortunate people have these types of views and do these types of acts. I'm going to go down there and enjoy myself."

The six-time major winner was comforted in making the trip knowing $500,000 had been spent on extra security, a figure detailed in a book by Robert Starnes, a special agent for the U.S. Department of Diplomatic Security Service, who was based in New Zealand. In *Dictators and Diplomats, A Special Agent's Memoir and Musings*, Starnes detailed how the author of that threatening letter held an opinion that Woods represented U.S. suppression and exploitation of the Islamic people of Southeast Asia.

Williams was not overly concerned, having dealt with Woods's security detail every working day of his life. Woods had a security entourage wherever he walked at tournaments. Occasionally, Woods and Williams were made aware of threats. "There were a lot of wacky people out there who sent some crazy messages or made threats but this NZ Open threat was kind of legitimate," Williams says.

Both the national police and army in New Zealand put a freeze on all vacation requests for staff for the weeks surrounding, and including, the NZ Open. Every public transport artery and entry point to Paraparaumu Beach Golf Course was watched. All food and beverages were monitored. Wellington assistant police commissioner Jon White also said the threats were directed at the tournament *because* Woods was playing, rather than at Woods himself.

"Whenever there was any kind of security threat relating to Tiger, my mind would always go back to the Monica Seles incident," Williams says. Seles was a prodigiously talented tennis player from the former Yugoslavia, who won eight grand slam singles titles as a teenager. In 1993, at a tournament in Hamburg, Germany, an obsessed fan of Seles's rival Steffi Graf stabbed Seles in the back with a nine-inch knife while she sat between games. Seles returned to tennis two years later and, while she managed to win a slam at the 1996 Australian Open, she never reproduced the tennis she was capable of. "There are a lot of crazy people and with crazy ideas but you'd never think someone would carry it out until that incident," Williams says.

Williams was himself intimidating, and at tournaments most fans were respectful. But the New Zealand threat awoke the caddie to the realization that professional golf tournaments, by nature, allowed fans to stand several feet away from players. On most tee boxes at tournaments, only a gallery rope separated fans from the pros and caddies. "There wasn't ever a time I felt unsafe, but often I would point out to security following Tiger that someone was showing odd behavior, or acting strangely, and they'd monitor that person," Williams says.

Williams felt the proximity to players was one of the best things about pro golf. In 2002, Woods was in his prime and it was easier to stand meters from him, while he hit a tee shot, than any other elite athlete in world sports. Fans could not get that close to tennis stars Andre Agassi and Roger Federer, New England Patriots' quarterback Tom Brady or 2002 World Cup soccer hero Ronaldinho. "Thankfully, the attention to detail of PGA Tour security personnel was world-class and they made you feel good about everything," Williams says. Security officials were scrupulous in analyzing the setup of a golf course, the flow and positioning of crowds between greens and tee boxes—where fans came closest to golfers.

Despite the concerns, Woods enjoyed a safe and smooth trip Down Under. His participation in the 2002 NZ Open was the payoff for a bet Williams, upon being hired by him in 1999, made with Woods. He'd challenged Woods to an informal bonus; a promise that, if Woods won a major in their first 12 months, he had to play in the NZ Open. It took two years after the 1999 PGA Championship win to clear Woods's schedule, but he settled his bet.

Woods and Williams arrived in Wellington on the morning of Tuesday, January 8, 2002, to an enormous reception—approximately 10,000 people—at the Wellington airport. That included fans, media and even Wellington's mayor. New Zealand Maori rituals were performed, such as Woods being greeted with a hongi, where two people touch noses. Later that afternoon, when Woods went out to Paraparaumu Beach Golf Club for a nine-hole practice round on the back nine that included Williams's club pro friend Bob Garza, Williams held back tears on the 10th tee at Paraparaumu. The hole was a tranquil short par 4, with a creek running along the left side, and was named Te Awa Iti, meaning "the Little Stream." "It was really emotional thinking about the course I grew up caddying on now had the best golfer on the planet playing the New Zealand Open," says Williams.

Woods, whose agency secured a reported NZ$4 million appearance fee for him to play, fought hard through heavy rain to impress the fans. He was in danger of missing the 36-hole cut, which would have been Woods's first missed cut worldwide since September 1997. But he survived poor weather and a day of bad putting to make the weekend with a 2-over 73. He came back with a 67 on day three, and then on Sunday Woods shot a 69 to tie for sixth behind the winner, Australia's Craig Parry. "Tiger had a four-putt on the second hole of the final round and I didn't see many four-putts in my time with Tiger," says Williams. The tournament was incredibly difficult to plan—Williams had worked on promotion and organization behind the scenes—and it was battered by rain. But Williams was still in awe of Woods. He'd summoned all his talents on the weekend to put on a show for the Kiwi crowds and finish in the top 10. "Some players treated paid appearances like a holiday, but Tiger took great pride in grinding it out," Williams says.

The golf tournament wasn't the only victim of the rain. On the Saturday night following the third round, Woods planned to watch Williams race in the Wellington Saloon Car Championships at the Te Mārua Speedway. The race, held on a dirt track, was canceled. Williams quickly learned that another track *was* running, a two-hour drive away at Palmerston North. Williams had his racing crew drive his car there, while he and Woods took a helicopter from Paraparaumu to Palmerston North. "Tiger sat in a corporate box and got his first look at racing; he loved the sport," Williams says.

Woods flew back to the U.S. and, in February, tied for 12th at the Pebble Beach Pro-Am before sharing fifth at his beloved Torrey Pines. Puzzlingly, he was knocked out in the first round of the World Golf Championships-Match Play event, losing to Australian journeyman Peter O'Malley. He recovered form at the Doral Open in Miami, finishing second.

Woods's form in the first two and a half months of 2002 was like early 2001, when he was conserving energy for a shot at winning four majors in a row at the Masters. The difference was, Woods was now scaling back the involvement of his swing coach, Butch Harmon.

Harmon, considered the greatest swing coach in golf history, had worked with Woods since 1993, when he was a 17-year-old amateur. But, according to Williams, Woods was growing frustrated with Harmon's gregarious personality and penchant for dropping Woods's name in conversation or on TV with throwaway lines like "I was practicing with Tiger the other day . . ." At the 2001 PGA Championship, Woods had expressed to Williams a desire to reduce Harmon's duties. That's exactly what Williams observed over the course of the next 12 months. They were occasionally seen as a group at the 2002 Masters and Open Championship, but Williams noticed Woods distancing himself from the legendary coach.

Williams adored Harmon and knew that coaching Woods would have been a complex role; expressing opinions over a golfer's technique was like walking a tightrope. Advice could be received poorly by any player operating under the stress of the cutthroat PGA Tour. But Woods's pressure was unlike his peers'; it was suffocating and came from all angles—from himself, fans and media. Rendering practice even more difficult were the waves of fellow pros, fans, officials, media and volunteers who wanted to chat with Woods.

Whether it was Harmon, or later Hank Haney (Woods's coach

from 2004 to 2010), each coach knew they needed to choose the right moment to say something to Woods about his technique or swing. "Sometimes, Butch or Hank would say something on the range at an inappropriate time," Williams says. He could tell when Woods was pissed off, because he wouldn't even look up when either spoke. Occasionally, if Harmon or Haney critiqued his swing at an inopportune time, "Tiger would purposefully hit a couple of really shit shots, like duck-hooking it way left," Williams says.

Williams, an earnest reader of body language, had learned the varying moods a professional golfer could move through. One of the most invaluable assets a caddie had was to know when to say something, and when to shut up. "I'd look for signs with Tiger, like his interaction, or eye contact, when he was talking to you, whether he was genuinely listening or not, and I'd adjust my approach to the factors affecting his performance," Williams says. Williams always pictured himself in Woods's shoes and asked himself, *Is the crowd more boisterous than usual? Have too many people been hanging around him today at the practice fairway? Do I need to get people away from him?* Woods's celebrity status added enormous obstacles, noise and distractions.

Woods formally split with Harmon in August 2002, several days before the PGA Championship at Hazeltine in Chaska, Minnesota. Woods called his longtime coach and said that, as it related to his swing, he'd be going it alone. He thanked Harmon for his time. Just like that, it was over. "Tiger loved Butch as a friend and coach, but he was also very private and low-profile and felt Butch had become too outgoing," Williams says.

Very few great golfers in history have gone without a coach for an extended period. The effort required to film and analyze one's swing is better spent on actual practice. A strong temptation for a pro is to go down rabbit holes reading and watching golf coaches who promise they own the secret to unlocking the golf swing. That presents a risk of trying new techniques that could ruin the swing that helped a pro get to the PGA Tour level in the first place. Harmon was old-school and kept it simple. "Butch had a great eye for detail in the golf swing; some people are born to do something, and Butch was born to be a golf coach," Williams says. "But Tiger was a great student of the game; he had an understanding of the golf swing and saw it as the right time for change."

Woods earned his first victory worldwide in seven months at the Arnold Palmer Invitational, his third straight year winning at Bay Hill. He defeated Williams's fellow Kiwi, Michael Campbell, by four shots. He was the first player to win at Bay Hill in three consecutive years and the only golfer to accomplish that feat at three different tournaments. Not even Bay Hill host Palmer managed that in his career. At 26, Woods became the youngest golfer to win his 30th PGA Tour title. Nicklaus was 29 when he bagged number 30. Bay Hill was also an important confidence booster heading into the majors season.

As the sporting world readied for the 2002 Masters, curiosity was high about how Augusta National would play under significant alterations to the course that were dubbed "Tiger proofing." Tom Fazio, a renowned golf course designer, worked with Augusta National to lengthen nine of the 18 holes. Overall, the course was stretched 285 yards. The Masters tees, which were farther back on every hole from the members' tees, measured 7,270 yards. The changes included:

No. 1: lengthened 25 yards to 435 yards.
No. 7: lengthened 45 yards to 410.
No. 8: lengthened 20 yards to 570.
No. 9: lengthened 30 yards to 460.

No. 10: lengthened 10 yards to 495.
No. 11: lengthened 35 yards to 490.
No. 13: lengthened 25 yards to 510.
No. 14: lengthened 35 yards to 440.
No. 18: lengthened 60 yards to 465.

Other alterations included the bunkers on holes 1, 8 and 18 being enlarged. More trees were planted. Woods's father, Earl, would later dismiss the impact of Augusta being beefed up on his son. "You want to Tiger-proof a course? Move the tee box to the ladies' tee. Eliminate the rough completely. Cut the greens to 8 or 9 [a slow reading from the usual 13 Augusta measures on the stimpmeter, which is a speed-measuring device for golf greens]. I'll guarantee you Tiger won't win. *This* course plays right into his hands." Williams didn't believe the changes affected Woods, either. They eliminated shorter players from competing, thus increasing his boss's chances at victory. "Tiger was swinging his best. Adding length didn't affect him."

Williams felt hole No. 1, which was lengthened by 25 yards to measure 435 yards, was a good example. It was a par 4 with a cavernous fairway bunker that—if players found it with their tee shots—created a very difficult shot. If a player was close to the lip, it was impossible to reach the green because they would have to hit a higher-lofted club just to escape the sand. With the change, most players had to play more conservatively to the left side of the fairway or even hit a 3-wood to land short of it. Woods could still carry the bunker easily with his driver and have a pitching wedge to the green.

Days before the tournament, Williams promised himself that if Woods went on to successfully defend his 2001 Masters title, a feat only achieved by Nicklaus and Nick Faldo, he would treat himself and Kirsty to a sun-splashed holiday later that year. For that reason, he chose "April Sun in Cuba" by New Zealand band Dragon as his theme song for the week. *Take me to the April sun in Cuba (whoa-oh-oh)!* Aside from the fact the rock tune's upbeat tone and drums were inspiring for the task ahead, Williams was motivated to celebrate such a milestone with Kirsty.

Woods began the 66th edition of the Masters at 10:53 A.M. on Thursday, April 11, 2002, playing with U.S. Amateur champion and Jacksonville native Bubba Dickerson, and Japan's Toshi Izawa. Woods shot 70, three shots behind first-round leader Davis Love III. On day two, Woods was among 39 golfers unable to finish their second round because of a rain delay. He managed only 10 holes as well as the tee shot on the 11th, before play was suspended at 5 P.M. with Woods in the 11th fairway. On Saturday morning, Woods awoke at four thirty to warm up for his early restart. Players who were resuming the second round were, under the rules, allowed to begin with a clean golf ball, meaning Woods could wipe off a huge clump of mud on the left side of his ball. The mud could have sent the ball flying sideways had he played the second shot the night before. Woods posted a second-round 69 to climb to 5 under. Arnold Palmer, 72, stole the show Saturday morning when the four-time Masters winner retired from the tournament.

When the third round commenced at 12:30 P.M. Saturday, Woods was four shots off the lead. Tournament officials sent players off the first and 10th tees in order to finish the round. Split tees hadn't been used in 20 years at Augusta National. Woods was paired with Spain's José Maria Olazábal, a close friend and a two-time Masters winner himself. By Saturday evening, Woods had fired a blistering 66 to share the lead at 11 under with South Africa's Retief Goosen. Woods had taken the Masters by the scruff of the neck during a 25.5-hole marathon—7.5 holes of his second round and 18 of his third. "Tiger was a supremely fit athlete and was probably better equipped to play additional holes than any player in the field," Williams says.

Woods's third-round 66 was the lowest of the day and was built on phenomenal driving; he found 13 of 14 fairways and had 27 putts while bagging seven birdies and just one bogey. Goosen, though, was arguably the hottest player on the planet leading into the 2002 Masters, winning six times in 24 starts. Overall, there was serious star power on Augusta National's famous white leaderboards going into the final day. 2000 Masters winner Singh was 9 under, while Ernie Els, Phil Mickelson and Sergio Garcia were two shots further back. Woods, though, had never lost a major championship when holding at least a share of the lead after 54 holes.

The weather gods opened the clouds over the Augusta area for the final round on Sunday, April 14. Williams noticed Woods was particularly quiet during his warm-up. When Woods was in peak performance mode, he tended to fall silent on the practice range before a final round. "We always talked on the range but in majors, when there was an opportunity to win, Tiger got quite nervous because he cared so much," Williams says. Woods would channel that anxiousness into laser-like focus on each shot during the warm-up. Woods was being chased and knew he had to bring his A game.

Woods teed off alongside Goosen in the final pairing at 2:10 P.M., getting off to a flyer with birdies at the par-5 second and short par-4 third. Goosen, meanwhile, had bogeyed No. 1. Woods had a three-shot lead over Goosen and Singh early on the final day and threatened to run away with the green jacket. "I thought we couldn't afford to get cocky; Augusta is such a difficult course that you can't ever get ahead of yourself," Williams says. He felt his job was to steer Woods away from obsessing over the leaderboard and keep him in the moment. He'd seen many a player fall victim to leaderboard watching, which could lead to choking under the pressure of the back nine.

Els charged to 10 under par through eight holes but imploded with a triple-bogey 8 at the par-5 13th. He never recovered, finishing tied fifth. Els, who won two U.S. Opens (1994, 1997) and would later claim two Open Championships (2002, 2012), would only ever manage two runner-up results at the Masters (2000, 2004), but never a win. "Ernie had a fantastic career, but at Augusta he just never hit that shot that you've got to hit at the right moment to steal the tournament," says Williams. "A champion always hit a career-defining shot, often at the par 5s like the 13th or 15th."

Woods's only real challenger, Singh, was three shots behind but also came undone spectacularly with a quadruple-bogey 9 at the 15th. Woods held his nerve so well he was able to bogey the 17th and still cruise to a 71. At 12 under (276), he won the Masters by three shots over Goosen (74). "Do I get the green pants for finishing second?" Goosen joked. Mickelson was third at 8 under. "This [Masters] was more of a physical test than last year, being a chance to win all four majors in a row and retain them all; that was a mental test to try and block everything out," Woods said.

Perhaps the weather and the delays were a grind, but Woods's performance suggested his seventh major championship victory was a cakewalk. He was on autopilot hitting 69 percent of fairways for four rounds and 75 percent of greens in regulation. He averaged 295 yards off the tee and made 19 birdies. He made just seven bogeys and had just one three-putt, at the difficult par-4 fifth on Sunday.

Williams was blown away that Woods had just one three-putt for 72 holes. His handwritten statistics detailed that in 1999, Woods had seven three-putts at Augusta, four three-putts in 2000 and four again in 2001, when he won by two shots.

After Woods's third green jacket victory, Earl Woods had suggested his son almost had a psychological weapon that forced competitors to falter, even though he'd only shot 71. "I don't care what any of these guys say about not looking at him or not noticing what he's doing," Earl said outside Augusta National's Butler Cabin. "Tiger intimidates through osmosis. You feel it. It freaks people out."

Williams agreed that Woods and Nicklaus were such dominant players their presence high on a leaderboard could force rivals to press too hard, especially at Augusta National, whose tricky back nine—particularly the par-3 12th and par 5s at Nos. 13 and 15—punished reckless aggression.

Woods was presented the green jacket for the second year in a row, just the third time a Masters champion had defended his title, after Nicklaus (1965, 1966) and Faldo (1989, 1990). Because Woods had won the previous Masters, there wasn't a champion to place the green jacket on Woods and instead it was the club's chairman, Hootie Johnson, who did the honor.

Williams never hung around for trophy presentations at the Masters. He had his own tradition; he would grab a beer out of the caddie shack, walk to the driving range, sit on the bleachers behind it and take it all in. The trophy presentation, and donning of the jacket, was several hundred yards away. Williams could hear fans leaving the course, cheering and verbally reliving Woods's latest Masters triumph. "There'd be no one there and I'd just listen; I found it very soothing," he says.

Woods's seventh major came at the age of 26 years, four months and 15 days. He was 13 months younger than Nicklaus was when he won his seventh major. No player had ever won seven majors as quickly as Woods, and there were still three more in 2002. Woods had won six of the 10 majors since the 1999 PGA, and half of the six Masters he'd played as a professional.

Relics of golfing history. Woods's Titleist staff golf bag from 1999 (*right*), and the Buick bag he began using in 2000 (*left*), now sit in the bar within Williams's house in New Zealand. Williams always carried in Woods's golf bag a wooden tee Woods didn't snap during the entire 2000 Open Championship at St. Andrews, which became a lucky charm; a Stanford University pouch; and two peanut butter and banana sandwiches for Woods.

The 1999 Bay Hill Invitational was Williams's first tournament with Woods. Note that Williams is wearing pants. After various trials in 1999, a rule mandating PGA Tour caddies wear pants was scrapped in September 2000.

The 1999 PGA Championship at Medinah was arguably the most important win for Williams and Woods. During the final round, Williams correctly overruled Woods's read of a pivotal par putt late on the back nine. Woods won a long-awaited second major and established "100 percent trust" in his caddie going forward.

Woods consulted Williams on the 18th green on the final day at the 2000 Open at St. Andrews because he needed to two-putt for par to break Nick Faldo's scoring record of 270. Woods did, and shot 269. He became the fifth golfer to complete the career grand slam. No golfer has achieved that feat in the twenty-five years since. Williams still has the 18th green flag from the Old Course that he is holding in this picture.

1 Handwritten messages of gratitude to Williams showed a caring and thoughtful side of Woods. On the 18th green flag from the 81st PGA (1999), their first major win together, Woods referenced Williams's par putt advice when he wrote, *"To Stevie, Nice read on 17!!"*

2 On the flag from Valhalla's 18th green from the 82nd PGA, Woods wrote, *"To Stevie, Well done!!!"*

3 Williams cherishes a flag from the 2001 Masters Tournament because Woods won an unprecedented fourth major in a row. An unspoken rule is that Masters champions are the only people allowed to sign inside of Augusta National's logo.

4 For the 2005 Open Championship, when Woods completed the career grand slam a second time, Woods wrote on the flag, *"To Stevie, Thanks for the putting advice!!!"*

5 A year later, after Woods won the 2006 Open, he wrote to Williams on Royal Liverpool's 18th green flag, *"To Stevie, You're the best. Thanks again for helping me attain my goals. Your friend always, Tiger Woods."* He also referenced his hole-out eagle on the 14th hole, *"P.S. Nice yardage on 14."*

6 On the flag Williams took from Southern Hills after the 2007 PGA Championship, Woods wrote his most heartfelt message. *"To Stevie, Thanks for your friendship. Love always, Tiger Woods."*

7 An injured yet relentless Woods won the 2008 U.S. Open in sudden death at the par-4 7th hole against Rocco Mediate.

In early 2002, Woods's team, including Williams and swing coach Butch Harmon, were confident Woods could win four majors in a calendar year. Critics spent 2001 debating whether Woods's four consecutive majors were a grand slam given they were won across two years. Williams and Harmon are pictured speaking at Augusta National during the 2002 Masters that Woods won.

When Williams joined Woods's team, he made a bet with the superstar: if he helped Woods to win a major in the first twelve months, he had to play in the New Zealand Open. More than two years after the 1999 PGA, Woods paid the bet and competed at the 2002 New Zealand Open at Paraparaumu Beach Golf Club. Here, Woods presses noses in an ancient Māori greeting, called a "hongi," with Kuia Mereiwa Broughton during an official Māori welcome (pōwhiri) at the Wellington airport.

The 2005 Ford Championship offered Woods, the winner, a rare Ford GT in addition to prize money. It was a remodeled version of the historic Ford GT40 MKII, which had won the 24 Hours of Le Mans race for four consecutive years from 1966. Woods threw the keys to Williams, a lifelong Ford fan and saloon car racer. More than twenty years later, Williams keeps the car in his garage in New Zealand with low miles on it.

Williams's outlet from the pressure cooker of caddying for Woods was saloon car racing in New Zealand. His race number is twenty-one, which inspired Woods to target twenty-one career majors when trying to overtake Jack Nicklaus's record eighteen. Valvoline was a sponsor of Williams, a logo he wore proudly on his golf shirts while caddying.

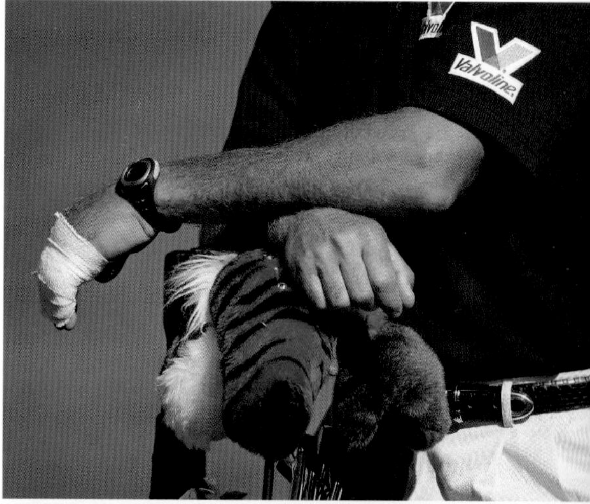

In early 2005, the worst saloon car racing accident Williams ever experienced caused broken ribs and a severed finger. Woods offered to send his private plane to New Zealand to bring Williams to the U.S. for medical attention. The ultra-tough Williams recovered from surgery and caddied for Woods at Riviera Country Club in February 2005, within three weeks of the accident.

Chris DiMarco, a three-time PGA Tour winner, was kind enough to share an image of the golf ball he kept from the 2005 Masters. DiMarco and Woods were the only players left on Augusta's practice range before the final round. DiMarco wrote "Go Gators!" on a ball to celebrate a recent University of Florida Gators basketball win at the SEC tournament. He chipped the ball to Woods, who scribbled out "Go" and replaced it with "F—k the." Woods later defeated DiMarco in a playoff.

The elation shown by Woods and Williams after defeating DiMarco to win the 2005 Masters was fueled by an almost three-year slump at the majors. It reignited Woods's pursuit of Nicklaus's record and triggered one of Woods's most remarkable runs.

Woods was always fascinated by Williams's car racing and took an interest in his caddie's lifelong passion. In 2006, after Williams's wedding, he and Woods held a press conference to discuss the golfer's participation in the Valvoline Celebrity Classic, a charity car race.

Early in the morning of Williams's wedding day, Woods caddied for Williams while he played with wedding guests and friends at his home golf course, the South Head Golf Club. The group ate afterward in the clubhouse in preparation for the big day.

Woods with Williams and his bride Kirsty and Jason Carter during Williams's 2006 wedding in New Zealand. Williams reflects fondly on the wedding as a rare moment when their golfing pursuits paused and the pair were simply friends.

Woods and Williams laugh during the ceremony, which was held in Kumeū, west of Auckland, only minutes from Williams's house.

Woods delivers his best man speech, which was littered with jokes but also meaningful observations. Woods said he felt Williams gained more perspective and work–life balance when he met Kirsty.

When Williams saw the Liverpool sun briefly appear on an overcast Sunday at the 2006 Open Championship, he said to Woods, "That's Pops, looking down on you." It caused Woods to break down in tears moments later with the emotion of the recent passing of his father, Earl. Williams had devised a game plan for Woods to hit driver just once in the four rounds, taking advantage of a firm, fast Hoylake course to win a third Claret Jug.

Woods won the 2008 U.S. Open on a broken leg. The instability of fairway bunker shots like this, during the 18-hole playoff with Rocco Mediate, put even more pressure on his injury. Williams calls Woods's fourteenth major win "one of the greatest accomplishments in sport."

Woods and Williams at the 2005 U.S. Open at Pinehurst, when he finished runner-up to New Zealander Michael Campbell. Williams is holding a headcover depicting a kiwi, a flightless bird endemic to New Zealand. Woods used it as a nod to Williams's New Zealand heritage.

Williams felt Woods's talent and work ethic were likely to yield at least one major a year. He was the best player in the world by a long stretch. The 2002 Masters was pivotal, Williams believed, in sustaining momentum after "an enormous comedown" from winning four majors in a row at the 2001 Masters. That manifested in Woods failing to finish in the top 10 in the next three majors of 2001. When Woods went a stretch of majors without winning, or even contending, Williams likened the difficulty in bouncing back for Woods to the difficulty of a normal tour pro trying to win a second major after securing their first. "That's the level of pressure he put himself under to chase Jack's record," Williams says.

Williams flew home to New Zealand the following day—given Woods was not playing again for almost a month—and delivered the good news to Kirsty, his girlfriend, they were going on a tropical holiday to Saint Martin in the Caribbean in December.

Woods's next two starts were the Byron Nelson event on the PGA Tour, and the European Tour's Deutsche Bank-SAP Open in Germany, where Woods received a reported $2 million appearance fee to defend his 2001 victory. While a hefty sum, it was an astute investment for tournament officials given almost 78,000 fans attended over four days and an unprecedented number of media credentials were issued.

European stalwart Colin Montgomerie and Woods were tied after 72 holes and went to a three-hole playoff at the Golf Club St. Leon-Rot near Heidelberg, in Germany. Woods defeated the smooth-swinging Montgomerie to record his third victory at the tournament in four years. "Tiger was up against Monty in a playoff, who was the top golfer in Europe, and he was very chuffed to have beaten him," Williams says. Woods said after defeating Montgomerie, "He is a great friend and a true champion."

The unfortunate streak for "Monty," as he was affectionately known, continued—he had never won a tournament with Woods in the field. Most of those were in the U.S., and the curmudgeonly Scotsman, who had won 26 events on the European Tour, had a love-hate relationship with the American golf crowds. He was heckled so badly at a PGA Tour event in February 2002 that he hinted he would no longer play tournaments in the U.S. It prompted one American golf magazine to write an editorial and hand out free buttons bearing the phrase "Be Nice to Monty," in an attempt to curb unruly fan behavior ahead of June's U.S. Open at Bethpage on Long Island.

After the Germany tournament, Woods and Williams were to fly back to the U.S. on a private jet out of a military air base in Heidelberg. Williams felt a wave of satisfaction wash over him, reflecting on the fact Woods had come to Europe for one of its biggest golf tournaments and defeated the continent's top golfer in a playoff. They closed out the trip in style, cruising in the two luxury vehicles tournament officials had loaned Woods's team. Williams was a car enthusiast and couldn't help being thrilled with the Lamborghini and Ferrari. Heading to the military air base, Williams drove Greg Nared—the former University of Maryland basketball player who worked as a Nike liaison for Woods's team—while Woods had Mark Steinberg in his car. "When I finally pulled onto the runway, it had a small dip that I couldn't see and my car got a little airborne," Williams says. "When I returned the car, it was a little bit worse for wear."

CHAPTER 8

THE PEOPLE'S OPEN

Woods walked off a private plane at Republic Airport on New York's Long Island early in the morning on Tuesday, May 28, 2002, and made the 10-minute drive to Bethpage State Park in Farmingdale, about 40 miles east of Manhattan. For a city that doesn't sleep, most New Yorkers were dozing when arguably the world's most famous sports star slipped through its back door and onto the third tee at the Bethpage Black Course, a half mile from the clubhouse and away from public golfers. Woods was joined by Mark O'Meara in scouting Bethpage, which was about to become the first municipal course to host the U.S. Open in its 107-year history. "It was so early the greenkeepers were only starting to cut the greens," O'Meara recalls. The pair had the course to themselves, while a state trooper, and Bethpage's superintendent, Craig Currier, joined them for a walk.

Recreational golfers would likely have recognized Woods's unmistakable figure at the clubhouse and caused a scene, so Woods started on No. 3, but played Nos. 1 and 2 at the end. No. 3 at the

Black Course was a 205-yard par 3. In the humid spring air, a local caddie, filling in for Williams, who did not make the quick trip to New York, handed Woods a 5-iron to hit his first-ever golf shot at Bethpage. Woods had hardly set foot on Long Island since he was an amateur playing the 1995 U.S. Open at Shinnecock Hills, out in the Hamptons.

The hype for the 2002 U.S. Open was unlike any buildup in the championship's history—likely only rivaled by the 100th U.S. Open at Pebble Beach in 2000. There were three reasons: First because Woods was aiming to become just the fifth player in history to win the first two majors of the year. Second, because Bethpage Black was the host. Although it was the 15th time America's national championship was being held in the State of New York, the other host courses were all private country clubs. Shinnecock Hills, an hour farther east into the affluent Hamptons, and Winged Foot Country Club near Westchester, and Garden City Country Club, also on Long Island, were among the country's most exclusive private golf clubs. The U.S. Open was now coming to an Average Joe's course. The Bethpage Park Authority owned the entire park, where five golf courses operated, three of which were designed or modified by celebrated Golden Age architect A. W. Tillinghast. He designed other major championship courses in the Tri-State Area, like Winged Foot and Baltusrol in New Jersey.

In 2002, the weekday green fee for the Black Course was $31 for anyone willing to wait. Plenty were willing, and there was plenty of waiting. Tee times were designated on a first-come, first-served basis. Only the first 24 golfers waiting each morning were assured of playing and it wasn't uncommon for golfers to show up 24 hours before their desired tee time. From 4 to 9 P.M. daily, bracelets were handed out to people in a car line for the following morning, with four people maximum allowed in a car (due to golf being played in groups of four). Tickets were given out at 5 A.M. and at least one person had to be in the car at all times. Tee times *could* be reserved weeks in advance via computer, but they booked out in minutes.

It was fitting, then, that the theme song Williams chose to sing all week was "Born in the U.S.A." by Bruce Springsteen. Williams would blast the song from his CD player every night before bed, feeling a surge of adrenaline while visualizing the crowds at Bethpage as the stadium-like drums and synthesizer rang through his headphones.

Williams felt the song had a strong connection to this U.S. Open; it was America's national championship. It was democratic; any golfer good enough could qualify. Springsteen was an all-American rock star who grew up two hours down the road from Bethpage in Asbury Park, New Jersey. This was the most American the U.S. Open had ever been. This was as blue-collar as a major championship in the U.S. could get. The fans were coming from all over Brooklyn, Manhattan, New Jersey, Connecticut and across New England. "Many of the fans were public golf course people and 'Born in the U.S.A.' was a blue-collar song," Williams says.

Woods took a liking to the news that Bethpage would host a major from the moment the USGA announced the news. Not only had Woods grown up playing golf on a modest navy course in Cypress, California, which had a similar sentiment to Bethpage, but Woods's golfing ancestry had deep connections to New York. Woods's father, Earl, had played his first game of golf near Bethpage, in Brooklyn, 30 years earlier while working for the military and was stationed at Brooklyn's Fort Hamilton. Earl was 40 in 1972 when he played the Dyker Beach Golf Course in Dyker Heights. He fell in love with the game, and borrowed golf instruction books, *Five Lessons* by Ben Hogan and *Golf My Way* by Jack Nicklaus, from a library. Earl also noticed a fellow lieutenant colonel, Daniel Lee, was a good golfer and played at Fountain Green Golf Course at Fort Dix in New Jersey, the nearest military course to New York. While playing with Lee, Earl would glean tips on how to improve. "As we played, he would attempt to get key points and go back and practice religiously," Lee told golf writer Hank Gola in 2002.

Earl even had a connection to Bethpage Black; soon after taking up golf, he played the Black Course one day as a single. He joked that "it took my manhood, my pride, everything." Earl added that he was "cocky" about his ability on the beastly course but after several holes of getting his butt kicked, he stopped playing, lay down underneath a tree and instead took in its beauty. "[Then] I went right to the snack bar and ordered a Heineken," he said.

The third, and perhaps most important, reason the 2002 U.S. Open was so anticipated was it offered something of a healing event in the form of a world-class sporting spectacle New York needed in the aftermath of the September 11 attacks in Manhattan, nine months earlier. Although the Buick Open was held at nearby Westchester Country Club the week before the 2002 U.S. Open, it was a regular PGA Tour event at an exclusive course. It was not in the same league as America's national golf open.

Chris DiMarco, although raised in Orlando, was originally from Huntington, New York, 10 miles from Bethpage. He felt New Yorkers, a proud bunch, were hurting deeply and deserved a distraction. "They needed big-time golf. For Tiger to win, in all honesty. They needed the best player in the world to do magical stuff and just take their minds off [9/11], if only for a week," DiMarco says. "There's a lot of pride in New York; to see it that week was amazing."

Families of some of the September 11 victims were coming out to watch the U.S. Open, including the children of Chief Peter J. Ganci, Jr., the highest-ranking uniformed officer in the New York

City Fire Department. There was also 12-year-old Christopher Otten, who was among a large group of children and their mothers taken to Bethpage by the Uniformed Firefighters Association to watch the Tuesday practice round. Christopher had lost his father, Michael Otten, of Ladder 35, on September 11. Christopher got several signatures from pro golfers before Woods learned of his story and came out to personally greet him, sign his hat and thank him for attending. "I distinctly remember Christopher was well-mannered and grateful; I hoped that helped his recovery a little," Williams recalls. Woods said at the time that, "This is going to be an exciting event for the people who live here and have had to see the [9/11] tragedy firsthand."

Williams felt it was an outstanding idea from U.S. Open officials to give New York City police officers and firefighters working or volunteering roles at Bethpage. He and Woods bantered with them all week. Williams recalls prior to the third round, when Woods was paired with Pádraig Harrington, the Irishman walked onto the practice putting green and began putting at a particular hole. A police officer who was in charge of the area all week said, "Hey! That's where Tiger starts his putting!"

The resilience shown by the families of September 11 victims was one of many reminders that to win a major in the State of New York, on a course as difficult as Bethpage Black, the champion was going to have to be gritty and tough. At 7,214 yards, Bethpage was the longest course in U.S. Open history. The rough came up to golfers' ankles and the greens were going to be quick. The most excruciating stretch was after the turn, specifically two long par 4s: the 492-yard 10th and 499-yard 12th. Bethpage Black, for the U.S. Open, was also a par 70, meaning the pros were given two strokes less to complete the round than with a typical par 72. The United States Golf Association had switched the seventh hole from the 553-yard par 5 it was for weekend golfers to a 489-yard par 4. Woods had never won a major on a par 70.

Bethpage had just two par 5s, instead of four on most courses, where pros had a better chance at making birdies. "After the scouting trip in May, Tiger knew that an even par total for four rounds [280] was going to be close to winning, maybe a couple shots under par at best," Williams says. Woods worked rigorously on his driving after the scouting mission.

Once at the U.S. Open, Ernie Els, who had won the championship twice, described the conditions at Bethpage as "a torture chamber." One celebrity who backed Woods to take it on was NBA legend Charles Barkley. At Woods's charity event, the Tiger Jam in Las Vegas, Barkley said of Woods's opponents, "Tiger is the greatest ever. I have played with Phil [Mickelson] and all those guys. Tiger does things they can't do. They are intimidated by Tiger."

Crowds of nearly 50,000 flocked to Bethpage on Wednesday, June 12, to watch Woods tee off in an early morning practice round. Standing on the tee waiting for Woods to hit his first shot on Wednesday, Williams rummaged around Woods's Buick bag and couldn't help but smile when he saw a 10-millimeter ring spanner he had recently purchased from a hardware store in New Zealand. Williams was an avid collector of flags from the 18th green at tournaments that his bosses—such as Ian Baker-Finch, Greg Norman, Ray Floyd and now Woods—had won. With Woods, though, Williams had been gathering the knitted polyester fabric flags at a rate he'd never envisioned. The ring spanner removed the flag from the flagstick rapidly, a necessity given the chaos that immediately followed a Woods victory. He'd use it to screw the cap off the top of the flag, which was always 10 millimeters wide. In 1999, Williams was on the bag for eight victories from 17 official tournaments. That didn't include unofficial events like the 1999 World

Cup of Golf, which Woods won with O'Meara. In 2000, Woods won 10 official tournaments from 22 starts. In 2001, he won six from 21. In the first half of 2002, Woods already owned three wins from 12 tournaments. The 18th green flag was a symbolic trophy for the winning caddie at a tournament and Williams was likely the only caddie who carried a ring spanner. "It was a tool of frequent use," Williams says, laughing. He was hoping to use it again in Bethpage in four days' time because he desperately wanted to take home the flag from the 18th green at a municipal host of the U.S. Open.

Wednesday's practice round wasn't exactly a love-in for Woods. It was clear New Yorkers wanted to see the world number one at least squirm under a challenge, and Phil Mickelson had become a national crowd favorite. "Lefty" was world number two but had not won a major in 39 tries and fans wanted to see him get over the hump. "Some of the stuff [they said] I can't repeat," Woods said that Wednesday. Mickelson said, "What I *have* heard a lot of is, 'Hey, I would like to see you play [Bethpage] after spending the night in your car!'"

Security was also tighter than at any previous U.S. Open; there were more pat-downs and extra guards on patrol while helicopters performed regular flyovers. There were 42,000 tickets sold for each of the four rounds. Woods was bracing for four days of Long Island mayhem.

* * *

Under dark clouds, falling mist and distant thunder, Woods began his U.S. Open campaign at 1:35 P.M. on Thursday, June 13, grouped with DiMarco and Northern Ireland's Darren Clarke. Woods was among a group of competitors who started from the 10th tee, after organizers broke from a 101-year tradition of every player teeing off the first hole to implement a two-tee start. Woods birdied the ninth, his last hole, to shoot 67. At 3 under par, he led Garcia, who teed off in the morning and posted a 68 while his girlfriend, Swiss tennis star Martina Hingis, watched from the gallery.

Williams's handwritten statistics highlighted how difficult it was to keep pace with Woods—one of only six players from 156 to finish under par on day one. Woods hit 11 of 14 fairways, and 13 of 18 greens in regulation. He needed only 28 putts.

Despite the near-perfect display, the Long Island fans were raucous and gave Woods a taste of what he was in for that weekend. After he slipped in and out of a portable toilet between the 14th green and 15th tee, the crowd erupted ironically in applause. "Are you guys clapping because I'm potty-trained?" Woods joked to the crowd. There was going to be no country club polish about these galleries.

At the 16th, Woods stood over a par putt when a fan yelled during his putting stroke, causing him to flinch and miss. The galleries were also ironically nice to Scottish star Colin Montgomerie, with his complicated history with hecklers in the U.S. The "Be nice to Monty" campaign had somewhat backfired; fans yelled cheeky phrases such as "Monty, you're a hottie" and "We've got love for you, Monty," as well as "Cheerio!" They eventually turned on him, though. After a bogey at the 12th, they yelled, "Hey, Monty, don't choke!"

Woods began his second round under rain on the first hole on Friday at 8:35 A.M., and played well for a 68. He found nine fairways, hit 12 greens in regulation and had 28 putts. DiMarco recalls being dumbfounded that his playing partner, Woods, "didn't mishit a shot for two days. It was unreal." In the afternoon, Garcia was caught in biblical rain and dropped four shots during a 74. Furious, he made a controversial suggestion that, "If Tiger had been out there, I think they [officials] would have called it [stopped play]." Williams says the remarks "were ludicrous."

Garcia was fuming after being heckled for hours by several fans who loudly counted the number of times he would waggle, or regrip, the club, while standing over the ball, a tendency for golfers looking to shake away tension or nerves from their swing before hitting the ball. At the 16th, reporters detailed how Garcia slammed clubs on the ground and raised his fist at the gallery. "It was like, shut up, I'm trying to get something going here," Garcia said of his gestures. "Sometimes they make some stupid comments."Rubbing salt in the wound, a reporter addressed Garcia as "Tiger" after the round. Garcia put his face in his hands, dropped his microphone and looked up to the clouds.

Williams and Woods, despite finding some of the crowd banter funny initially, admitted the fans had likely gone too far. They felt for Garcia.

At 5 under, Woods led Harrington by three shots after two rounds and was paired with the Irishman for the third day. Harrington was exposed to the bizarre circus that was Tigermania: While Woods waited on the fifth tee, he tossed a banana peel into the trash. A fan waited until Woods moved down the hole and took the discarded fruit skin. "Tiger and I both saw and heard that because I can remember the fan screaming 'I've got it!' to his friends," says Williams. Incidents like that happened regularly at tournaments; often fans would run onto the tee on a par 3 after Woods walked off and pocket his wooden tee if he had not picked it up. Sometimes, when Woods hit a tee shot into rough, Williams saw fans take Woods's divots if the clumps of grass landed near them.

Woods felt uncomfortable with his swing and putting in round three but fought for an even-par 70, to remain at 5 under. Garcia, meanwhile, clawed his score back with a gutsy 67. He dealt with more severe heckling from the crowd, particularly on the last four holes as the beer flowed among the galleries. Garcia, who at one stage waggled 29 times over a shot, was called Whiner and Waggle Boy. At 1 under, Garcia sat second and booked a spot in Sunday's final pairing with Woods.

Fans and media were anticipating the pairing to be a made-for-television showdown. That was exacerbated when Woods and Williams left the range at 8:40 P.M. and returned to the locker room, where Woods found a letter of apology from Garcia regarding his rain remarks the previous day. Woods and Williams smiled, but they had bigger fish to fry. He was about to face tens of thousands of fans who wanted to watch him at least struggle. "Tiger was more excited than daunted thinking about a big Sunday against a crowd that wanted Mickelson to win and he knew he'd have some support as New Yorkers knew Tiger came from a public golf background," Williams says. He and Woods discussed before the final round that victory wasn't a certainty, and anyone could catch him. Williams's advice to Woods was that Greg Norman had a theory that any player could win a major championship starting from eight shots back on a Sunday. They still needed to play well.

Woods and Garcia teed off in the final round at 3:30 P.M. on Sunday, June 16. Fans hoping for a close contest were licking their lips when Woods, who'd been unflappable the first three days, three-putted for bogey on each of the first two holes. His lead was cut in half. "I wasn't worried, and neither was Tiger," Williams says.

A calming birdie finally arrived at the 489-yard, par-4 seventh. After a perfect drive, Woods fired a 2-iron approach to close range and made the birdie putt. After nine holes, Woods had restored his four-shot lead with Mickelson his nearest chaser.

After a great iron shot to the 11th green, Mickelson made birdie and was three shots back. The crowd was overwhelmingly on the left-hander's side, cheering his every step with, "LET'S GO, MICK-EL-SON!" They also sang "Happy Birthday" to Mickelson, who turned 32 that Sunday. Conversely, they spared no insult, with one heckler even yelling about Mickelson's weight, "Hey, Phil! Are those A cups?"

Mickelson's momentum, however, was stalled only a few minutes later, as Woods was finishing the 11th, when a weather delay was called. Mickelson appeared relaxed and laughed with officials during those 49 minutes. He even joked that if Woods resumed play before officials sounded the horn, they should "slap him with two," meaning a two-shot penalty. Williams recalls the weather delay was likely an advantage to Mickelson. "The New York fans had enjoyed a few beers that afternoon and what do you think they were going to do during a delay? Drink more beer." When Woods and Williams returned to play, the crowd was supercharged in their support for Mickelson. New Yorkers wanted to see an underdog win his first major on their course, which their city owned. He was the people's champion.

None of it bothered Woods. His first shot back from the delay was a missile with a driver from the 12th tee. At the par-5 13th, Mickelson closed to within two strokes, courtesy of a brilliant fairway metal for his second shot that set up a birdie.

Woods responded with a breathtaking long iron from 263 yards for his second shot at No. 13 and narrowly missed the eagle putt. Moments later, Mickelson bogeyed No. 16 and made another at No. 17—savagely ending his run.

Woods had enough of a cushion to bogey No. 18 and win by three shots. Woods's Sunday 72 gave him a 3-under total (277), with Mickelson runner-up at even par (280). Jeff Maggert was third at 2 over (282) and Garcia fourth at 3 over (283).

"It was an incredibly resilient performance from Tiger because he wasn't putting well," Williams says, consulting his statistics. Woods hit 12 fairways and 17 greens, his best tee to green stats all week. But on Sunday, he had three three-putts. His 38 total putts for the day was the highest number Williams ever saw from Woods in a single round at the majors. The only statistic that mattered, though, was the win. It was Woods's eighth major championship at the age of 26. As a partnership, Woods and Williams had won seven of 11 majors.

Well after dark at Bethpage, when the U.S. Open champion's obligations had wrapped up, Woods and his girlfriend, Elin Nordegren, as well as Williams, filed into Woods's private jet to fly back to Orlando. Williams recalls it was one of the rare occasions where the group did have a small celebration with a couple of drinks, instead of instantly planning the assault on the next major. "It wasn't a massive celebration, but by Tiger's standards it was good," Williams says. "There was a different air of excitement; a lot of laughter, banter and a few beers." For most of Woods's victories, including majors, there wasn't a lot of stopping to smell the roses. Victory was expected and his attention turned immediately to the next major. Williams guessed the cause for celebration this time was because Woods, by winning a major in the area where Earl had first played golf, felt he was tipping the cap to his dad.

Williams felt two aspects of the 2002 U.S. Open stood out. First, that Woods won a major later nicknamed The People's Open—played at the first municipal course to stage a U.S. Open—strengthened his legacy. Woods, a working-class guy, wanted that on his résumé. "It was also in New York, which feels like the people's city," Williams says. Second was a certain bittersweet feeling Williams experienced after Woods's win; it was the first time he could imagine an eventual end of his caddie career with Woods.

He felt that, while Woods was an amazing player to work for, and the Nicklaus quest was thrilling, the pressure was also a burden. "I didn't realize until I finished caddying for him what sort of toll it took on me, caddying for a global superstar like that," Williams says. "I began to think, *The quicker we can get to this career goal of breaking Jack's record, the quicker I could relieve myself of my duties*. It's not like I wanted it to end, but I knew from a mental standpoint, I needed to picture the finish line."

If Williams was beginning to feel like chasing Nicklaus's record was a marathon, then they were not even at the halfway mark. They did have momentum, though. In winning the 2002 Masters and U.S. Open, Woods had become the first player to win the first two majors of the year since Nicklaus in 1972. The 2002 Open Championship and PGA were still to come and the sporting world began to consider Woods reaching Nicklaus's 18 majors a fait accompli. As a partnership, Woods and Williams had won a major in 1999, and at least one in 2000, 2001 and 2002. That span also included the Tiger Slam.

Woods took a month off and returned to competition at the Open, where he was 4 under through two rounds and only two shots off the pace at Muirfield golf links. On the morning of Saturday, July 20, the weather was warm, for Gullane, on the east coast of Scotland, and the sun was shining over the Firth of Forth when Williams went for a run along Gullane Beach. It was hot enough that Williams ran without a shirt. Woods was in contention and not playing until 2:30 P.M., paired with O'Meara for the third round.

By the afternoon, the weather had turned miserable with strong gusts, cold temperatures and driving rain. In the worst weather Woods had ever played in as a professional, he shot 10-over 81. Nine other players shot in the 80s, while the four golfers who posted rounds in the 60s played before the wild weather rolled in. On Sunday, Woods rebounded with a 65 and tied for 28th, while Els won the Open for his third major. Failure to win the Open meant Woods's quest to win the calendar slam was over.

"I put my hand up for Tiger's 81 and I apologized to him," Williams says. Williams had an unusual habit of keeping Woods's golf bag as light as possible. Because the weather was perfect in the morning, he'd packed less protective gear—fresh gloves, rain gloves, extra towels and layers of warm clothing—than was needed out on the course. Under-packing made both their jobs wildly difficult. Williams admits it contributed to Woods's horrific score, although it may have only accounted for a few strokes of the 81. Williams was amazed at how unfazed Woods was by his caddie's mistake, given he could have blamed his entire round on Williams. "He was so mentally tough, he didn't get flustered with something minor like that or direct blame," Williams says.

Williams's penchant for keeping the bag light, which could weigh between 40 to 45 pounds, inconvenienced Woods on two other occasions. The Players Championship, at TPC Sawgrass, was prone to unstable northeast Florida weather in mid-March. One year, the weather had been perfect before Woods teed off, so Williams didn't pack the umbrella and rain gear. On the par-5 16th, rain moved in quickly and drenched the area. Knowing Woods had to play the nerve-racking par-3 17th over water, and the difficult par-4 18th, with very little protective apparel, Williams borrowed a fan's umbrella and gave it back to him after the round—with a signed glove from Woods. The third instance Williams was caught flat-footed was one year at Bay Hill, when the weather was perfect as Woods and his caddie left his Isleworth home for the day. Once out on the course, rain began to pour, and Woods asked Williams if someone from his wider team could fetch his umbrella from the car in the parking lot. "The umbrella is back at your house in the garage, mate," Williams said.

Woods never showed frustration at Williams for packing light, knowing a caddie's job, having to lug a heavy bag around—often in hot and humid weather—was physically taxing. Part of the reason, too, was that Woods relished the challenge of playing in foul weather and certainly wasn't going to moan if his caddie forgot protective gear. His father had encouraged Woods to push through rain, saying that the mentality he developed serving in the Special Forces was, "You can only get wet once." Williams considered Woods the best foul-weather player who had ever played on tour. He thought Woods's 68 on day two at the U.S. Open at Bethpage was the best foul-weather round he saw in his entire time with Woods. Woods had battled heavy rain, wind, thick rough and small, sloping greens to shoot a 2-under score that crushed the spirit of those high on the leaderboard.

One of Williams's habits did irk Woods, though. He was notorious for forgetting to zip up the pockets on the golf bag, even prior to working for Woods. "It really annoyed Tiger because the front pocket was where players put their valuables," Williams says. Caddies often lay a player's bag beside the green and picking it up could cause a watch or a phone to fall out. "Tiger's cell phone fell out once or twice, but thankfully I noticed quickly," Williams says.

* * *

The final major of 2002, the PGA Championship, was held at Hazeltine in Chaska, Minnesota, an outer-ring suburb of the Twin Cities. Woods began the final day five shots off the lead but cut the deficit to one after nine holes. Woods turned to Williams in the 15th fairway and declared that if he birdied the final four holes, he could win. Sure enough, he rattled off four straight birdies to post the clubhouse lead at 9 under—meaning he finished with the lowest total score while other golfers were still playing. Woods had found a level of concentration that rendered his caddie speechless. Williams didn't know Woods had any more gears.

It wasn't enough for Woods to win, though. Instead, he earned his first runner-up in a major. Journeyman Rich Beem held his nerve in the final group to win his only major, one shot ahead of Woods. Beem had quit professional golf years earlier, due to poor play, and worked as a car stereo salesman before returning to the PGA Tour in 1999 for one last-ditch effort. "I mean this in a nice way, but not only did Tiger hate losing when he was in contention at a major, he didn't want to be the guy to lose to a player no one expected to win [Beem]," Williams says.

A month later, Woods returned to one of his favorite countries, Ireland, for the World Golf Championships-American Express tournament at the Mount Juliet course in Kilkenny. Despite having been a regular visitor to the Emerald Isle, it was Woods's first 72-hole professional tournament in the lush links country. It was also the first tournament where Woods began using Nike golf clubs—drivers, irons and wedges. "The greens at Mount Juliet were the best greens we had ever seen, and Tiger putted beautifully," Williams says. Woods had 110 putts for the tournament—the equal lowest total Woods had for 72 holes during Williams's time.

Woods won the tournament and its US$1 million first-place prize. Remarkably, it was the best chance Woods had ever experienced to go a 72-hole tournament without a bogey. He hadn't dropped a single shot in 71 holes before smoking a drive down the fairway on the final hole, the par-4 18th at Mount Juliet.

"Tiger was well aware he hadn't made bogey and really wanted to achieve it but, on the 18th, he was in the final group and officials let the crowd walk behind us like the 72nd hole at the Open Championship," Williams says. As Woods began his backswing for his second shot, a photographer audibly took photos from behind him. Woods backed off, glared, and Williams engaged in a verbal exchange with the snapper. Woods was visibly frustrated once he returned to the golf ball and flared the shot to the right. He then missed his par putt and said afterward the moment had disturbed his focus. "He was devastated with that bogey," Williams says. In fact, Woods never played a PGA Tour event in his entire career without making a bogey. Ironically, he managed 110 holes without a bogey across two tournaments—from his fourth hole in the second round of the 2000 Bell Canadian Open (51 holes) through the fifth hole in round three at the 2000 National Car Rental Classic at Disney (59 holes).

The 2002 WGC-American Express also came the week prior to the 2002 Ryder Cup in England. Headlines flowed after Woods's tense exchange with a reporter after round one.

In your view, what would be more important for you, to win this week or the Ryder Cup next week?

Woods: "Here this week."

Why is it rather than next week?

Woods: "I can think of a million reasons why." [laughter]

Is it no contest for you, then, the question of which is more important?

Woods: "This is a big event [with] the best players in the world; you're playing stroke-play on a great golf course. I'm not saying the Ryder Cup is not important, it's a completely different animal. You can go out there and play lousy and the team can win, or play great and win all five matches, and lose the Ryder Cup."

Williams says Woods joked about the WGC's million-dollar winner's check to deflect from the Ryder Cup topic, but British tabloids didn't care. They had a field day with the quote. "Tiger never, ever played for prize money," he says. Williams understood Woods's opinion on the Ryder Cup; every pro golfer had a carefully orchestrated routine to perform at their best. At Ryder Cups, that routine went out the window as team members rarely got to bed before midnight due to commitments and functions.

Woods, and several other players in the 1990s and 2000s, weren't thrilled that the PGA of America, which runs the American team and Ryder Cup editions held in the U.S., made significant money but the golfers were the unpaid stars. The issue of not paying players was still a sore point 20 years later at the 2023 Ryder Cup in Rome.

The 2002 Ryder Cup was held at The Belfry, an elegant golf resort in Warwickshire, England, September 27 to 29. The biennial home-and-away event sees 12 Americans take on 12 Europeans in a three-day competition with 28 matches. The first team to 14.5 points wins the Cup, although the defending champions can retain it with a 14-to-14 tie. In 2002, the Europeans won 15.5 to 12.5.

On the Thursday practice session, Woods and U.S. teammate Mark Calcavecchia played a nine-hole practice round at 7 A.M. and were done before nine. The first practice-round tee time wasn't until ten, and many fans had bought a one-day ticket just to see Woods play. When there was no sign of him, a crowd marched to the hotel, which was on the property, and chanted for Woods to play. "Curtis Strange, the U.S. captain, made Tiger and 'Calc' go back out and play another nine holes," Williams says.

Woods rounded out his 2002 schedule by finishing in the top 10 in his last three official tournaments. After that, Woods had his second knee surgery, but the first of his professional career, on December 13. The procedure was done at the HealthSouth Surgical Center in Park City, Utah. Fluid was drained from inside and outside his knee ligament while benign cysts were also removed. Woods later revealed on his website that he had been "playing in pain for most of the year and felt it was time to take care of it." Woods's first knee surgery came in 1994, when he was at Stanford University and had a benign tumor removed from his left knee.

As far as Woods's relationship with Williams, they were firing on all cylinders. "We had that distinct line perfected for when we were friends, and when we were working," Williams says. The pair would need to lean on that friendship, on and off the course, because Woods was about to undergo a two-year slump that had him seriously contemplating walking away from the game.

CHAPTER 9

MASTERING THE SLUMP

On Saturday evening, May 17, 2003, Woods and Williams snuck onto the practice fairway at the Gut Kaden golf course outside Heidelberg in Germany, determined not to be seen by media and, especially, by photographers. The sun in northern Germany didn't set until nine thirty at this time of year, so Woods had to be discreet. He wanted to test a rival equipment company's driver.

Woods had just played the third round of the Deutsche Bank-SAP Open with the French golfer Marc Farry, a Parisian who turned pro in 1979 and had spent the early part of his career teaching golf in Florida. Internally, Woods was rattled. He'd spent the entire round being outdriven by Farry by at least 10 yards on almost every hole. But he was 16 years younger than Farry, who smoked cigarettes on the course. Although a prolific winner on the French domestic circuit, Farry's only career victory on the European Tour came in 1996—two months before Woods had even turned pro. Woods was 27, lifted heavy weights and ran eight miles a day. He looked like an NFL player. Woods and Williams were baffled, repeatedly whispering to each other, "Can you f——g believe this?"

The two could only conclude that TaylorMade's new R510 TP driver, which Farry used, was how he'd outmuscled Woods on almost every par 4 and 5. The R510 TP had a 390cc clubhead that was 60cc larger than its previous version. The Carlsbad company had created technology that maximized the energy transfer from a traveling clubhead into the ball, helping golfers, from pros to weekend hackers, boost their distance. Woods, meanwhile, was using the first driver Nike had ever manufactured, the Forged Titanium. "I asked around, among the players who had one, and got a TaylorMade driver that Saturday night in Germany because Tiger wanted to hit it," Williams says.

There was a tree in the middle of the driving range that was perfect for Woods to stand in front of and hit balls in private. Williams walked out to the end of the practice fairway, at around 295 yards from Woods, and waited for his boss to hit several balls with the Nike driver. Williams would watch the ball flight and move out of the way if it headed toward him. Woods then held up his arm to indicate he'd switched to the TaylorMade driver, and hit between five and 10 shots. "Tiger averaged about 292 yards off the tee in 2003, but the TaylorMade driver was almost 20 yards longer in that range session," Williams says.

While Woods was paid $20 million a year to be a Nike ambassador, he wasn't contractually obliged to use their clubs. In fact, he used Titleist for his 3-wood, wedges and putter. But he knew switching drivers would cause headlines, and he wanted Nike's golf division to be a success. Still, distance was distance, so Woods decided to use the TaylorMade driver, with 7.5 degrees of loft, for the final round in Germany. He finished T29, but shot 68 and jumped nine places on the leaderboard. As renowned golf equipment journalist Mike Johnson wrote, "It sent gearheads into overdrive." Photos quickly circulated, but by the time Woods was back in the U.S. and playing the Memorial Tournament, he had reverted to a Nike driver. Two months later, though, Woods informed Nike he would put an old Titleist driver, the 975D, back in the bag for the Buick Open. It was not a great look for Nike Golf, even though Woods had won two majors with their driver. But Nike's design team worked eagerly to meet Woods's driver needs and he eventually settled with a club he liked off the tee.

Despite switching drivers, Woods was protective of the Nike brand and its efforts to get into golf. He was, according to Williams, honored that a mainstream sports apparel giant was showing an interest in golf. It was an opportunity to introduce Nike fans of other sports to golf, not necessarily golf fans to Nike.

Curiosity was high that elite tour pros such as Woods and Duval were using Nike equipment when most players were aligned with brands like TaylorMade, Callaway and Titleist. Nike Golf became its own division in 2001 and had more than 200 employees. By 2002, Nike clubs were available in retail stores. A bizarre incident occurred toward the end of 2002 when, according to *Sports Illustrated*, Woods was at the Target World Challenge at Sherwood Country Club, in Thousand Oaks, California, when several wedges went missing from his golf bag in the locker room during the pro-am dinner. "Tiger never, ever, left his clubs in the locker room at a tournament but at this event he hadn't completed his host duties for the evening, so they were put in the locker," Williams says. Tour pros treated their equipment like gold, having spent years dialing in their specifications, especially with wedges. Wedges, which range in loft from 48 to 62 degrees, are temperamental because of the way their sharp leading edges (the bottom of the club) interact with turf. Wedges are also at the coalface for scoring on the course; they help golfers make birdies on par 5s when laying up or when they miss the green in two shots, and are a vital tool to save par on par 4s when failing to hit the green.

Even at tournaments where the locker room was patrolled by security guards, Woods refused to leave his clubs. Most tour pros, though, typically left their clubs in the locker at the host course from the Tuesday practice round until the end of the tournament Sunday (earlier if they missed the cut). Woods's Nike clubs were so meticulously calibrated to his needs that Williams guarded them like the Fabergé egg, transporting them to and from Woods's car in the parking lot to his accommodation. That was every day of every tournament Woods played. "There was one other occasion, in 2003, when Tiger definitely knew someone had tinkered with his clubs, or had taken some out to have a look, because they weren't put back in the order we kept them in the bag," Williams says.

Considering the research and development Nike had invested in crafting golf balls for Woods, such as the Tour Accuracy ball in 2000, he didn't leave those at the course, either. "There were players who thought that, whilst he was playing a Nike ball, it wasn't actually a Nike ball," Williams recalls.

The daily ritual made for a funny scene, and Williams laughed when Woods called himself the "car park pro." Woods played out of the back of his car and almost took pride in changing his shoes in the parking lot. At many private golf courses, it was considered tasteful and good etiquette for a golfer to change their shoes inside the clubhouse rather than at their car. Williams would either be with Woods in the tournament courtesy car or travel separately and meet him in the parking lot. He would take the clubs to the range or putting green, while Woods would eat inside the clubhouse. "It was meaningful that Tiger played out of his car, given he had grown up playing municipal courses, and that's how it was done," Williams says.

Months before Woods was outmuscled by Farry in Germany, his Nike equipment had been mocked by Phil Mickelson in an interview with *Golf Magazine*. The left-hander, who hadn't won a major, poured fuel on their rivalry when he said Woods "hates that I can fly it past him now." Mickelson gave a backhanded compliment when he noted Woods had a faster swing speed but used "inferior equipment." Williams felt Mickelson's remarks had likely set Nike Golf back. Woods was deeply offended. He and Williams reminded themselves Mickelson was likely trying to get inside Woods's head at the beginning of a season. "But Tiger was too smart and mentally tough; it was nearly impossible to throw him off his game," Williams says.

It was getting more difficult, though, to withstand critics while Woods endured a majors slump that eventually seeped into his results on the PGA Tour regular. The majors drought began in the second half of 2002 and lasted until the end of 2004. In 2003 and 2004, he registered only two top 10s at the majors, one at each Open Championship. This was a player who was expected to win at least one a year. Woods won five PGA Tour titles in 2003 and finished in the top 10 in 12 of his 18 tournaments. But in 2004, he won just once.

The root cause of the slump could clearly be traced back to when he parted ways with longtime swing coach Butch Harmon in August 2002. Apart from the occasional telephone conversation with Harmon, Woods was largely coaching himself in 2003. He would have Williams check his posture and alignment at tournaments and, whenever Woods was rehearsing a certain move within the swing, confirm he was executing it to his intention. At home at Isleworth, Woods would occasionally ask O'Meara or John Cook to look at his swing.

As his results suffered, there were brief moments of tension, instability and even professional restlessness inside Woods's camp. Externally, there was ongoing media coverage of Woods's rough patch, fueled by one very public spat between Woods and Williams in April 2003.

The most heated and visible argument Woods and Williams ever had boiled over on the ninth hole at Augusta National during the final round of the 2003 Masters. It epitomized the ongoing scrutiny and pressure Woods and his team faced. The two had disagreed over club selection on the tee at the third hole at Augusta, a short par 4. Williams urged Woods to hit driver; he was only three shots behind the lead, and it was time to attempt to drive the green and possibly make birdie or an eagle. Woods, though, wanted to lay up safely from the tee with an iron. Williams convinced Woods to hit driver, which he flared out to the right and had to play his second shot from against a tree, left-handed. He walked away with a double-bogey 6. Considering many would birdie the hole, his tournament was effectively over. Woods was as pissed off as Williams had ever seen him.

"Tiger had not said a word to me for over five holes, or 90 minutes, when I finally read him the riot act in the ninth fairway," Williams says. He gave Woods both barrels: "You hit a s——t shot! Stop acting like a child! I didn't give you bad advice; you were only three back and needed to press! Driver was the right call!" Woods bit back, and the pair hashed it out, loudly. Williams was hoping the dressing-down would fire his boss up for the back nine, because he still believed Woods could shoot 30 (6 under) and steal a win.

At the completion of the round, Woods told his caddie he was glad he spoke up and that it was petty not to talk to him for so long. The two moved on, but a reporter had picked up on the exchange and it made headlines. Woods addressed the story on his website via a statement, which also doubled down on his desire to play conservatively on No. 3. "Contrary to some reports, Stevie and I are getting along fine," Woods wrote.

Woods went on to shoot 75 and tied for 15th at 2 over while Mike Weir won, becoming the first Canadian champion at Augusta. Woods had bookended the Masters with an opening round of 76 (4 over) and a 75. According to Williams's statistics, Woods's first round at the 2003 Masters featured no birdies. Only twice in 12 years working for Woods did Williams witness him fail to make a single birdie in a round at the majors. The other occasion was the third round at the 1999 Open Championship at Carnoustie.

The Masters was only the tip of the iceberg. Woods finished tied 20th at the U.S. Open at Olympia Fields. He had a golden opportunity on the final day of the Open Championship a month later, at Royal St. George's, when he started Sunday two shots off the pace. But he failed to mount a charge and tied fourth. At the 2003 PGA at Oak Hill, he was 12 over par and tied 39th.

In 2003, it was the only time during Williams's tenure that Woods finished each of the four majors over par. In 1999, his cumulative total across the four majors was 1 over par, but he had shot 11 under during his 1999 PGA win. In 2000, his cumulative score was 53 under, winning three majors. In 2001, he was 15 under with one victory. In 2002, he was 24 under and won two. In 2003, he was 18 over and all four majors were over par. "Things had really unraveled in all parts of the game," Williams says. While Woods's ball-striking was off, his putting was also beneath his standards. At the U.S. Open at Olympia Fields, he had a total of 131 putts for four rounds—the most of any tournament Williams worked for Woods.

Williams was working overtime trying to find information that could help him react and adjust his strategy. He would observe the way Woods moved around at a tournament and make notes in a book after each round:

What was Tiger like playing in the morning versus in the afternoon?

"Everyone liked playing in the morning for the first two rounds because the weather was normally calmer. Some guys scored better in the afternoon because they were more awake and alert. But Tiger warmed up enough to be ready for any tee time."

What was his mood when he's not in contention versus when he was in contention?

"Tiger was always focused, but when he was in contention, his concentration elevated to such a degree that it was very common to say something to him, and he didn't even hear it. When I had to repeat myself, I knew he was in the zone."

What was his focus level playing in the final group versus second-to-last group?

"In final rounds, he was as intense when playing in the last pairing as he was from, say, five shots back with an earlier tee time. He always believed he could win as long as he started the final day within eight shots."

Williams never wanted to be thrown into a situation he hadn't seen before. He noticed trends, too. If Woods walked toward a certain area of the practice facilities at a normal or slow speed, that indicated he was comfortable with that part of his game. When he walked quickly, that signaled Woods wasn't satisfied and knew that facet of golf needed work, hence the urgency. When Woods walked onto a driving range, he'd always begin his warm-up with a sand wedge. He never had a target for those first few shots. Williams would watch intently for tension in the swings, and whether the timing was rhythmic, like a metronome. "When Tiger was 100 percent confident, those first few swings were effortless and almost lazy-looking and he wouldn't even bother watching where the ball landed," Williams says. But on days when Woods was out of sync, those initial swings had a forced commitment. He'd watch the ball flight intently.

Professionally, it was a tough time for Williams. Majors were really all Woods cared about. He chose to focus on small positives, like a milestone he had been waiting for his entire career. Until the end of 2003, Williams had rarely flown business class to tournaments. Despite being one of the highest-earning sportspeople in New Zealand—collecting approximately $3.4 million from his share of Woods's prize money between 1999 and 2003—Williams refused to fly up front until he reached the age of 40. He wanted to earn the privilege and was looking forward to it more than any perk of caddying for a top-tier golfer. Of course, he did travel to most tournaments on Woods's private plane—but only once he was in Orlando. Most of his flights in and out of the U.S., and around the world, were in coach class.

Holding off allowed Williams some normality while working for a global superstar. Woods didn't mind that Williams was based in New Zealand as long as he showed up at tournaments on the correct day. Plus, that's what he'd done his entire career, caddying around Australia, Europe, Asia and the U.S. "Tiger's staff were always fascinated that I didn't want to fly business class," Williams says.

Williams had gone into caddying in 1978 as a way to see the world, regardless of the seat on the plane. After 1999, it became a regular occurrence for airline passengers to ask Williams, "Hey, aren't you Tiger Woods's caddie?" with a confused expression as to why the megastar's bagman was in coach. Williams found it funny, and so would the passengers once he'd explain he was waiting for

December 29, 2003—his 40th birthday—to move to the front of the plane. Most fans thought Williams lived the high life, but he was not a flashy person. He didn't buy gifts for himself, other than pouring money into his saloon car racing. "For a long time while I caddied for Tiger, I drove a Ford Laser until I couldn't drive it anymore," says Williams. Occasionally, Williams would fly business to European editions of the Ryder Cup, on the American team's chartered plane. In the 1980s, while caddying for Norman, who was an ambassador for the Australian airline Qantas, he'd occasionally be gifted a business ticket.

Williams finally took up regular business-class travel on the eight-hour flight from Auckland to Honolulu, Hawaii, on Monday, January 5, 2004, for the Mercedes Championships at Kapalua. While he enjoyed the new flying accommodation, he continued to find himself worried about the new season and what it would bring.

* * *

The year 2004 yielded even fewer victories. Woods was a nonfactor in the three American majors but was in contention at the Open Championship at Troon. In the regular events, Woods's results were respectable, but he struggled to close out wins for the first time in eight years as a pro. Woods went almost the entire year without winning a 72-hole stroke-play event, given his victory at the World Golf Championships-Match Play was in the head-to-head format. He finally won a stroke-play tournament at the Dunlop Phoenix in Japan in November.

Woods was even ripped by his adopted home newspaper in a sassy column in 2004. He and Williams walked off the 18th green at Bay Hill in Orlando, fuming, after a third straight round over par, at a golf course where he had won the previous four years. Woods, who finished in a lousy tie for 46th, stopped at the request of a pack of reporters. One asked how he felt with the Players Championship the following week. "I feel like going and having a nice little beer right now and I should be all right," Woods joked.

His attempt to lighten the mood was pounced on by a column in the sports section of the *Orlando Sentinel* the next day. It was occasionally funny, but mostly curmudgeonly and definitely brutal.

From the Tiger Slam in the four majors to Tiger slamming down a sixer to drown his sorrows. New Tiger motto: "When your game goes to pooh, go have a brew."

The almighty serve caught Woods flat-footed. Woods felt his start to 2004, Bay Hill excluded, was exemplary. He'd tied for fourth, 10th and seventh in his first three starts, before winning the Match Play and earning a T5 in Dubai. The column continued:

Is it too early to start asking, "Is Tiger in a slump?" . . . We may just have to accept Tiger for what he has become—still the best golfer on the planet, just not the best golfer from another planet.

Woods was hurting, and the column wasn't the only event that rubbed salt into that wound. Mickelson won the 2004 Masters, finally breaking through the major barrier at age 33, after 46 previous attempts. Woods was nowhere near contention at Augusta, while Mickelson shot a back nine of 31 (5 under) to win by one. It stung Woods deeply. "Tiger wanted to be in contention when Phil won his first major, as though he'd have to go *through* Tiger," Williams says. Woods knew Mickelson had the talent to open the floodgates and be a headache in the majors. He thought the San Diego native's short game was unlike that of any other player in history.

While pressure was mounting, Woods decided to overhaul his swing for the second time in his career. He would often tell Williams he wanted to "own his swing, and not just rent it." That meant he wanted complete control and to reduce, if not eradicate, periods that could last days, weeks or months where his swing felt less than 100 percent. In golf, that was essentially impossible. Woods also wanted to build a swing that was easier on his knee, and so in March 2004 he hired renowned guru Hank Haney. The McKinney, Texas–based coach knew Woods from his time coaching O'Meara.

Haney had a different coaching style from Harmon's; he was more of a reserved personality but thought deeply about Woods's goal of owning his swing. He'd often share those thoughts in emails to Woods. "If Tiger had a bad round under Hank, Hank would go back and study every shot and really try to understand, technically, why each poor swing happened, while Butch would have a nice meal with friends and colleagues regardless of how Tiger played," Williams says. "Hank wanted to achieve perfection in the golf swing as strongly as Tiger."

Williams was still a huge fan of Harmon's coaching. "To this day, I still think he's the best golf coach in history," Williams says. But Williams had a stronger bond with Haney, helped by the fact Haney was only eight years Williams's senior, whereas Harmon was 20 years older. Williams also spent considerably more time with Haney than Harmon, given the latter had a stable that included other top golfers. Over the years, that list included Greg Norman, Adam Scott, José Maria Olazábal, Fred Couples and Phil Mickelson, to name only a handful. "Hank was focused solely on working with Tiger and that made a big difference to the team dynamic," Williams says. Williams and Haney developed a ritual once Woods started winning under Haney's tutelage: Williams would call Haney after a victory and review the final-round heroics as a way to enjoy the moment.

Haney was a proponent of using ball flight—the trajectory and sidespin—to diagnose faults within a golf swing. It was almost working in reverse from other coaches, who started with a golfer's swing technique to change their ball flight.

Once he'd assessed Woods, Haney wanted him, at the top of his backswing, to get the club more "laid off," or pointing left of the target, as opposed to pointing at, or to the right of, the target. Doing so would prevent Woods's dreaded hooks and produce a more predictable left-to-right shape, or a "fade." "That stopped the left miss and Tiger was essentially able to eliminate the left side of the golf course," Williams says. Haney also wanted less wrist action in Woods's swing, arguing that caused inconsistencies in the strike and distance control. "There was a noticeable difference in the force Tiger would swing his irons; it seemed more rhythmical and controlled and that subtle change brought out some of his best iron play," Williams says.

The swing changes took more than five months to trust in the heat of a major championship. In August, at the 2004 PGA Championship, Woods confirmed another year without a major win, when he finished T24 at Whistling Straits in Wisconsin. This came after a T22 and T17 at the Masters and U.S. Open, respectively, and a T9 at the Open Championship.

For the second time in his career, Woods faced questions over why he would change a swing that was clearly good enough to win majors. Woods overhauled the swing that produced a 12-shot Masters victory in 1997 and spent the next two years without success at the majors. The next iteration of his swing yielded another seven majors, many of them record-setting. Williams never verbalized this to Woods, but he believed the swing changes were more for the mind than the body. "Tiger tinkered with his swing over the years as a way to completely reset his career," Williams says. "If he took his swing apart, and restarted, it gave him something extra to get up for every day. Overcoming a swing change was an added challenge, and another reason to put extra time into practice."

It also provided Woods with a small chip on his shoulder, rendering his victories more satisfying. It was not unlike the way Michael Jordan used perceived slights by NBA rivals as fuel to perform. In golf, though, there were no teammates urging Woods on and no coach or high-performance manager creating strict training schedules. If a golfer decides to take a day off practice, they can. After all, a pro golfer is the boss of his support team. With the unfathomable riches pouring into golf from Woods's popularity, it would have been difficult for the man himself to maintain his inconceivable intensity, from the practice range and regular PGA Tour events to the events that defined him: the majors. "Tiger needed something to be taken away, his form, to then want to get it back and continue winning majors," Williams says.

Despite a litany of headlines suggesting he was in a slump, Woods had won the PGA Tour event at Torrey Pines, as well as the WGC-Match Play, the Bay Hill Invitational, the Western Open and the WGC-American Express in 2003, as well as the WGC-Match Play in 2004. Some PGA Tour pros win six times in their career and rightfully consider it a good haul. But Woods was held to a higher standard. Williams was certainly feeling the pinch, especially at the majors. "The pressure was obvious, and Tiger's fuse was getting shorter at the majors," Williams says.

Woods was hitting poor shots far more frequently than he was used to, which would compel him to slam a club in the ground or toss it toward the golf bag, and swear, more often after errant swings. "During 2003 and 2004, his frustration level at bad shots was incredibly high," Williams says.

Woods was discreetly relieving some of that stress by leaning into his lifelong military obsession. At the 2004 U.S. Open, he and Williams were driving back to their rented house in the Hamptons on Thursday afternoon when Woods pulled the car over some 200 yards before the driveway. He confessed to Williams he was contemplating walking away from golf and joining the Navy SEALs. Woods had a fascination with the military in general, given his father was a Green Beret and served in the Vietnam War. After the 2004 Masters, Woods and Earl took a tour of Fort Bragg in North Carolina, where Earl had been stationed at one point. Woods did two tandem jumps with the army's parachute team. Williams, although shocked at the revelation, told Woods if that's what he wanted to do, then he wasn't going to talk him out of it. He was happy for Woods, and if anything, Williams himself was relieved at the idea of retiring. Woods's obsession didn't in the end lead him to enlist, but it would lead him to years of training sessions with San Diego–based Navy SEALs. He would take part in combat exercises that Woods's trainer, Keith Kleven, worried might reinjure his left knee, which he'd had surgery on in late 2002. Those training exercises included skydiving and simulations where the SEALs would clear rooms in houses and rescue hostages. The obsession led to an hour-long talk, three years later, with Mark Steinberg at his Cleveland house during the week of the WGC-Bridgestone. Despite the risk of injury, Williams saw some value in Woods's hobby. "I think, overall, Tiger's obsession with the SEALs was a distraction from the stress of being the world's best golfer and, if anything, it probably kept his golf career going because he felt he'd scratched an itch. He also realized how good he had it in golf," Williams says.

Williams had his own outlet in car racing. But that wasn't enough to prevent cracking under the scrutiny and pressure of everything that came with caddying for Woods. Fans, photographers and officials occasionally bore the brunt of Williams's stress. An ongoing frustration for Woods, and by extension Williams, was clumsy photographers. Williams admired the regular snappers whom he got to know on tour, but those with limited experience, or who didn't regularly shoot golf tournaments, often took pictures during Woods's backswing. At the end of 2002, Woods was playing the Skins Game in California with $200,000 on the line. A camera clicked 20 feet from Woods during a bunker shot, causing Woods to flinch and lose the final skin (a designated jackpot on a hole). Williams grabbed the photographer's camera and threw it into a lake. At the 2004 U.S. Open at Shinnecock Hills, Williams walked across the 10th tee and kicked the lens of a camera belonging to a New York *Daily News* photographer. In the final round, Williams went into the gallery on the second hole, having spotted a man taking pictures, and grabbed the camera. The fan happened to be an off-duty police officer. Williams was later labeled a "bully" in a scathing article, although Woods later defended his caddie via a post on his official website.

Looking back, Williams was disappointed at how he was perceived. He feels accusations of being a thug were not a true indication of his warm and friendly personality. With Woods, he was under stress trying to caddie for the world's best golfer—who was hell-bent on a mission to win majors—while policing ever-growing crowds and soaring media interest. That meant a rising number of media members inside the ropes, on the driving range and on the course during tournaments. Williams felt his responsibility was to provide a level playing field not only for Woods but his playing partners. "We had a few incidents that attracted some attention, and some people were critical of my actions. My response to them was, 'Come to the golf course with me on Monday and walk every step for the next seven days with me and Tiger. See what it's like.'"

In October, a welcomed distraction arrived for Woods and Williams in the form of Woods's wedding in Barbados. Woods, who flew straight in from Ireland, where he'd finished ninth at the WGC-American Express in Kilkenny, married Elin Nordegren in an elegant ceremony on Tuesday, October 5. Kirsty, now Williams's fiancee, was already in Barbados, given Elin invited her to spend the entire week leading up to the ceremony. The festivities were held at Sandy Lane, a lavish resort on Barbados's west coast that counted Dermot Desmond and J. P. McManus, friends of Woods, among its co-owners. Armed security patrolled the hotel and beach during the wedding, as the couple married under an arch of flowers just before 6 P.M. while the sun set over the blue Caribbean. Like Woods's house in Isleworth, Williams found the wedding understated and tasteful. "One thing I admired about Tiger, including his wedding, was that it was down to earth and not much different than any other wedding, with the exception of the guest list," Williams says. That guest list included Michael Jordan and his fellow basketball icon Charles Barkley, as well as Oprah Winfrey and Microsoft founder Bill Gates. Woods's friend Darius Rucker, and his band, Hootie and the Blowfish, played at the reception.

* * *

The driving range at Big Canyon Country Club, located just inland from the luxurious Newport Beach and Balboa Island, was about 270 yards long and bordered by residential housing. And not just any residential housing; the type of towering mansions that inspired the hit TV series *The O.C.* The teen drama was set in the affluent beachside community of Newport and became one of the most popular shows of 2003 and 2004. The streets surrounding Big Canyon's practice fairway were named after major championship venues and top American golf courses, like Oakmont Lane to the left, and Augusta and Cypress Lanes to the right. At the very end of the range, beyond a row of trees, was Royal St. George Road.

It was here, in November 2004, that Woods had a eureka moment that snapped him out of one of the worst, and most turbulent, slumps of his career. Woods was beginning to feel comfortable executing the swing changes he'd made in competition, having finished T2, T2, 9 and 2 in the four starts after the final major of 2004. Woods was preparing at Big Canyon for the Dunlop Phoenix tournament in Japan, his last start of the year. On the range, he struck an 8-iron that soared high above the turf and gave Woods a familiar satisfaction of proprioception; when he swung it perfectly, he couldn't even feel his swing.

In Japan, Woods issued a warning that he was back to his brilliant best, taking a 10-shot lead into the final round and winning by eight at the Phoenix Country Club in Miyazaki. Weeks later, Woods birdied three of the last five holes to defeat Pádraig Harrington at Sherwood during Woods's own Hero World Challenge, an unofficial event. Although he did not win a stroke-play event on the PGA Tour in 2004, he had closed out the year with eight consecutive rounds in the 60s. "Tiger was starting to feel his new swing was ready to withstand big pressure and, as 2004 rolled over into 2005, there was a real air of confidence in the team," Williams says.

The Masters was months away, and the Open Championship was returning to St. Andrews.

CHAPTER 10

THE ROARS RETURN

The wheels of Williams's race car left the dirt track at the Baypark Speedway at Tauranga, on New Zealand's North Island, on January 28, 2005. The saloon car, which looks like a cross between a NASCAR and an F1 vehicle, but with a more exposed roll cage, hurtled through the air and smashed into a safety fence. Williams, in shock, looked down at his hand. It was grim. There was plenty of blood, and he could see bone. "It was the worst accident I've ever had in racing," Williams says.

Williams broke several ribs, and his left hand was de-gloved, with some of the skin sheared off. His left index finger was torn off and, after he was taken to the hospital, surgically reattached. Only days earlier, Williams had been in San Diego working for Woods while he won the Buick Invitational at Torrey Pines for a third time in six years. Now he was in danger of being sidelined from caddying. "Tiger offered to send his plane all the way from America to New Zealand to pick me up," Williams recalls. Williams remembers he wanted to project confidence, so he called Woods and said, "Don't worry, I won't miss an event." Woods believed it, later telling media in a separate press conference that Williams would be ready to go within weeks. "If anyone can overcome an injury, it's Stevie," Woods said.

Miraculously, Williams made a quick recovery and was back on the bag three weeks later on February 17 at the Nissan Open at Riviera in Los Angeles. Williams traveled from New Zealand to California, arriving the Sunday before the tournament. He had been ordered by doctors to avoid flying, due to the fractured ribs, and to avoid swimming due to the surgery. But on Sunday, February 13, Williams boarded a flight from Auckland to Los Angeles. The first thing he did upon arrival in L.A., while he waited for his hotel to allow check-in, was to go for a swim at Santa Monica Beach. It was freezing, but he needed the jolt from the cold of the Pacific Ocean to stay awake.

Williams then walked to Woods's hotel to catch up and talk about his injuries and the upcoming tournament. He told Woods, "I wasn't supposed to fly or swim, mate. But I've completed those two tasks." Woods let out a roaring laugh, louder than anything Williams had heard in six years. "Stevie, you are the most hardheaded prick I've ever met. That is so idiotic and stubborn. *Only you* would swim," Woods said. Williams couldn't help but laugh, too. Maybe he was hardheaded, but it only added to the similarities he shared with his boss. O'Meara often joked Woods seemed to "live vicariously through Steve" on some of these high-octane stories. He loved that his caddie was a tough, rugby-playing, race car–driving adrenaline junkie.

A month later, at the Ford Championship, Woods faced arguably his greatest-ever battle against Mickelson. More than 35,000 Miami fans packed into the Doral resort's Blue Monster Course for the final round. Fans were eager to watch golf's two biggest stars—

and bitter rivals—go head-to-head in the final group on a beautiful resort course. Doral's Blue Monster was lined with palm trees and fraught with water danger. Drama was guaranteed.

Mickelson led going into the final day, but when Woods reached the green at the 603-yard, par-5 12th in two shots, he drained a 25-foot eagle putt to leap two shots ahead of Mickelson. Lefty responded with birdies on Nos. 13 and 14. On the last hole, Mickelson had a chip that, if he holed it, could have forced a playoff. But the ball hit the cup and lipped out. Woods secured a one-shot victory.

Along with the $990,000 in prize money, Woods was given a 2005 Ford GT. It was the most beautiful car Williams had ever seen. The GT was a bright tone of racing red with a white stripe down its center. It held a lot of significance for Ford: it was a sleek, modern redesign of the Ford GT40 MKII, which had won the Le Mans 24-hour race for four consecutive years from 1966 to 1969. It was valued at $139,995 but was certain to appreciate in value given only a limited number were built (in 2024, the resale value of the car online was around $500,000). Woods was an ambassador for Buick, a company of Ford's great rival, General Motors, and likely couldn't accept the car. But he cared less about that and more about his caddie's obsession with Ford cars. Woods, with a twinkle in his eye, tossed the keys to Williams, who knew he would hold on to this collector's item forever.

Williams was moved and knew Woods's smirk was an acknowledgment of a joke from exactly one year earlier. In 2004, he and Woods were in a hotel gym during the Dubai Desert Classic. Above their exercise bikes was a TV showing the Ford Championship on the PGA Tour in Miami. Craig Parry, an Australian, holed a 6-iron from the fairway for eagle in a playoff to win. He collected the prize money but, for the first time at the event, also received the GT. Williams, sweating, turned to Woods and said, half laughing, half serious, "Tiger, what the f——k are we doing in Dubai, when you could be at Doral winning me that Ford."

The GT was a dream prize for Williams. The 1966 Le Mans race was a momentous victory for Ford in its battle with Ferrari, which is depicted in the film *Ford v Ferrari*, while the drivers, Bruce McLaren and Chris Amon, were New Zealanders. "It didn't have any trunk space and had two racing seats, so it looked like some of the Ford saloon cars I raced," Williams says.

He had the car delivered from Detroit, where the motor company was headquartered, to a Ford dealership in Oregon. His good friend Bob Garza picked the car up for Williams, who was in New Zealand when it arrived, and drove it to his house at Sunriver. Williams went for one extended joyride in the car in Oregon. But the next time it was driven was to a port in Portland, Oregon, so it could be put on a container and shipped to New Zealand, where it sits in Williams's garage to this day. "I knew I would be keeping it at home forever with very low miles on it," Williams says proudly.

The Ford victory was Woods's second PGA Tour title for 2005. Williams headed to the Masters in April knowing something special was going to happen.

* * *

Williams arrived with Woods on a chartered plane at the Daniel Field private airport in Augusta, Georgia, on the morning of Monday, April 4. Williams spent most of the 90-minute flight listening to the jangling guitar riffs of Australian rock band INXS and the bluesy voice of its front man, Michael Hutchence, as their hit song "This Time" pounded through his headphones. Williams had chosen the uplifting song to manifest the end to Woods's majors slump with one of his favorite '80s rock tunes, which he listened to all week. The tune details a longing for a change: *This time will be the last time, that we will fight like this*. Williams adored INXS, and the lyrics felt right for the 2005 Masters. "Golf is just a game, and people were saying Tiger wasn't going to come back to the winner's circle in the majors, but I felt this was the last time he would have to answer those doubts," Williams says.

As they walked off the plane, Williams had to lug two sets of golf clubs: Woods's sticks and those of fellow pro Jesper Parnevik. Parnevik, whose wife, Mia, had originally introduced Woods to his own wife, Elin, had accidentally left his clubs at home in Florida. "I'm the only one to come to the Masters and leave his clubs in his garage," Parnevik said.

Woods's team made the four-mile journey from Daniel Field to Augusta National on that warm spring morning and, after registering for the Masters as player No. 67, Woods marched to the practice fairway. In 2005, Augusta National's warm-up area was west of Magnolia Lane, a famous driveway into the club marked only by a tiny, blink-and-you-miss-it "Augusta National Golf Club" sign on Washington Road. In 2010, a new, state-of-the-art practice facility spanning 18 acres would be built only a short walk from the first hole. But in 2005, the range was just 260 yards long, with a net standing 105 feet tall at the end, in between the golf course and Washington Road, a busy stretch with fast-food chains, motels and bars. Woods didn't hit many wedges or iron shots during his warm-up before taking out his Nike Ignite 460cc driver. He hit six monstrous shots, two of which flew over the net. It was almost a message to the other 92 Masters competitors that Woods was going to overpower Augusta once again. "He was quite chuffed that he had the power to crank a drive when he needed to," Williams says.

In the best weather Augusta would experience all week, Woods played only a light practice round of nine holes with O'Meara. "Tiger holed out for eagle with a sand wedge on the par-4 ninth and the crowd went wild; he was striking the ball exceptionally well," Williams says. In his pretournament press conference, Woods explained how bullish he was about his 2004 swing rebuild under coach Haney. He felt a sense of déjà vu to the beginning of 1999, when his swing changes under Harmon had finally become muscle memory. "That went pretty good for two years," Woods joked, referring to five major wins from late 1999 to early 2001. But Woods also stressed his 2004 overhaul wasn't to rekindle his 2000 form. "I want to become better than that," he said in an ominous statement to rivals.

Some 40,000 fans turned out to watch Monday at Augusta, the first official day of practice rounds. Security was beefed up considerably from previous years. Fans were required to walk through metal detectors for the first time, speeding up security processing and preventing cell phones from being brought into the ultra-private club. On Tuesday, Woods played a full 18-hole round with O'Meara and Australian Rod Pampling.

The 69th Masters began on the afternoon of Thursday, April 7, with a spluttering start delayed five hours due to severe thunderstorms. Biblical rain lashed the Augusta area. Masters officials instituted a two-tee start for competitors, a rare move from a tournament that likes all players starting at hole No. 1. Fans were not allowed on the grounds all morning and waited in cars. With wet, sloshy fairways, balls were plugging in muddy turf once they hit the ground. Conditions led to some dire results for some of the older players and shorter hitters. Notably, 1970 Masters champion Billy Casper. The 73-year-old put five balls in the water at the par-3 16th, using a 9-wood for the 185-yard shot. He made a 14 (11 over) on the hole. Casper shot 57 for nine holes (21 over) and 106 for the round (34 over).

Woods, meanwhile, was grouped with Northern Ireland's Darren Clarke and Carlos Franco for the opening two rounds and the trio teed off No. 10. Despite the promising practice rounds, Woods invited critics to predict another poor major result when he opened with a 2-over 74 to sit seven shots behind leader Chris DiMarco. The greens remained lightning quick while the fairways were soaked, a horrible combination. A bizarre snapshot of Woods's round came at the par-5 13th; after an impressive second shot from the trees, his eagle attempt rolled off the green into the water. "It was a very difficult putt," Williams recalls. Woods took a penalty and walked away with a bogey.

Separately from Woods's group, 2000 Masters winner Vijay Singh had played the opening rounds in the group behind defending Augusta champion Phil Mickelson. In round two, a Masters tournament official asked to examine Mickelson's spikes because a fellow player had reported they were too long. Mickelson was cleared, but that didn't stop him from having a heated verbal confrontation with Singh in the clubhouse after the round, believing he had reported the spikes. Mickelson later issued a statement: "I was extremely distracted and would have appreciated if it would have been handled differently." In a karmic twist, two days later, Mickelson's and Singh's scores meant they were paired for the final round.

Due to weather delays, Woods managed just one hole of his second round on Friday. On Saturday, Woods finished the remaining 17 holes in 6 under par, posting a 66. That lifted him to 4 under, while DiMarco climbed to 10 under, increasing his lead to four. Sent back out late Saturday afternoon for his third round, Woods was 5 under through nine holes when play was called due to darkness. At 9 under, Woods trailed DiMarco by four shots. He'd made 12 birdies in 26 holes on Saturday.

"He was bombing driver like he had done Monday on the practice fairway," Williams says. Conditions were soft, and players' drives were plugging where they landed. It offered a distinct advantage to Woods, who carried the ball more than 300 yards and was left with plenty of short irons into greens.

The discrepancy in length off the tee between DiMarco and Woods was laid bare on Saturday. At the par-4 11th, one of the most difficult holes at Augusta, Woods hit a pitching wedge to the green while DiMarco needed a 3-iron. They were playing a different game.

On Sunday morning, with nine holes still to play in his third round, Woods arrived at the course wearing a black shirt. It was a change from his usual Sunday red polo. "I said to him, 'Why have you got New Zealand rugby colors on?'" Williams says. "Tiger said, 'You and your f——ng All Blacks. Hopefully we play like them today.'" Woods resumed his third round in the 10th fairway, hitting his second shot close and making birdie. The chase was on.

Woods eventually shot 65, taking the 54-hole lead at 11 under par. DiMarco, meanwhile, shot a 5-over back nine of 41 and plummeted to 8 under. Trailing in second place, DiMarco knew history was against him; Woods had converted all eight 54-hole leads he'd held in the majors. "Tiger didn't ever sit on a lead and try to protect it," Williams says. "If he was leading by one, he'd wanted to lead by two, then three and so on."

Woods and DiMarco were the only ones left on the range before their final pairing when DiMarco, a playful trash-talker, wanted to have some fun. DiMarco had played at the University of Florida and was an avid fan of the Gators football and basketball teams. The latter had recently defeated Kentucky to win the SEC Tournament. DiMarco picked up one of the range balls at Augusta National, a Titleist Pro V1x with a red 2, and scribbled *Go Gators!*

on the ball. He chipped it down to Woods, the ball hitting his bag. Woods picked it up, laughed and with a Sharpie scratched out *Go* and wrote *F——K THE* and chipped it back to DiMarco. "That was how we were; he liked a bit of competitiveness and I wanted to laugh and see if he had a pulse," DiMarco says. "I also kept that ball." It was going to be a fun battle.

On Sunday afternoon, April 10, Woods began the Masters final round with two birdies. A bogey at the difficult par-4 fifth was his only stumble on the front side. DiMarco played an error-free front nine with a birdie at the second and ninth holes, reducing his deficit to three. On No. 9, Woods hit a pitching wedge to eight feet. But DiMarco had already hit his 4-iron even closer. "It was clear the Masters had become match play between Tiger and me," DiMarco says.

Woods bogeyed No. 10, and at No. 11, DiMarco hit an iron close to the hole. He sensed an opportunity to needle his playing partner, just like he'd done on the range. "Aren't you tired of putting first [being farther from the hole]?" DiMarco said. Woods laughed, but looked at DiMarco with an expression that said, *That was funny, but go f——k yourself.* DiMarco sank the birdie putt, cutting Woods's lead to one.

Despite a bogey at the par-3 12th, DiMarco made birdies at No. 14, where he hit his second shot to one foot, and No. 15. He reminded himself Woods was 13 months into a swing rebuild with Haney. "He was kind of struggling and not hitting his usual shots; I was hitting every shot how I wanted," DiMarco says.

At the par-5 15th, DiMarco, who laid up for his second shot but still matched Woods's birdie, had to back off his third, interrupted by a roar on the next hole. South African Trevor Immelman had made a hole in one at the par-3 16th. The ace only warmed up the gallery's vocal cords for what was about to happen.

* * *

Woods, for a few minutes, looked human. It would be a stretch to say he looked beatable, although he was in serious trouble at No. 16, Augusta National's fourth and final par 3. Although the 170-yard tee shot requires a carry over water, it's a simple 8-iron for elite pros—until they face the nerves of the Masters' finale.

DiMarco had hit an ideal tee shot that left a midrange, uphill birdie putt. DiMarco's landing target was about 160 yards, which would allow the ball to feed down a slope and to the left, where the hole was cut. He deliberately used too much club in hitting a 7-iron. With a pure strike, DiMarco's 7-iron carried 170 yards. But he could also carry it 140 yards, depending on the shot. He would often do that to mess with playing partners and this time, he had the "honor," meaning he was hitting first on No. 16. "They'd look in my bag and think, *Holy shit! 7-iron? It's only 156 yards!* It was fun to do," DiMarco says. "Typically, they'd hit the ball harder and land it 25 feet past the hole." It didn't work this time, though; Woods was far too focused and didn't even look inside DiMarco's bag.

Woods held a one-shot lead on the 16th tee but made a poor swing with an 8-iron. His tee shot sailed left and over the back of the green. It was the only time he missed the putting surface on No. 16 all week. DiMarco had noticed Woods was struggling with his swing for the first 15 holes. He was also curious about Woods's strategy; was he trying to draw the tee shot into the left pin or was he trying to hold the shot against a breeze? "It was a very uncharacteristic shot for Tiger. If that went a little further left, it was in the water," DiMarco says.

Williams found it excruciating how many times his emotions changed while the ball was in the air. The first thing he thought when Woods struck the ball was, *Oh god, Tiger!* Then, *That's in the bunker . . . No, that's in the water . . . No, that's over the back of the green!*

Woods hounded Williams on the walk up to the green, "Stevie, what's over there?! What's over there?! Do I have a shot?!" Williams piped back, "Tiger, I have no f——ng clue, mate! I've never been over there!" He had seen just about every inch of Augusta since he first caddied at the 1987 Masters, for Norman. But he'd never laid eyes on the area long and left of the green at No. 16—the worst spot to leave the ball in view of the fact that the traditional final-round pin placement was in the middle of the green and on the left side. It was extremely difficult to chip it close since golfers had to negotiate a steep side slope from that angle.

Woods and Williams walked behind a strutting DiMarco, who held a putter under his arm as if to rub in the fact *he* was on the green. Once the pair reached Woods's ball, they realized its position was not pretty. It sat where the end of the manicured fairway met the longer rough in a violent step up. The long grass behind the ball made the club's entry difficult. That forced Woods to come in steep, which would squirt the ball out in a low trajectory. He would then need to land the ball left of the hole, catch the sidehill and take a severe turn to the right toward the cup.

As Woods assessed the shot, CBS cameras zoomed in on the ball's Nike swoosh so that millions of viewers around the world could see the lie. "There's a good chance he doesn't get this inside [closer than] DiMarco's ball," former player Lanny Wadkins said on the broadcast.

Williams felt the tension; if Woods didn't save par, they would, at best, be tied going into the 17th. DiMarco could also make his birdie to go one ahead. The worst-case scenario, Williams believed, was Woods's ball could pick up too much speed coming back down the slope and roll into the greenside bunker.

Woods took considerable time stalking the shot and said, "Stevie, see *that* old pitch mark up there? If I land it *there*, the ball should only get halfway up that hill, and it shouldn't be traveling too fast coming back." The silence among the gallery was eerie when Woods lined up the shot, placing his black leather Nike shoes close together for extra finesse and balance.

Woods stabbed at the ball with his 60-degree wedge, the ball shooting low off the clubface, landing on the pitch mark and skipping about 15 feet left of the hole. "I heard the sound, and he nipped it off the turf so perfectly, you could hear it as soon as he hit it," DiMarco says. The ball took a vicious right turn and crept toward the hole at a glacial pace, the black Nike swoosh flashing with every revolution.

Commentator Verne Lundquist set the scene by half shouting with his deep, rich voice, "Oh my goodness!" Woods raised both arms toward his chest, as though he were performing a biceps curl, staring at the hole while Williams did the same. The ball paused on the edge of the cup dramatically when the Nike swoosh appeared once again, this time for a full second. Then it dropped into the hole like a whale falling backward into the ocean after breaching the surface.

"IN YOUR LIFE, HAVE YOU SEEN ANYTHING LIKE THAT?!" Lundquist screamed on the broadcast while the crowd erupted.

DiMarco had been working with performance psychologist Dr. Gio Valiante, who had urged him to expect the unexpected. DiMarco prepared for all outcomes, including the best case—where Woods failed to save par and DiMarco made birdie, which would invite the nerves of leading by one while standing on the 17th tee. Admittedly, DiMarco didn't spend much time visualizing Woods chipping in. "I had the best vantage point of anybody, standing right down by the bunker," DiMarco says. "I was blowing air on that thing as hard as I could the other way to stop it." He laughed, and briefly let himself think, *Are you f——ng kidding me?* "He was very calculated with that chip and pulled it off perfectly. I think he could have sat there with 100 more balls and never done it again. But he did Tiger-like things in the biggest moments."

Those heart-stopping 16 seconds—from when Woods struck the ball to when it fell in—were worth an estimated US$125,000 in free advertising for Nike Golf. The company's marketing director, Chris Mike, who was watching at home on TV with his family, screamed so loudly his children ran out of the house. The timing couldn't have been better for the company, which was just about to release the One Platinum ball that viewers were seeing into the golf ball market, which was worth $4 billion annually. "Great for Tiger, great for us," Mike said.

O'Meara, meanwhile, had missed the cut and was watching from his couch when J. P. McManus called and said, "Oh my god! That could have been the worst thing that could have happened." O'Meara, confused, listened as McManus explained that Woods could get emotional and hyped up. He had a bad feeling about the next two holes.

Indeed, the comedown from the chip-in was severe. Woods hit a poor tee shot on 17, and a poor approach on 18, causing two closing bogeys. "JP saw that coming," O'Meara says. Williams felt that three of Woods's last four shots were unusually poor. This was the first time his new swing was put under the immense scrutiny of leading a major championship final round and he was not yet completely comfortable with the more laid-off position at the top of the backswing.

Woods shot 71 while DiMarco, whose chip on No. 18 rattled the flag and nearly dropped for birdie and the victory, posted a

68. They were tied in regulation at 12 under par (276). Woods now had to enter a sudden-death playoff with DiMarco. Williams whispered to Woods, "You're the f——g number one player in the world. You're playing against Chris DiMarco. Show *him* who's number one and show *me* who's number one."

The two began sudden death at No. 18, the first year Augusta started a playoff there. Historically, overtime began from the 10th hole. Woods obliterated his 3-wood up the fairway and stuck an 8-iron close on the green. DiMarco missed the green but chipped his third up to a foot for par. "Tiger hit his best two shots all week in the playoff," Williams says. Woods drained the birdie, let out a spirited fist pump and hugged Williams. He'd won the 2005 Masters. "I think Tiger was one of the most underrated putters ever; people don't realize how many five- to 12-footers he made during that stretch," DiMarco says about Woods's prime.

Woods had withstood almost 1,000 days of questions about his majors slump that, while reasonable, were persistent. He had defied the critics with a fourth Masters win and a ninth major overall. He was officially halfway to equaling Nicklaus's record, although Woods himself called it "a long way to go."

Haney conceded he was "shaken" by both Woods's tee shot on No. 17 and second shot on No. 18 in regulation, but had a comforting realization. From his point of view, Woods's two-shot lead with two to play was almost too big a cushion for an athlete who feasted on the adrenaline of being under pressure. The proof was in the sudden-death playoff, when there was no room for error. Woods executed a perfect 3-wood, iron shot and putt when he had to—and that was the difference.

Williams's own stats highlight how Woods's iron play had improved enough under Haney to win the Masters. He hit 10 of 18 greens in regulation, then 16, 15 and 13. Williams also noticed Woods's driving remained an issue. He'd hit nine of 14 fairways in round one, then six, 10 and seven.

"His putting was also phenomenal; 115 putts for the 72 holes, plus the one birdie putt in the playoff," Williams says. Woods had 30 putts in rounds one and two, and 26 and 29 in the third and fourth rounds, respectively.

Williams also points to the mini stories within his notes. Woods missed the green on No. 18 in all four rounds but saved par the first three days. The only time he didn't save par was when it mattered most, on the 72nd hole when par would have either prevented a playoff and won the title or, if DiMarco's chip had dropped for birdie, salvaged a playoff. Woods had hit two of seven fairways on the back nine on Sunday, under the most pressure. That led to three bogeys on the homestretch. Woods also hit five bunkers for the week and saved par only twice. He did not hit the fairway on No. 15 all four days. That is typically a pivotal hole in closely contested Masters given it's the final par 5. Woods had to work harder for birdie and did manage to in rounds one, two and four. But he made bogey on No. 15 in round three. Nos. 5 and 7 were the only holes Woods hit the fairway in all four rounds, while he fared much better in approach shots. On Nos. 3, 4, 5, 9, 13 and 14, he hit green in regulation all four days. His putting was also exemplary.

"Tiger only had three three-putts for the week, at No. 5 in round four, and No. 14 in rounds two and three," Williams says.

But there were no pictures on the scorecards, and no replays of the poor swings on the final day. Only a shot many argue became the most famous shot in Masters' history. Woods's chip-in went as viral as videos could in 2005, before Twitter's creation. It joined an exclusive group of sporting moments that transcend the sport in which they happened and permeate pop culture. Woods's chip lives on in highlight reels and documentaries, like Michael Jordan's "The Shot" in the 1989 NBA Eastern Conference first round, when his Chicago Bulls were down by one point and Jordan took an inbound pass to fire a buzzer beater. He gave the Bulls a 101–100 win and they advanced to the next round of playoffs. Woods's chip-in was golf's equivalent of The Shot, but arguably more dramatic. It was conjured in the dying moments of the final day, not the Eastern Conference first round. As O'Meara puts it, "That moment was etched in history, forever. Tiger had this way of conjuring magic. Jack [Nicklaus] had the same thing."

In the six years Williams worked for Woods after that chip-in, he never saw his boss drop a spare golf ball in that same spot on No. 16. He had no interest in re-creating it for fun during a practice round. DiMarco did, out of pure curiosity. "Tiger didn't, because he never wanted to hit it there again," Williams says.

Winning the Masters in such dramatic fashion, after a 10-major drought, released an enormous pressure valve for Woods and Williams. It was a relief to see evidence of the team's internal belief that rebuilding Woods's swing was the right move despite taking a two-year haircut on his results.

Woods had read the headlines and remarked that he'd been getting "ripped" for the changes he'd made. "To play as beautifully as I did this entire week is pretty cool," he said. Woods blew his shot at winning the 2003 PGA Championship, while at the Open Championship that year, and in 2004, he couldn't find the extra gear he normally possessed. Almost referencing Williams's choice of the INXS song "This Time," Woods said, while he had failed in those attempts, "This time, I got the job done."

It was Woods's first genuine opportunity in almost three years at the majors and while he hadn't quite stuck the landing, it was clear Woods was still capable of closing them out. "The win was enormous for building confidence, and it was probably the second-most-important major victory in our partnership," Williams says. The other crucial major win was the 1999 PGA Championship, which cemented Woods and Williams's dynamic under the gun.

Williams felt the victory validated Woods's trust in him; that he wasn't contributing to the slump. It also demonstrated the team hadn't altered the course of his career by tinkering with the swing. "It stopped the continuous reporting of Tiger's slump in the majors, but more importantly it added great credibility to Hank and Tiger's relationship," Williams says. More broadly, the 2005 Masters was a turning point that reinforced the belief, after two and a half years of doubt, that Woods was capable of reeling in Nicklaus.

As he always did immediately after the Masters, Williams drove two and a half hours to Atlanta that Sunday night, and the next morning flew home to New Zealand. On the journey over the Pacific Ocean, Williams reviewed some of the shots Woods hit at Augusta, particularly his iron play and the proximity to the hole. "His new swing looked capable of being fine-tuned to peak for each major, just like in 2000 and 2001."

* * *

On Sunday, July 10, 2005, Williams sat in a plush chair inside Woods's Gulfstream GV as it approached St. Andrews, Scotland, and he looked around at the mahogany interior of the private plane. He was incredibly proud of his boss; he felt Woods had earned the right to fly so luxuriously around the world. The plane was unmistakably Woods's property, with napkins and drinking glasses all branded with the TW initials on them. Still, Williams felt it was understated, a trait of Woods's, who didn't ever raise the topic of flying private. "Tiger didn't see the use of a private jet as a way to show off wealth; it was all about efficiency in preparing for tournaments," Williams says. "Tiger was certainly not a flashy guy, in any sense."

Woods saw the jet as a necessity and a competitive advantage. With his level of superstardom, it was simply not possible to prepare for a major with the detail and execution he craved if he flew on commercial airlines. Given Woods's businesslike attitude toward private travel, Williams was confused when a sports magazine ran a poll, asking 50 PGA Tour pros, *Who had the coolest private jet on tour?* Greg Norman's Gulfstream G550 won 40 percent of the vote, followed by Els's and Woods's Gulfstream GVs. Williams wondered why anyone would want to pit private jets against one another. They were all a privilege, in his mind. In fact, Williams often felt he didn't belong on Woods's plane; occasionally, when Woods had friends on board who were having a drink, Williams would go right to the back and stay out of view.

Private jets were a status symbol to some, especially in a sport beloved by millionaires and billionaires. Golf was expensive to play and that was reflected in everything from companies that chartered private planes for small groups of wealthy weekend golfers, to equipment manufacturers who catered to the uber-rich. In 2005, the Japanese golf club maker Honma Golf released a gold-plated set of irons called the Twin Marks MG-818. Golfers could pay as much as £20,000 for a 24-karat gold-plated, platinum-finished set, which was custom-built in Sakata.

Woods, Williams, Haney and O'Meara had flown in from Ireland, where they had played J. P. McManus's charity pro-am at the opulent Adare Manor before another trip to Waterville Golf Links in County Kerry. They helicoptered to other links courses like Ballybunion. Woods brought his friends Jerry Chang and Bryon

Bell, as well as J. P. McManus and PGA Tour winner John Cook. "The preparation in Ireland went extremely well," Williams says. "At Waterville, Tiger teed off very early in the morning and by the back nine, the locals had heard Tiger was playing. He had a decent crowd for the last few holes." The Irish coastal winds were whipping, and Woods wanted to wow the impromptu gallery. He put on a masterful display of beautifully struck low shots that he kept under the breeze. The locals cheered and Woods smiled. "I knew Tiger was going to play well at the Open, given how well he was striking it in Ireland," Williams says.

Moments before Williams stepped off the plane, he chose his theme song for the week from his rock playlist. "Feels Like the First Time" by Foreigner was the theme for the 2005 Open Championship at St. Andrews's Old Course. The upbeat, catchy pop song, and the way Woods had been playing in the summer of 2005, reminded Williams of the feeling he had prior to the 2000 U.S. Open at Pebble Beach. That week, he felt it was a fait accompli that Woods would win, with how well he was swinging the club and putting. Once off the plane in St. Andrews, he had a similar confidence to Pebble Beach. The lyrics of "Feels Like the First Time" put Williams in a great mood as he walked through town and into his rented house: *Together we'll make history*.

The sporting world was so confident in Woods, one gambler laid down £100,000 on Woods to win with a major bookmaker. Woods and Williams arrived at the Old Course early Sunday evening for a practice round with O'Meara and Fred Couples. The weather was warm, and the Old Course was firm. Woods couldn't wait to ask Williams to fetch his beloved pitch mark repairer from his Stanford pouch inside the golf bag. It was a two-pronged fork that fixed impressions on the green made by a golf ball. During a practice round at each course he played, Woods would throw the repairer straight down into the green on the first hole to test how firm it was. "He'd panic ever so slightly if that repairer fell out of the pouch and into the bottom of the bag," Williams says. Woods threw it into the first green at St. Andrews. It barely pierced the turf. The greens were rock hard and were going to be fast, which was not typical at British Opens. The links greens were slightly slower than at other majors to offset the challenge the wind and weather provided.

At the Old Course, Woods was flanked by four local security guards, while he was also assigned two police officers in addition to his usual security detail at tournaments. Concerns were high over a repeat attack to the July 7 bombings in London the previous Thursday. Terrorists had detonated three homemade bombs on the London Underground and one on a double-decker bus. The blasts happened on the Circle line near Aldgate and at Edgware Road, as well as the Piccadilly line near Russell Square. Fifty-two U.K. residents were killed and more than 700 injured. Woods's mother, Kultida, was vacationing in London at the time and stayed at a hotel across the street from one of the blasts. "My mom was in the building right across the street from where the bomb blew up, I was very thankful [she] is still here," Woods said. "It very easily could have been pretty tragic for me, personally. I can only imagine what everyone else who was involved, what they might have been going through."

New Zealander Michael Campbell, who had defeated Woods at the U.S. Open at Pinehurst a month earlier, was driving to Heathrow Airport to pick up his parents when the attacks happened. He admitted he was "concerned about security and safety for the British Open."

Woods and the 155 other competitors forged ahead with their practice for the 134th Open. Woods's main security concern was the dense crowds that followed his every move at tournaments.

On a calm and warm morning, Monday, July 11, Woods was on the second tee at 6:33—before the course had officially opened for practice—ready for a round with O'Meara and 2003 U.S. Open champion Jim Furyk. Woods stuck to his trick of teeing off on No. 2 but more than 100 people anticipated it, and gathered to watch. He raced around the 17 holes in three and a half hours, despite a large throng of media, photographers, security guards and police.

On the par-4 18th, Woods hit an errant drive that hurtled toward the road right of the fairway, toward the Old Course official merchandise shop. O'Meara pounced on the opportunity to needle Woods. "You should grab a cashmere sweater from the Tom Morris Golf Shop while you look for your ball," O'Meara said. The jab was revenge: During a practice round three months earlier at Augusta National, O'Meara hit a terribly wayward drive from the seventh tee that flew well right of the fairway. "Tiger said to me, 'Hey, why don't you grab me a chicken sandwich from the concession stand when you look for that.' So, in St. Andrews, I got him back a beauty."

After the round, Woods chatted on the clubhouse steps with Nicklaus, who at 65 decided to come out of retirement in 2005 for the Masters and the Open. His grandson, Jake, the son of Steve Nicklaus, had drowned in a devastating accident a month before Augusta and Nicklaus felt the family needed a distraction via two tournaments, and courses, that were special to them. Jack Nicklaus, Jr. caddied for his father at the Masters, while Steve was looping at St. Andrews, the final tournament of Nicklaus's career. There was a mutual love between Nicklaus and the St. Andrews fans; he'd won two of his three Open titles at the Old Course, in 1970 and 1978. To mark Nicklaus's retirement, the Royal Bank of Scotland minted a special five-pound banknote with him on it. "I bought several and got Jack to sign them," Williams says.

Woods's practice rounds had gone well enough for the superstar to outwardly declare, at his pretournament press conference, that he could improve on his eight-shot win at the 2000 Open at St. Andrews. "Last time I was conservative; this year I might be more aggressive," Woods said.

British broadcaster BBC, celebrating its 50th anniversary televising the Open, gambled that while Woods would play aggressively, he would at least tone down his occasional expletive outbursts. At the U.S. Open a month earlier, coverage of Woods was put on a delay after he unleashed a loud "F——k!" at Pinehurst, heard by viewers. However, a BBC spokesperson said, "After that incident, we understand NBC delayed their broadcasts by four seconds. But we have no plans to do the same." Although three-time Open winner Hale Irwin said, "I don't know Tiger very well but . . . how can you be a leader when you hit a bad shot and yell, 'Motherf——er'? You would never see Jack Nicklaus or Arnold Palmer do that," Williams says cursing was integral to Woods's play as it allowed him to blow off steam. "Tiger did not have a bad temper. When he hit a poor shot, he was able to get that frustration out and shake it off, instantly. That was just his way of doing it."

Woods began his quest for a second Open title at eight twenty on a cool, gray and drizzling Thursday morning, July 14, 2005. He was paired with Robert Allenby and José Maria Olazábal. Nicklaus, preparing for his Open swan song, was three groups ahead. While Woods didn't hit into a single bunker all week at St. Andrews during his 2000 victory, on day one in 2005, he found three. But it didn't matter. He fired a blistering 66 to lead at 6 under.

Woods and Allenby were Isleworth neighbors and had been on several Ireland trips together. Perhaps that's why the Australian wasn't nervous about the pandemonium of being grouped with Woods on the first two days of an Open at St. Andrews. "It could be a daunting experience for some," he says. It was the opposite for Allenby, however, who believed the enormous galleries spurred him on. Woods and Allenby had played hundreds of times together, in tournaments and when they raced around 18 holes at Isleworth using golf carts. He had seen Woods's absolute best golf in Orlando, when there was no pressure. "But the way Tiger played those first two days at St. Andrews, I wondered if anyone had ever struck it that good," Allenby says.

Round one saw a two-minute silence held at noon to honor the victims of the London bombings. The Open, which was first played in 1860, had never been temporarily paused to honor victims of a tragedy. Golfers, caddies and officials stopped play while tens of thousands of fans also remained mute. "We were on the par-5 14th and the silence was eerie," Williams says. Woods appeared to be in a meditative state. As he told reporters after the round, he had only found out a day earlier that his mother was staying in a hotel near one of the blasts. "I've talked to her about it, but she hasn't said a whole lot," Woods said.

On day two, Woods continued to blow away the field with a bogey-free 67. He drove the green at the 380-yard, par-4 10th and two-putted for birdie. As Woods approached the 16th, he could hear the bedlam on No. 18 as Nicklaus waved goodbye to the Open, the majors and all competitive golf, forever. The commotion was still going around the 18th hole when Woods teed off. Attempting to drive the green from 357 yards, he hooked it so far left the ball ran across to the far side of the adjacent first hole. Woods recovered and finished 36 holes at 11 under par (133)—the exact same halfway score as his 2000 Open at St. Andrews. Woods led by four shots and had never lost a major when holding the 36-hole lead.

On day three, though, Woods invited his fellow stars back into the tournament when he struggled to a 71. At 12 under, he led by two over Olazábal. Scottish native Colin Montgomerie was 9 under alongside two-time major winner Retief Goosen. Monty threw down the gauntlet by saying, "Tiger is not bulletproof. If I can [shoot] a 66, I have every chance of winning."

On Sunday, Woods teed off at 2 P.M. in the final group with two-time Masters winner Olazábal, while Goosen and Montgomerie were in the penultimate group ahead. Olazábal was chasing the Cinderella story of the year; the Spaniard had failed to qualify for the Open Championship and was listed as an alternate. But he was given an 11th-hour reprieve when his friend, idol and countryman Seve Ballesteros withdrew. Ballesteros had won the 1984 Open at St. Andrews among five career majors.

Woods, at 13 under, allowed Montgomerie to come within one shot of his lead when only eight holes remained. With uplifting support from the Scottish crowds, Montgomerie made three birdies and no bogeys in the first 10 holes while Woods dropped a shot at the par-4 10th. Montgomerie, though, soon fell apart with three bogeys over the last seven holes. Woods went 1 under in that span.

When Woods tapped in for par on the 18th and signed for a 70, he'd finished at 14 under par (274), thrashing Montgomerie by five shots. Olazábal and Couples finished tied for third a shot further back. Woods had won his 10th major, and ninth with Williams, in six years together.

Victory also meant Woods had completed the career slam for a second time. He'd won each of the four majors—the PGA Championship in 2000, the Masters in 2001, 2002 and 2005, the U.S. Open in 2002 and the Open Championship in 2005—at least once more since capturing his first career slam with his 2000 Open win at St. Andrews. "It's a dream come true," Woods said of his second claret jug. "It's the home of golf. This is as good as it gets. Honestly, even in my wildest dreams, I never thought I would win 10 major championships, let alone two career Grand Slams, before the age of 30."

Williams was astonished by one statistic: Woods only three-putted once all week, at the par-4 12th on Friday, when he drove the green and walked off with a par. "Considering seven of the 18 greens at St. Andrews are enormous double greens [two holes occupy the same green], it is far easier to three-putt."

After the Open champion's obligations had wrapped up, Williams boarded Woods's plane back to Florida. "The flight home was a little more subdued than the first time he won the claret jug in 2000," Williams says. The first Open win came with a great sense of fulfillment, but the second was validation that Woods's skills transferred to the ground game played on U.K. links courses. The group ate well and had "only a drink or two," according to Williams. "Tiger was truly humbled by winning the Open in Jack's last-ever competitive appearance," he says.

Indeed, Woods had won all four of the majors where Nicklaus teed up for the final time: the U.S. Open at Pebble Beach and the PGA at Valhalla in 2000, as well as the Masters and the Open at St. Andrews in 2005.

On the flight to Orlando, Williams reflected on how Woods's status among the greats had changed significantly. While he had claimed nine majors before St. Andrews, only one had been an Open Championship. Even among the most prolific major winners in golf history, there was extra respect for those who had claimed multiple Opens. That club included Tom Watson (five Opens among eight majors), Nicklaus (three Opens among 18 majors), Arnold Palmer (two Opens among seven majors) and Nick Faldo (three Opens among six majors). "The 2005 Open will be remembered for Tiger capturing the Open for the second time," Williams says. "Given both of them were at St. Andrews, Tiger's image changed as a golfer. It was a monumental occasion. He didn't want to be a great player with just one Open title."

Woods's game was suited to Augusta, but to be successful in winning all the major championships, one had to have every shot in the bag—especially at St. Andrews. A heightened level of imagination was required to play links golf. Considering Woods held the scoring record outright at St. Andrews (for 22 years, until Cameron Smith shot 20 under [268] to win in 2022), Woods could make a claim as being among the greatest-ever links golfers.

Bagging two major wins after a long slump also reduced an incredible amount of stress for Williams. From mid-2002 to late 2004, there were anxious moments as Woods's drought continued. Some caddies might have felt they were walking on thin ice. "But Tiger never made me feel like that, although personally I felt stress," Williams says. After changing coaches and making some adjustments to the swing, things were back to normal. Woods and Williams's relationship was better than ever.

Finally, Williams dared to dream of Woods eclipsing Nicklaus's 18 majors, given Woods had jumped over the mental hurdle of double digits. "Now we were more than halfway to Jack's 18 and almost halfway to our personal goal of 21, it was all becoming feasible," he says.

For the first time, Williams began to picture *when* that might be. If Woods, at 29, could win one out of every three majors for the next seven years—which was equal to eight major wins from the next 24—he could be knocking on the door of Nicklaus's 18 by 2012. It was a tall order, but with Woods's work ethic and talent, not implausible. "I had a feeling that at around 36 or 37 years of age, Tiger could overtake Jack," Williams says.

CHAPTER 11

THIS ONE'S FOR POPS

The members at South Head Golf Club, an hour northwest of Auckland, gathered around the parking lot and clubhouse on a sunny Friday morning on April 21, 2006. The gorgeous yet humble course costs visitors just $30 for 18 holes, which are laid out along rolling green hills at the doorstep of Kaipara Harbour. Members knew the famous Kiwi caddie, Williams, lived nearby and belonged to the club. But word had spread that Woods himself was in town, and had swapped roles to carry Williams's clubs on the morning of his caddie's wedding. "Tiger was adamant he wanted to caddie for me and didn't want to play, so I put a few bricks in the bag," Williams says. "He noticed straightaway and threw them out."

Williams and Woods arrived at the short par-4 12th, which was near South Head's parking lot. After 11 holes of Williams's friends begging Woods to hit a shot, any shot, the 10-time major winner caved. The 12th was 300 yards long and slightly uphill. "Without even a practice swing, Tiger took my driver and blasted a tee shot onto the green," Williams says. Woods whipped around and said, "Is that how you're supposed to play this hole?" The members laughed and cheered Woods, who was grateful that they had largely left him alone to enjoy the day.

Woods was in New Zealand, four years after his maiden visit, to be the best man at Williams's wedding to Kirsty Miller. Woods adored their relationship. In November 2002, he had urged his caddie to pop the question one night during the Dunlop Phoenix tournament in Japan. He called Williams's hotel room phone in the middle of the night and summoned him to his room. "Stevie, are you thinking about asking Kirsty to marry you?" Woods asked. "She's the one for you. I'm thinking about proposing to Elin, but you should ask Kirsty first." Williams laughed at the sudden and surprising suggestion. While Woods had taken a keen interest in learning about Kirsty, and Williams often reciprocated by asking how Elin was doing, the pair never exchanged relationship advice. But Williams did consider Woods's suggestion at the time. In 2003, Williams was racing in New Zealand when he held out a sign from his car during a warm-up lap that read "WILL YOU MARRY ME, KIRSTY?" Although Williams did ask properly moments after it, Woods later said to Williams about his proposal, "Stevie, I always knew you were a redneck."

Woods and his wife, Elin Nordegren, arrived in New Zealand two weeks after the 2006 Masters, where Woods had tied third at Augusta, three shots behind the winner, Phil Mickelson. After Woods's rare caddie appearance that Friday morning, Williams and Miller married that afternoon, April 21, in Kumeu, west of Auckland. It was a rustic, country wedding where Miller arrived in a long-haul truck and her bridesmaids in a gray utility vehicle while a bagpiper played "Amazing Grace." The bagpipes were a nice touch given Miller's father is Scottish.

The newlyweds had extra security because it became national news that Woods was in the country. Not that he tried to hide his presence; Williams and Woods frequently jogged along the roads around Kumeu. "The whole wedding was a great day; Tiger and Elin were absolutely amazing with all our friends, my parents and Kirsty's parents," Williams recalls.

Woods made a moving best man's speech, the contents of which Williams has never previously revealed. Woods spoke about how funny he found the way Williams had proposed from his race car, and about how much grayer his hair had turned since joining Woods in 1999. He joked about his caddie being a "petrolhead" and a "reckless hard nut." But it was also heartfelt and meaningful; Woods observed that since meeting Kirsty, his caddie had more purpose and perspective in his life. He thought Williams, while incredibly driven, had realized family was more important than Woods's own grand golfing ambitions. "His speech was very gracious," Williams says. "He's quite articulate, Tiger. His words made me realize while my hard work had earned his respect, I'd also gained his admiration as a friend. It was a rare moment when our pursuit of major wins paused and it was just about friendship."

Woods and Elin had a unique friendship with the Williams couple that went as far as Nordegren making trips to New Zealand, without Woods, to spend time with Kirsty. Williams believes Woods and Elin found them refreshing because they weren't "yes people." They were genuine and honest. If Woods and Elin asked them out to dinner, and Williams and Kirsty didn't feel like it that particular night, they would decline. "I think a lot of people were afraid to say no to someone like Tiger," Williams says.

Days after the wedding, Woods and Williams took part in a charity speedway race. On Monday, April 24, Woods led one of two five-man teams in a 12-lap competition on a dirt track at Huntly

International Speedway, 60 miles south of Auckland. The stock car was a class of vehicle that allowed contact with other cars. Woods hadn't needed much convincing; whenever Williams had shown his boss videos of stock car racing, which was different from his usual saloon car racing, Woods had said, "I'd love to try that!" So Williams put together a charity event and invited New Zealand celebrities, such as Tana Umaga, the rugby star and recently retired captain of the national All Blacks team, as well as Greg Murphy, the country's leading V8 Supercars racer.

"This is a bit more physical [than golf]," Woods joked at a press conference in Auckland. "If they knock me off, I can knock them off. The idea is to have fun."

There was only one hiccup leading up to the race. With rain lashing Auckland in the lead-up, the city's notorious traffic was especially slow on race day. Woods and Williams were stuck on a highway only hours before the race was due to start. "We left the car on the side road and got a helicopter from my pilot friend," Williams says. "Taking a chopper into the event added a lot of excitement." Woods picked the skills up quickly while acting as a "blocker" for the other cars on his team in the first race of 12 laps. In the second race, Woods came from the back of the grid to win. The money raised from the night was donated to the Steve Williams Foundation, which started out providing sporting opportunities and grants for junior golfers in New Zealand but evolved into raising money for sick children.

Williams had set out in 1999 not to become too close with Woods after a similar error a decade earlier cost him his job with Norman. But the bond between him and Woods had snuck up on Williams. He tried to convince himself he had successfully maintained the player-caddie distance, but three months before Williams's wedding, he took a phone call from Woods that moved him.

Williams had won the New Zealand Super Saloon Championship at the Baypark Speedway, near Mount Maunganui, on Tuesday, January 3. The following morning, a hungover Williams was walking into a café overlooking the gorgeous waterfront in the Bay of Plenty when his cell phone buzzed. It was Woods calling from the U.S. He had learned, at an impressive speed, that his caddie had achieved a lifelong dream. Williams ducked outside the café, took the call and gazed up at the Mauao volcano, a special landmark for the Maori people. Mauao rises 232 meters from the sea and its name translates to "caught by the dawn." Williams smiled and couldn't help but think of dawn thirty. "Tiger was the very first person to call," Williams says. "I don't know how he knew, but for him to call and congratulate me on something where *I* had reached the pinnacle was very special."

Woods knew every detail; that there were two qualifying runs. He knew Williams was on the inside of the front row, that he took the lead on the third of 25 laps and that he'd led from there until the end. What he didn't know was that while celebrating, Williams was running and slipped, injuring himself. "That's why Kirsty and I were getting a recovery breakfast when Tiger called; I had been spraying and drinking champagne all over the track," Williams says.

Woods could be surprisingly encyclopedic about a range of topics. In Williams's saloon car racing world, he had learned what a "clean sweep" was. It's when a driver tops the qualifying, wins the heat race and the feature race. When his caddie would go back to New Zealand for a big race meet, Woods would often joke, "Stevie, if you can get us a clean sweep, there'll be a financial incentive."

Racing wasn't the only sport in which Woods could throw around lingo. With a Kiwi caddie, he knew a little rugby, which was more of a religion in New Zealand than a football code. Williams's domestic rugby team was the Waikato Chiefs. The men's national team, the All Blacks, were megastars. Woods knew a lot of the rules and the plays, including the ruck, which was when the ball was on the ground and players from either team surrounded it. Woods also knew several players' names. He could even talk about the Tri Nations tournament, when New Zealand, Australia and South Africa played each other in a series.

In fact, the two had a ritual—mostly driven by Williams—on the Saturday morning before the third round at the Open Championship each year. Mid-July was always in the thick of Test rugby season and the All Blacks often had a big match that kicked off on TV around 8:30 A.M. U.K. time—7:30 P.M. that same day in New Zealand. Williams did not want to leave the rented house where he was staying before the game finished, usually after 10 A.M. He would joke to Woods, "You need to get your ass in contention because we need an afternoon tee time Saturday." More often than not, Woods did.

At the 2004 Open at Royal Troon in Scotland, Woods and Williams were in the gym Saturday morning and were riding stationary bikes, side by side, with the rugby tournament on TV. New Zealand was playing Australia, a big rivalry, and the Wallabies scored in the dying minutes. One of the All Blacks, Joe Rokocoko, dropped a high ball under the goalposts and Australia scored a try, a touchdown equivalent. Williams screamed "F——k!" at the top of his lungs. "I'd forgotten where I was; a few people in the gym looked around at me," Williams says.

Woods was fascinated by the passion in rugby. He'd often sit down and watch matches with his caddie. He was particularly enamored with the emotion and symbolism of the Haka, a war dance the Maori people of New Zealand performed on special occasions. It's an intense and poetic display of pride and strength, and there are different choreographed versions for varying occasions.

Woods had also taken a keen interest in some of the players, including Umaga, whom he'd met in New Zealand. Woods could see he was a leader on the field, and Williams explained to Woods that Maori people had a word for Umaga's charisma, *mana*. He commanded immense *mana* from rugby fans for his courageousness on the field. "Tiger loved watching Tana play," Williams says.

The rivalry between New Zealand and South Africa also intrigued Woods, which he saw through banter between Williams and Ernie Els, who grew up in Johannesburg. The two had a standing bet: every time the All Blacks played the South African team, the Springboks, the loser had to pay $100. In the early and mid-2000s, the All Blacks regularly dominated the Springboks, including an eight-Test winning streak that spanned July 2001 to August 2004. At one stage, Williams recalls Els's wife, Liezl, telling Els he was simply "donating" money to Williams. "Tiger took pleasure in telling Ernie to hand over the $100," Williams says. Occasionally, Williams and several others would have Test rugby viewing parties in the fitness trailer on the PGA Tour. Phil Tataurangi, a New Zealander who won on the PGA Tour in 2002, had the keys to the trailer, which had the satellite dish required to watch rugby Tests. Anthony "Antman" Knight, who had caddied for Sergio Garcia and Michael Campbell among others, was usually the organizer of these viewing parties, which would see Tataurangi, as well as major winners Trevor Immelman and Els, pack into the trailer with caddies like Antman, Williams and Els's South African bagman, Ricci Roberts.

* * *

On the course, Woods and Williams were humming. Woods's PGA Tour results in early 2006 hinted he was in for another stellar season. He triumphed at the Buick Invitational at Torrey Pines and the Ford Championship at Doral, as well as the Dubai Desert Classic. Woods's success was a welcomed distraction from a tough topic: his father Earl's battle with prostate cancer. It had returned in 2004. That was in addition to heart problems, diabetes and poor circulation in his legs. Earl's health began to decline when Woods's majors season kicked off at the Masters. Woods conceded he tried too hard at Augusta, knowing it was likely the last major Earl would ever see. "He was forcing it and getting a little bit out of sync on the greens and his overall strategy changed," Williams says. "His putting was maybe too aggressive for Augusta National. He wanted so deeply to win the Masters for Earl."

Earl died on May 3, 2006, leaving Woods shattered. He and his father had shared a unique, strong and honest relationship. Earl had taught him how to play golf as a toddler and, along with Kultida, gave Woods every opportunity to succeed in golf and school. Earl and his son were proud of their open, two-way dialogue that better resembled that of best friends than a typical father-son dynamic. As Woods's amateur career began to take off, and even into his professional era, Earl constantly used a phrase to encourage his son: "Let the legend grow."

Woods posted on his website about Earl's passing: "My dad was my best friend and greatest role model. He was an amazing dad, coach, mentor, soldier, husband and friend."

Williams was home in Auckland when Elin called Kirsty and delivered the sad news. Days later, they flew from New Zealand to Southern California for the funeral. Williams himself was saddened. "Earl was someone I looked up to," Williams says.

From May to June, Woods took nearly a month off competing to grieve. The week prior to the 2006 U.S. Open at Winged Foot, an ultra-exclusive club in Mamaroneck, a harborfront town in Westchester County, New York, Woods had his yacht, *Privacy*, taken up from Florida. Woods often used the yacht at any tournament that was near a harbor or port. After he bought it in 2004, Woods would use it as his own personal hotel. At the Players Championship, he'd dock the vessel at Mayport in Jacksonville; while at the Ford Championship at Doral near Miami, he'd dock it off Key Biscayne. Williams would stay on the yacht, too.

At the 2006 U.S. Open, *Privacy* was worth every dollar, given a grieving Woods wanted to avoid crowds, questions and New York's notorious traffic. Williams noticed instantly that it was too soon for Woods to return to competition. In the practice rounds, he was wildly inaccurate with the driver, often missing in both directions, and Winged Foot had gnarly, deep rough. "In the entire time I'd caddied for Tiger, I'd not seen him that out of sync," Williams says.

Woods shot 76-76 to miss the cut by three shots and found a measly four fairways on both days. It was his first missed cut at the majors as a professional. "He hadn't had time to grieve," Williams says. In a dramatic final round, Australian Geoff Ogilvy won his only major when Mickelson, who was leading, imploded on the final hole with a double-bogey 6 to share second with Colin Montgomerie and Jim Furyk.

"I knew Tiger would be fine; he was far too tough," Williams says. "I just wondered if the overall timeline of his goal of breaking Jack's record might be pushed back."

Fortuitously, the Open Championship was heading to Royal Liverpool, nicknamed Hoylake after its local town, a month after the U.S. Open. The Open had a rota of 10 courses across Scotland and England that shared host duties. But the Open had not been held at Hoylake in 39 years. Very few among the 156 competitors had seen the course, including Woods. So, he skipped his usual Ireland trip to study Hoylake. "The new challenge of Hoylake fired up Tiger," Williams says. "He needed that after Earl's death. Links golf at the Open inspired Tiger more than any of the other three majors and their venues."

England was suffering a heat wave by its standards; the country's hottest July day on record was registered when the mercury hit 98.6 degrees (37 Celsius) near London. The heat was guaranteed to dry the course out. Williams was champing at the bit; he knew Woods's creative mind would relish the challenge of firm and fast courses. Golfers had to think about how the ball would react when it hit the ground. That's not common in the U.S., where golf is played mainly through the air on damp, soft courses. Liverpool, as a city, was buzzing; sports fans' attention wasn't on English soccer, given July was during the offseason. Liverpool's connection to The Beatles also added excitement with plenty of sites special to Beatles fans. They included the Cavern Club, where The Beatles frequently played in their early days.

World number one Woods had spent most of July at home in Florida, throwing himself into practicing a "links swing" that was shallower and didn't dig into the turf as steeply. The shallower swing allowed Woods to better control spin in the coastal winds common at links courses, while it also prevented wrist injuries, given that the U.K. turf was rock hard. "Tiger loved to pick the ball cleanly off the turf on links courses," Williams says. "He would get frustrated if he took a single divot in a practice session." Woods's great rival and Masters champion Mickelson had spent three weeks in the U.K., staying close to Hoylake to fine-tune his links play.

Woods and Williams arrived at the John Lennon Airport in Liverpool, England, on the morning of Saturday, July 15. Williams typically drove at tournaments, especially in England, where cars traveled on the left side of the road, as in New Zealand. But Woods wanted to take the wheel as the pair made the 21-mile drive through Liverpool, across the River Mersey and into the quaint English seaside town of Hoylake, where Royal Liverpool sat at the northwest corner of the Wirral Peninsula. En route to Hoylake, Williams wanted to stop at a corner shop to get water and snacks, so Woods pulled in off the highway but scraped the wheels of the car along the curb. "I laughed and told Tiger, maybe I should drive while we're in England," Williams says. In Hoylake, Williams made a beeline to the course for a three-hour walk during which he'd formulate a game plan. He knew most of the Open venues, like St. Andrews, Carnoustie and Royal Troon, like the back of his hand. "But I'd never been to Hoylake, so I had no notes," Williams says. His first impression was Hoylake was similar to St. Andrews—a flat links heavily exposed to the wind.

Woods had tied for second at the Western Open in Chicago, his last start before the Open. Williams believed it was the best Woods had ever struck his long irons (2-iron through 5-iron). Hoylake, like most links courses, had extremely difficult pot bunkers. Williams believed if his boss eliminated the bunkers, and avoided three-putting, he would be very difficult to beat.

Williams came up with a bold strategy. He felt Woods should not use driver the entire tournament and instead hit irons or fairway metals from the tee. He would have more control with direction, and at certain distances from the tee (laying up) there were no bunkers. Woods was the 10th longest driver on the PGA Tour, averaging 304.3 yards per tee shot. But he was longer than any of the elite players at the time; the nine above him in distance were not in his league.

Williams was aware the strategy was like asking Woods's friend Roger Federer, the tennis star, to try and win Wimbledon from his second serve. Woods would at times be hitting 5-iron to a green when his peers would hit 8- or 9-iron. But the conditions called for it. Hitting one bunker was forgivable, but more than two or three could derail his entire tournament. Plus, the fairways had been baked to a crust, meaning Woods's 3-iron could land 220 yards and roll out 60 yards. In fact, the fairways were so firm and dry, Open organizers planned to park two fire engines on the course for the opening rounds, fearing ground fires.

Over lunch, Williams told Woods the strategy. He agreed instantly. "Tiger completely trusted my judgment," Williams says. On Saturday afternoon, Woods hit a couple of drivers during a practice round. But the risk was too high. For the entire tournament, Woods hit one driver—on the par-5 16th in round one.

On Monday, Woods reverted to a 6:45 A.M. practice-round tee time as his quest for a third Open title began. With his strategy in mind, Williams couldn't help but pick the song "Reckless" by Australian Crawl as his soundtrack for the week. He felt its lyrics applied directly to Woods in Liverpool, as the song admonished him to "throw down" his guns and not be "so reckless."

He knew it wasn't palatable, in fact it could be seen as a bold risk, to take driver out of Woods's hands. "But it would have been so reckless to change the game plan," Williams says. "I knew it was going to work."

For Woods, the loss of his father was still a cloud hanging over an otherwise warm and sunny Liverpool. But he was clearly choosing to use it as inspiration. "There's not a day I go through without thinking about my dad," Woods said.

When the tee times were released, Woods was grouped with Japan's Shingo Katayama, who was known for regularly wearing cowboy hats, and golf great Nick Faldo, whose six majors included three Opens.

Reporters sensed an awkwardness to the grouping, given Faldo, 49 and semiretired, criticized Woods's swing while working as a commentator for ABC on the coverage of the Buick Invitational at

Torrey Pines in early 2005. Woods reportedly didn't speak to the Englishman for more than a year.

"I'm paid for my opinion, and I'm entitled to my opinion," Faldo said. Williams thought the grouping was odd, given Woods was world number one and Faldo was nearly retired, having failed to make the cut in all six events he'd played before the Open. Faldo predicted the atmosphere "won't be much fun; head down, blinkers on. I need just a smidgen more than a week's practice to take on Tiger."

The pair were about to spend more than eight hours together, over two rounds. But Woods didn't even attempt to hide the feud. "We really don't talk much; I've only played with him two times since I've been a pro and there wasn't a lot of talking there, either," he said. Asked if the pair would speak at all on Thursday at Royal Liverpool, Woods believed it was up to Faldo. He promised to be in his own world competing, rather than socializing. Quizzed what his reaction would be if Faldo did chat, Woods smiled and answered, "Surprised."

Bookmakers had listed Woods a 5-to-1 favorite to win the 135th Open, with world number two Mickelson at 10 to 1. Woods struck his first shot just after 2:39 P.M. on Thursday, July 20. Predictably, there was tension on the first tee when Faldo and Woods exchanged a frosty handshake. Faldo reportedly wheeled around to the crowd and touched his cheek, seemingly joking that he was anticipating a kiss from the defending Open champion. Woods was not amused, and he three-putted the first green for a bogey.

Four birdies steadied the ship for Woods, before he produced an eagle at the par-5 18th for a 67. He was one shot behind the lead. Woods and Faldo briefly talked on the 15th. "We were grinding, trying to turn things around," Woods said.

On Friday, at Hoylake's most difficult hole, the 456-yard, par-4 14th, Woods had confused spectators when he hit 2-iron from the tee. But he sent shock waves through the tournament when he drilled a 4-iron from 212 yards in the fairway and into the hole for eagle. It was the longest competitive hole-out of his career. Woods went on to shoot 65 and took the lead at 12 under par. His 65 set the course record at Royal Liverpool, but it was matched later that day by Chris DiMarco and Ernie Els. As Woods and Faldo left the 18th green Friday, they exchanged a joke and Faldo said the pair buried the hatchet. "Tiger needed no motivation, but he probably played better Thursday and Friday because he wanted to send a message to Faldo that, 'This golf swing is fine the way it is,'" Williams says.

Woods and Els were paired in the final group Saturday, though both were flat and carded lackluster 71s. Woods had two three-putts on the back nine alone. He hung tough and birdied the last to lock a final group pairing Sunday with Sergio Garcia. Still, at 13 under, he led by one over DiMarco, Els and Garcia, who had holed a 9-iron from 167 yards for eagle during his third-round 65.

By Saturday night, the Liverpool fans had grown rowdy as the beer flowed and the championship came to a head. The crowds knew how to put on a show; they were used to cheering on Liverpool FC and Everton across town. They were unlike the more respectful, reserved Scottish crowds. "Hoylake had some of the best atmosphere I ever saw at an Open," Williams says. "The chants sounded like we were at Anfield [Liverpool FC's stadium]."

Although the Open had been to Royal Birkdale and Royal Lytham, 40 minutes away, fans hadn't witnessed a major in Liverpool for almost 40 years.

Williams also gave Woods some putting advice that Saturday evening; his head was not still enough during the stroke and he was looking up too early. Woods practiced the putting tip furiously that night.

Woods, who'd won all 10 of his majors when leading after 54 holes, had a date with destiny: 2:30 P.M. in the final group with

Garcia. Woods started steady with four straight pars, but Garcia, who shocked the excited fans by wearing a canary-yellow outfit, three-putted for bogey at the second and third holes. "I don't think Liverpool, England, was the right place for that outfit," Williams says.

Els was having more success, joining Woods in the lead after four holes. It was brief, though, as Woods responded with an eagle at the par-5 fifth to seize control of the tournament. When Els faded, DiMarco emerged as the biggest challenger. The Floridian was playing with a similar grief to Woods; he had lost his mother, Norma, to a heart attack on July 4. DiMarco was close with his mother; she had driven him to all his tournaments growing up and never missed one.

"I wasn't going to play the 2006 Open, at all," DiMarco recalls. "I had just lost Mom two weeks earlier. Both my brothers were like, 'You need to go.' So, I took my father, my father-in-law and my son, Cristian, and a buddy of mine to caddie. We needed to get my dad out of the house. I had zero expectations going in. I shot 70, 65, 69 and I was one shot back of Tiger going into Sunday."

In the final round, DiMarco felt a spirituality in the air. "I walked onto the first tee and my walking scorer's name was Norma. I got goose bumps. I realized my mom was with me, watching, and I played with a peace that day that I hadn't really played with too often." DiMarco showed his competitive fire when he came within one shot of Woods's lead, courtesy of a birdie on the par-3 13th while Woods bogeyed the 12th. But Woods responded with three straight birdies from the 14th. "When the moment meant the most to Tiger, he always found a way to hit an extraordinary shot under pressure," Williams says.

A par on 17 ensured Woods had a three-shot lead teeing off on the par-5 18th. Then came the defining moment of the championship, and the most emotional scene Williams ever witnessed from Woods. He and Woods made their way up the 18th fairway, a cathartic walk for the grieving superstar, when they exchanged a high five. Woods, though, held on to Williams's hand after the handshake and grabbed his caddie around the shoulders. "I could see there was a lot going through his head," Williams says. As Woods and Williams approached the 18th green, they could see over the enormous navy-blue grandstands that the sun had shone through the clouds on a heavily overcast Sunday. The English sun pierced the thick gray clouds for two minutes, before they closed back up. Being in Liverpool, and with Williams an avid rock music fan, The Beatles were on his mind. He leaned into Woods and said, "Mate, look at that. Here comes the sun. That's Pops looking down on you. That's him; he's telling you he's watching you and he's proud. He'll always be watching." Woods was too consumed with trying to hold off his emotions to respond, but nodded and distracted himself by staring at his upcoming putt.

They arrived on the green, and Woods two-putted for par to win by two shots. Woods was trembling and grabbed his caddie. He was an emotional wreck. Throughout Woods's career, even his inner sanctum had rarely seen his emotional side. He was always stoic, almost robotic, even in victory. But on golf's grandest stage—the 18th green at the Open—Woods began to bawl his eyes out. The memories of his father came streaming out when he realized he'd won a major, but for the first time, Earl wasn't alive to see it. Williams pointed to the sky and said, "This one's for Pops, mate. Major No. 11 was for Pops."

Woods's impressive final-round 67 left him at 18 under par (270), one shot shy of his Open Championship 72-hole scoring record. DiMarco was second, two shots behind, while Els was third. When Woods finished, DiMarco was in the scoring tent having just signed his card. The winner and runner-up shared an embrace. "Tiger said, 'Your mom would be proud.' I was crying," DiMarco says. "I said, 'Well, your dad would definitely be proud of you.' The hug was probably two seconds longer than we intended, but we were both going through something pretty traumatic," DiMarco says.

Woods's 11th career major win—10 of which had come in the previous seven years alongside Williams—drew him equal with Walter Hagen, second on the all-time list. Eight majors remained to overtake Nicklaus. Two and a half months after Earl's death, Woods was back in the major winner's circle.

Remarkably, using Williams's conservative strategy, Woods had hit 86 percent of fairways (48 of 56) and had found just three bunkers in 72 holes (the 10th hole in round one, and the second and seventh holes in round three). "To win a major championship using driver once will go down in history; I don't think it had ever happened, or ever will again," Williams says.

According to his own statistics, Williams noticed Woods didn't make a double-bogey the entire tournament. His ball-striking was one of the best tournaments Williams ever witnessed. On the front nine, Woods only missed three fairways all week (25 of 28), along with five on the back nine. He hit 58 of 72 greens in regulation, which was 12 greens on day one, 16 on day two, and 15 greens in both the third and fourth rounds. Woods's short game was also incredible. He saved par nine times in the 14 greens he missed all week—including a perfect 6 of 6 on day one.

The numbers were outrageously impressive in the pressure cooker of a major, unlike Woods's typical roller coaster of anxiety, wild drives and thrilling escapes. This win was strategic, controlled and relatively stress-free. His opponents probably felt it was death by 1,000 cuts. But the numbers are not what Williams remembers most vividly. To this day, he gets slightly emotional if he stumbles upon highlights of the 2006 Open, which were shown frequently in the lead-up to the 2014 and 2023 Open championships when the Open returned to Hoylake. "I think about that tournament often because the 72nd hole was the most spiritual moment I've ever witnessed in a tournament," Williams says.

Naturally, as Woods cradled the claret jug, Earl was on his mind during the trophy presentation. He described how his dad's memory had kept him calm all day, but walking up the final hole, the energy and the moment got to him. "I wish he could have seen this one last time; I love my dad and I miss him very much," Woods said to applause.

Within hours after Woods's win, he signed Williams's caddie trophy, the bright gold flag from Royal Liverpool's 18th green:

> *Dear Stevie,*
> *You're the best. Thanks again for helping me attain my goals. Your friend always,*
> *Tiger Woods*

On the right-hand side of the flag, underneath the Open Championship logo—a claret jug silhouette—Woods added a postscript that related to his stunning eagle hole-out from 212 yards during the second round:

> *P.S.*
>
> *Nice Yardage on 14.*

For the first time in his career, Woods was beginning to let people in. Even his defeated rivals found it difficult not to sympathize with a guy grieving the loss of his father.

Almost 20 years on, DiMarco says a moment during Woods's acceptance speech still lives with him. "He turned toward me and addressed my dad, me and my son," DiMarco recalls, his voice cracking with emotion. "Tiger said to both of them, 'Chris went through a hard time and everyone sends their best for what you're going through.' He didn't have to say that, but he did. That was pretty cool."

CHAPTER 12

WORDS THAT WON

By the summer of 2006, Williams and Woods had become incredible communicators. Their dialogue was unlike that of any other player-caddie combination on tour. It was underscored by Williams's old-school, analog approach and Woods's upbringing—a father who conversed with him like an adult, and a mother who ensured her son's education was put before golf. At the center of their dynamic was a fondness for writing each other notes of encouragement, constructive feedback and inspiration, regularly, during tournaments.

Exchanging notes started in early 2000, once their partnership had solidified. Originally, Williams began writing them because he didn't have a cell phone. He was from a different era. For most of 1999 and 2000, Woods would have to call Williams's hotel and be connected to his room if he wanted to communicate a change of plans regarding Woods's practice times. But he grew tired of risking hotel staff figuring out golf's biggest star was on the line, and so he bought Williams a cell phone in early 2000. "Even then, we still continued the handwritten notes; they were really meaningful to his performances," Williams says.

The notes weren't exchanged after *every* round, but they were frequent. Williams would grab the notepad beside his hotel bed, pen a message on paper and take it to Woods's hotel room when he dropped the golf clubs back. Williams once wrote after a round:

> *TW,*
> *Today was a great day.*
> *Your driving was superb!*
> *Tomorrow, we need to think about better wedge play.*
> *Stevie*

They could be more specific, too. While always encouraging, Williams's notes were frank when needed. He felt Woods had enough people in the world telling him what he wanted to hear. Only a truthful approach would improve Woods's results. Another note Williams wrote after one round was:

> *TW,*
> *Today you had six shots inside 60 yards, but you only got up and down three times.*
> *Your chipping action was beautiful.*
> *But you need to leave the ball on a more conservative side of the hole.*
> *Today you left yourself with a few downhill, difficult putts.*
> *We are going to be fantastic tomorrow!*
> *Stevie*

Woods would read a note when he returned from the golf course or dinner, and he might read it again the following morning. When

Williams picked the clubs back up, Woods often left a note in reply. "Tiger had very tidy handwriting, and most times he made a real effort to respond to the content in my messages," Williams says.

Their most memorable note exchange came during one of Woods's most publicized showdowns with a fellow pro golfer. In February 2006, at the World Golf Championships-Match Play event at La Costa resort in Carlsbad, California, Woods was drawn in the first round to play against Stephen Ames, a Trinidad-born golfer raised in Canada. Match play is a format where two players go head-to-head and, instead of recording the total strokes over 18 holes, the lowest score wins a hole. If two players record the same score on a hole, they "halve" it. The WGC-Match Play tournament used a single elimination format for the top 64 players in the world. Asked about facing Woods, Ames referenced the world number one's Achilles' heel—his occasionally wayward driver—to suggest Woods was beatable. "Anything can happen, especially where he's hitting the ball," Ames said. Woods was deeply disappointed with Ames's comments. "Tiger found them incredibly disrespectful, so, I left him a note in his hotel room the night before the match," Williams says.

The note urged Woods to go out the following day and show Ames—who had just one PGA Tour victory to his name—that Woods was unequivocally the best player in the world:

> *TW,*
> *Your job is to not lose a single hole.*
> *Go out and get the job done!*
>
> *Stevie*

Against Ames, Woods birdied seven of his first eight holes during a demoralizing 9-and-8 victory. That meant Woods had won nine holes from 10, but only eight holes remained. Hence, Ames mathematically could not win, nor halve (tie) the match. Woods, who had set a record for the largest-ever margin of victory at the WGC-Match Play, was asked about the showdown. He barely answered the reporter's question, instead blurting out, "Nine and eight." Woods also said of Ames, "I think he understands now." Australian Geoff Ogilvy, who won the tournament days later, said Ames's original jab "wasn't the smartest thing he said."

The following morning, Woods wrote back to Williams. He usually used a ballpoint pen, but for this note he grabbed a Sharpie and, in capital letters, scribbled:

> *STEVIE,*
> *JOB DONE!*
> *HA HA HA*

Woods could not understand why rivals wanted to take public shots at him. He never initiated such exchanges and often took the high road unless a barb had acutely upset him. Kultida had raised him with the phrase "Let the clubs do the talking." This time, his clubs had shouted a message loud and clear: don't mess with a Tiger. Williams believed the exchange with Ames had strengthened Woods's resolve in time for another public jab months later at the 2006 PGA Championship in Chicago.

The week before the PGA Championship, Woods won his 50th PGA Tour title at the Buick Open in Michigan. As Woods's putt dropped on the final hole, Williams pulled off his caddie bib and flashed the logo of Valvoline, his personal sponsor, to the TV cameras and photographers. A deal had been struck by Woods's team to allow Williams to stitch the Valvoline logo on his shirt. Williams admired Valvoline and used their oil in his race cars. "Steve's a savvy pro at his job and as a marketer," Barry Bronson, a Valvoline spokesman, said at the time.

Williams had a burning passion to improve working conditions for caddies, which had come a long way since the PGA Championship was last held at Medinah in 1999. Woods's steadfast defense of Williams's rights—such as refusing to play the 1999 *Showdown at Sherwood* unless his bagman could caddie in shorts—forced tournament organizers to view bagmen differently. Tournaments began providing caddies with meals, a place to relax and allowed them to park on-site. At Medinah Country Club, caddies were parking at the course and eating in their own dining area. Williams might have celebrated Woods's winning putts like he was the star, but he was just excitable and competitive. He certainly didn't overestimate his importance. "You're always going to be in the limelight because you're beside Tiger; I'm his caddie and he's the star," he told the *New York Times* in 2006.

* * *

Williams turned over the *Chicago Tribune* to the sports section on the morning of Tuesday, August 15, in 2006, to see what had been written in previews of the 2006 PGA Championship. Williams was in a good mood, having returned to Medinah's No. 3 course, the site of his first major win with Woods. But he let out an audible laugh after reading the back-page sports story.

World number two Phil Mickelson's short-game coach, Dave Pelz, had made bold claims about his student, who'd recently won his second Masters title. For the opening rounds at Medinah, Mickelson had been grouped with Woods and newly crowned U.S. Open champion Ogilvy.

"When Phil's at his best, I'm thinking nobody can beat him,"

Pelz told the *Tribune*. Asked if that included Woods, Pelz said, "You bet it does." He added, "I'm not saying Tiger's short game is bad. He has a great short game. But I think Phil putts more consistently than Tiger. He has more imagination and a few more shots around the green."

Williams and Woods saw right through the intention of the comments; they thought Pelz and Mickelson were just playing mind games. Woods and Mickelson had not often been paired together in majors, so it was likely intended to throw Woods off, knowing reporters would pounce. In his pretournament press conference, Woods joked, "I think I'm pretty tough to beat when I'm playing well, too." Williams, if anything, found it funny. He and Woods *knew* Mickelson's short game was the best in the world. It was not something they denied. But Woods's short game was also elite, and it was one of many tools in his arsenal. Woods was one of the longest drivers, one of the best iron players, ever, and, in Williams's mind, the greatest clutch putter in history. As for the mental game, Woods was peerless. "Tiger was not the guy you wanted to direct a comment like that at," Williams says. "It would backfire 100 percent of the time."

Only a day later, an opinion piece in the same newspaper wrote that "bad ideas in life" included "trying to floss a pitbull's teeth . . . and firing up Tiger Woods." Woods's last two starts included an 11th major win at the Open at Hoylake and a victory at the Buick Open. Williams was chuffed when he learned about both the groupings and Pelz's comments. If the WGC-Match Play was any hint, Woods thrived on public barbs. Williams knew Woods was already intense and would be even more fired up to win. "Tiger, all of a sudden, had a more stoic and calmer look on his face than he usually did at majors," Williams says.

Woods, Mickelson and Ogilvy had been grouped by PGA Championship organizers simply because the trio had won the first three majors of 2006. Ogilvy was curious to see how the two stars would get along, pointing out a sports-mad city like Chicago would only produce a more electric atmosphere if there was player beef. "I'm sure it will be a zoo; I don't know the last time they played together in a big spectator market like [Chicago]," Ogilvy said.

The 2006 PGA was only the fourth time Woods and Mickelson had played together at a major championship, following the 1997 PGA Championship (final round), the 1999 U.S. Open (third round) and the 2001 Masters (final round). At almost every event, groupings for the first two rounds were arranged pretournament, while the third- and fourth-round pairings were based off scores. Williams believed broadcast TV, which had significant influence, played a major role in Woods's and Mickelson's lack of major pairings together in opening rounds because TV rights provided the biggest funding for the tour and organizing bodies of the majors. "If you have your two most valuable players, in terms of TV ratings, playing together in the morning wave, then nobody would watch in the afternoon and vice versa," Williams says. In the majors, there were several traditional groupings, such as the Masters, where it was customary for the reigning U.S. Amateur champion to play with the defending Masters champion on the first two days. Williams knew Woods's hunger to beat Mickelson was a tournament within a tournament.

Adding to the hype was that Mickelson, since he last played with Woods in a major, had broken through the barrier and was now a bona fide threat. He'd won three majors in two and a half years: the 2004 and 2006 Masters, as well as the 2005 PGA Championship at Baltusrol in New Jersey. He'd blown the unwanted tag of "best player without a major" out of the water. "It is nice that I was able to pass that mantle on to somebody," joked Mickelson.

Mickelson took an unusual step of practicing at another golf course in the Chicago area before the tournament started, to escape the crowds and commotion. Williams says that was because Mickelson was usually so gracious with his time for fans at regular PGA Tour stops and it was likely the Californian wanted to conserve energy at a major. "He was like the Arnold Palmer of the modern day, constantly signing autographs and giving thumbs-ups to fans, and that could be mentally draining," Williams says.

Woods, Mickelson and Ogilvy teed off at 8:30 A.M. on Thursday, August 17, from Medinah Country Club's 10th tee. The bedlam predicted from Chicago fans seemed to be immediately apparent: one golf writer observed a fan buying his first beer near the 10th tee at 7:45 A.M. and returning moments later carrying two more brews.

Mickelson came out swinging with a birdie on the par-5 10th while Woods fell two shots behind him with a bogey. He steadied and both Mickelson and Woods finished the day with 3-under-par 69s—three shots behind the leaders. "Neither one of them was trying to avoid the other, but no one was walking across the fairway to talk to each other, either," a diplomatic Ogilvy said.

Mickelson wasn't expecting anything to change for Friday's second round. "I enjoy playing with Tiger," Mickelson said. "He gets in his own world. We take care of business on the course and then we shake hands after."

On day two, Woods surged to within one shot of the lead, rolling in a birdie putt on the 18th for a 4-under 68. That was helped, marginally, by a fan on the first hole. When his opening tee shot hooked well left and was tracking for the gallery, a spectator used his arm to hit the ball back toward the fairway. Woods joked, "It was nice to have Shaquille O'Neal out there knocking them back." Williams wasn't surprised; he felt Woods was prone to hitting some of the worst opening tee shots among great players because he took such pride in his performance it often triggered first-tee jitters.

Woods demonstrated the inaccurate driver Ames had joked about back in February; he hit just 15 of 28 fairways during the first two rounds in Chicago. But Williams says the stats were misleading. On every tee shot, Woods aimed at a certain side of the hole based on trouble and hazards. "It wasn't just the fairway that he accepted as a good result," Williams says. Instead, if a hole was a dogleg left or had a hazard left, Woods would aim well to the right side of the fairway and even toward the rough. Landing in the first cut of rough was still considered hitting the overall target. Rough was better than out of bounds or lost balls, especially with Woods's strength and speed hitting out of long grass.

On a dramatic third day, Woods shot 65 to take a share of the 54-hole lead at 14 under par with Englishman Luke Donald. Mike Weir was 12 under and Ogilvy 11 under. Woods was 11 for 11 in converting 54-hole leads at the majors. Donald, aiming for his maiden major win, lived in Chicago and became something of a hometown hero, having played college golf at Northwestern University. In 2000, he was the first amateur to win the Chicago Open. "Luke was a fantastic iron player and short-game wizard," Williams says of the smooth-swinging lad from Hertfordshire. But Donald was also a shorter hitter, and not overly accurate. A golfer trying to win his first major, in his adopted backyard, while playing with Woods, was possible but certainly a tall order. "I did not think Luke was going to trouble Tiger, although we were ready for the crowd to be cheering heavily for Luke," Williams says.

On Saturday night, Woods had a practice putting session and made a crucial technique adjustment: Williams says Woods didn't have his eyes directly over the ball, but after the tweak he could see his starting lines perfectly. "Sunday was perhaps the best 18 holes of putting he had at a major," Williams says.

Woods sank a 12-foot birdie on the first hole to take sole

possession of the lead and never looked back, adding another birdie within the first five holes. He then drained 40-foot birdie bombs on Nos. 6 and 8 to increase his lead to four. A birdie at No. 11 pushed his advantage to five. "When Tiger was on top of the leaderboard, it put an unbelievable amount of pressure on the other guys because they often tried to force it," Williams says. Woods cruised to a tidy 68 and, at 18 under par (270), he won by five shots over Shaun Micheel. Donald, Sergio Garcia and Adam Scott tied third.

Woods made just three bogeys for the entire tournament, securing his 12th major and third PGA Championship title. He became the first player ever to win the PGA twice on the same golf course. Mickelson fizzled out with a closing 74 and tied 16th. "Pelz had ticked off Tiger, in a good way," Williams says. Mickelson was asked to describe Woods adding to his majors tally. "It's pretty good," he said.

Woods was utterly dominant for the remainder of 2006. The week after the PGA, he returned to his happy hunting ground of Firestone Country Club in Akron and won. Two weeks after that, a scintillating final round earned him a victory at the Deutsche Bank Championship outside Boston, his seventh PGA Tour title of 2006.

Despite his success, Woods was not happy with his swing in Boston through three rounds. Haney subsequently gave his student some instructions via phone to work on in front of the mirror in his hotel room. Woods practiced Haney's instructions for two hours before bed, then for 90 minutes in the middle of the night after a bathroom trip. Woods spent another hour Sunday morning swinging in front of the mirror. He closed with a 63 and clipped Vijay Singh by two shots. Williams marveled at Woods's ability to rehearse a feel in his swing without needing to hit a golf ball.

The Deutsche Bank was Woods's fifth consecutive PGA Tour win. In his final four starts of 2006, he finished no worse than tied ninth. In that stretch, he won the WGC-American Express and finished second, twice. The win came at The Grove in Rickmansworth, England, and Haney wrote in *The Big Miss* that Woods's swing was the closest it ever looked to perfection. Williams agreed: "He was on a stretch from the Open Championship and into the fall, where he just wanted to keep winning and winning," Williams says.

Overall, 2006 was cemented as one of Woods's greatest-ever seasons. From 19 official events worldwide, he recorded nine victories and three runner-up results. Two of his nine wins were majors and two were elite World Golf Championships events. "It was probably the most overlooked year of Tiger's career," Williams says. Earl's passing could have forced an understandable delay in Woods's pursuit of Nicklaus's 18 majors, but he had dug deep and turned it into one of his best seasons. The year 2007 couldn't come quick enough.

Toward the end of 2006, the Ryder Cup was held at Ireland's luxurious K Club in Kildare, a lush, green golf sanctuary with a grand hotel that resembled a noble manor. It was an emotionally charged cup, given that Northern Ireland's Darren Clarke was on the European team and his wife, Heather, had tragically died of cancer that summer. Despite Woods winning three of his five matches, the Europeans rallied for a stirring victory over the Americans.

There was a moment of comic relief, though, when Williams was holding Woods's 9-iron during his Sunday singles match against Sweden's Robert Karlsson and was standing near the water at the K Club's seventh green. Williams went to soak a towel in the lake but lost his footing and dropped the club into the pond. The club sank to the bottom. Woods saw it and laughed. "You f——g clown. Really?" Woods chirped at Williams. Later, a diver retrieved Woods's club.

* * *

Williams sat in his room in Woods's rented house in Tulsa, Oklahoma, on Wednesday, August 8, 2007, and listened to the plucky guitar notes and vocal falsetto of Bruce Springsteen's "I'm on Fire" and cracked a smile. He'd found the perfect song to sing all week at the 89th PGA Championship at Southern Hills Country Club. Hours earlier, Woods had told Williams he felt confident of winning, the only time the caddie had ever heard Woods explicitly say that aloud before a major. Usually, his form, body language or cryptic words to the media spoke for him. This time, it was coming straight from the source. "In the afternoon, Tiger said he was on fire, and he knew he was going to win. Naturally, I thought of Springsteen," Williams says. Woods's 2007 results leading into the PGA included four wins and joint runner-up results at the Masters and U.S. Open. He'd certainly earned the right to be cocky. But despite his sensational first seven months, there seemed to be a group of emerging challengers wanting their pound of flesh. Woods had given them hope, too, blowing golden chances at the Masters and U.S. Open. Now, they were in Tulsa, and apart from the 155 other players, Woods was also going to be battling a heat wave if he wanted to take out the last major of the year. The heat index was expected to be well over 100 every day.

The challengers had thrown their hats into the ring from the early part of 2007. Nick O'Hern, a relatively unheralded left-handed Australian golfer who used a broomstick putter, earned himself a rare statistic at the World Golf Championships-Match Play. On February 25, 2007, O'Hern made history—or at least, a brilliant trivia question—when he became the first player to beat Woods twice in professional match play. O'Hern, who was also one of Woods's Isleworth neighbors, capped an upset win, in extra holes, over Woods during the third round of the WGC-Accenture Match Play at The Gallery's South Course in Marana, Arizona, near Tucson. It was O'Hern's second match play win over Woods, having first defeated him in 2004. O'Hern also ended Woods's seven-event winning streak on the PGA Tour, which began at the 2006 Open Championship at Hoylake and continued into 2007 at the Buick Invitational at Torrey Pines. "It's something to tell the grandkids," O'Hern said.

Woods typically relished match play competition, having won the WGC-Match Play twice before facing O'Hern. Williams began to notice Woods's peers were getting used to his intimidation factor, which had taken 11 years to develop since he turned pro. Now, a handful of hungry players wanted to face him one-on-one. That included at the WGC-Match Play, the Ryder Cup and the Presidents Cup. "The other guys were starting to see it as an opportunity to beat him because match play is only played over a maximum of 18 holes. Tiger's game was so well-rounded that it was very difficult to hang with him over 72 holes," Williams says. In match play, an opponent could have a blowout, pick up his ball and concede that hole to Woods. In stroke-play, if Woods was leading and a chasing opponent came unstuck, there wasn't any limit to how many strokes one could drop. It was difficult to recover.

In all formats, Williams could see that in 2007 a handful of mentally strong players had developed a degree of immunity to the circus that came with playing with Woods. Being grouped with Woods meant oversized crowds, unrelenting noise, extra officials inside the ropes and a stampede after each of Woods's shots, especially when he finished putting. Some players knew they would, occasionally, have to back off their shot and regroup if fans yelled during their backswings. They were evolving.

The subject of challengers was one topic Williams recalls being brought up during an informal dinner Woods had with his friend Roger Federer at the WGC event at Doral in March. Williams was staying on *Privacy* with Woods at Key Biscayne in Miami when his boss invited the Swiss champion onto the yacht. Federer had walked a nine-hole practice round with them earlier that day. The previous summer, at the U.S. Open in New York, Federer faced English tennis pro Tim Henman in the second round. Henman was asked about taking on Federer—the top seed and defending champion—when he used Woods's stranglehold on golf, and the growing confidence of Woods's rivals, as motivation. "It's as tough a test as you can have," Henman said. "I was watching golf the other day and one of the golfers said, 'Tiger Woods is the best in the world, but he is beatable.' I think that is the same with Roger. He is the best in the world . . . but you hope he has a bit of an off day." Federer went on to win that match, and the 2006 U.S. Open. Before the final, Woods, who was in attendance, met Federer for the first time and struck up a friendship. On the yacht in 2007, Williams marveled at the two sporting giants sharing stories about dealing with rivals, practice and preparation. Woods and Federer concluded that physical training allowed them to face any tough situation, but their mentality and competitive drive was how they dominated rivals. "One thing that struck me was how down to earth and laid-back Federer seemed. He was very comfortable with who he was," Williams says.

In April, Zach Johnson, a short-hitting but accurate golfer from Iowa, certainly wasn't intimidated when he was in contention during the final round of the 2007 Masters. As nasty rain and wind lashed Augusta National, Woods and Australian golfer Stuart Appleby played in the final group. Two groups ahead, Johnson birdied three of his final six holes to win. Although Woods had not topped the leaderboard after 54 holes, he lost a major for the first time in which he held the lead *during* the final day. Early on, Woods led outright and was later tied through seven holes. Woods tied second with Rory Sabbatini, two shots back. After four wins in 10 Masters as a pro, 2007 was Woods's first runner-up.

In the first half of 2007, another golfer who did not seem intimidated by Woods was Sabbatini, a talented South African who lived in Florida. In May, at the PGA Tour event at Quail Hollow in Charlotte, Sabbatini led Woods by one shot going into the final round. The night before, Sabbatini said he was eager for the chance to duel with the American superstar, because he felt some critics had undermined his win at the 2006 Nissan Open at Riviera. In that tournament, Woods had withdrawn with the flu. "He's here [in Charlotte] this week [and it is the] best opportunity I've had to put any of that criticism or doubt aside," Sabbatini said. Despite his bravado, Sabbatini shot 74 in the final round at Quail Hollow. Woods thrashed him by five shots and won. The following week, at the Players Championship at TPC Sawgrass, Sabbatini jokingly threw shade at Woods, claiming he was more beatable than ever. "He had to battle for that [Quail Hollow] win. I've seen him when he figures it out; it's scary. I don't want to see that anymore. I like the new Tiger. I'm waiting for him to have kids to really test his patience."

Woods took the unusual measure of biting back, telling reporters, "I've won three times this year, the same amount he's won in his career. So, I like the new Tiger as well."

Williams, perhaps having a soft spot for a South African, saw the funny side. He considered Sabbatini a character who simply danced to the beat of his own drum. He also felt a lot of tour players were starting to speak in clichés to avoid controversy, with their images being carefully managed by agents and corporate sponsors. Sabbatini was a colorful player voicing an opinion. At the very least, he was entertaining. The only thing Williams couldn't understand was wanting to poke the bear. "With Tiger's record, he *always* had the last laugh," Williams says.

On June 18, 2007, Woods and Elin welcomed their first child, a baby girl they named Sam Alexis. Woods told organizers of the upcoming PGA Championship his daughter's birth had helped him overcome his grief at the loss of Earl a year prior. "From losing a father to becoming a father, my life is in two totally different places." Woods and Elin named their daughter Sam to honor Earl. Woods's father had created a nickname for him as a child, in addition to Tiger, because he often joked Woods looked "more like a Sam." Earl would call out "Sam!" at junior golf tournaments as a code word to let Woods know he was proud, regardless of how he played. Woods wanted to transfer that bond to his own daughter by naming her Sam.

At the 2007 U.S. Open at Oakmont Country Club near Pittsburgh, Woods was in the final group on Sunday and was tied for the lead with 11 holes to play. On the final hole, he couldn't make birdie to force a playoff as Argentine Angel Cabrera won his first major. Woods tied second. "Tiger put up a tremendous fight right to the very end," Williams says. "The 17th hole was pivotal because it was a short par 4 where Tiger could have driven the green, but he couldn't hit the hero shot he needed."

After a stellar 2006 season, Woods had failed to capitalize on great chances at the first two majors of 2007. Only the Open Championship at Carnoustie and PGA Championship at Southern Hills in Tulsa remained, and Woods had never started a majors season with consecutive runner-up results. "There was extra pressure on the next two majors, without a doubt, given how well and consistent he was playing, and how productive the work had been with Hank," Williams says.

Woods tied 12th at Carnoustie, meaning that, for the fourth time since Williams had joined his team in 1999, Woods was going into the final major of the year having not won one. "Once Tiger had got to 10 majors at the 2005 Open, each additional major was such a big step toward the ultimate goal. Even if he won one major a year, going past 18 was looking very obtainable."

On August 5, the week prior to the PGA Championship, Woods won the WGC-Bridgestone Invitational by a whopping eight shots over Justin Rose and, of course, Sabbatini. Woods had won at Firestone for the third year in a row, his sixth time overall. He was the only player to finish under par, with the fewest number of players in red figures at a PGA Tour event since the 1995 Tour Championship. "At Firestone, he had every part of his game dialed in; he was putting very well, and his iron play was superb," Williams says. The irons were going to come in handy at Southern Hills, a course with plenty of dogleg holes, meaning Woods was not going to hit driver as often as he'd like.

There was no rest for Woods, though, who flew to Tulsa that Sunday night. On Monday morning, Woods teed off at dawn thirty for his first practice round at Southern Hills. "I wasn't really expecting him, but his work ethic is pretty good," Colombia's Camilo Villegas joked.

Around Tulsa, promotional posters were hyping the 89th PGA Championship as "Tiger versus Southern Hills." Tulsa was buzzing that literally the world's biggest sports star was in town. Woods garnered more votes than LeBron James, Peyton Manning and England football icon David Beckham in ESPN's "Who's Now," a U.S. television and internet popularity contest. As for "versing"

Southern Hills, Tulsa was chuffed their championship course in 1996 had relegated a rookie Woods to a tie for 21st at the Tour Championship held there. He fared marginally better at the 2001 U.S. Open at Southern Hills, sharing 12th, although that was his first major start after winning the Tiger Slam. "It's definitely one of the best tests we will ever play," Woods said. "You have to place the golf ball correctly off the tees as well as firing at the pins."

Perhaps a more accurate promotion would have pitted Woods against a thermometer. "It felt like this was the closest golf course to the sun," Williams says. The 2007 PGA Championship was expected to be the hottest major ever played. Excessive heat warnings were in effect, with temperatures expected to reach 102 degrees (39 Celsius) each day, and drop no lower than 80 degrees (27 Celsius) at night. Coincidentally, the highest daily temperatures ever recorded at a major were at Southern Hills when temperatures averaged above 100 degrees (37 Celsius) at the 1970 PGA Championship. Williams says the clear blue skies, Oklahoma humidity and penetrating sun meant he didn't go to the bathroom during each of the first three rounds, which lasted about five hours. He and Woods drank a bottle of water per hole. "Tiger had a deal with Gatorade and he would empty a sachet of Gatorade into every fourth bottle of water or so," Williams says. Woods took additional measures to avoid the heat, playing the majority of their practice rounds at 6 A.M. to conserve energy. "Tiger had won the week before, so he did very little practice on the driving range," Williams says. He adds that Woods, apart from going to the golf course, didn't leave the rented house all week. "He just stayed in the air-conditioning in the house and rested," says Williams, who only left the accommodation twice to see a New Zealand friend who lived in Tulsa, and to watch speedway racing on the weekend.

Woods's extreme workouts, and living in central Florida, had prepared him for the brutal Tulsa test: "It's one of the reasons I train as hard as I do—you go all-out, every day. As far as concentration waning, I don't see how that can ever be a problem." Rather than an obstacle, Williams says Woods saw an advantage in the scorching temperatures. He was desperate to be remembered as winning the hottest major ever played. "Tiger felt he'd beaten at least half the field before he teed off, just given the physical shape he was in; most players would not be as sharp, especially come Sunday," Williams says. Woods took enormous pride in playing well in extreme weather, and the heat just gave him extra motivation.

As the course's name suggested, Southern Hills had some aggressive undulations that were also going to be a challenge for Williams as he lugged around a 35-pound professional golf bag in the heat. "During my career I caddied in some extremely hot weeks. If you hydrated from the time you get up in the morning it was manageable," Williams says. He would regularly walk ahead of Woods and in the rough, under Southern Hills' many trees, for shade breaks.

Fortunately for Woods, he got *one* round in the slightly cooler morning temperatures that week. He was grouped with Bob Tway and Rich Beem for the opening rounds and the trio teed off at 8:45 on Thursday. Beem had clipped Woods by one to win the 2002 PGA Championship.

For all the talk of welcoming the heat, Woods seemed to back it up early with birdies on three of his first six holes. But he blamed tricky wind gusts for his unraveling over the next 12 holes with a 1-over 71. He was six shots off the lead. The following day, Woods teed off in the extreme afternoon heat and it seemed to narrow his focus. He obliterated the field with one of the finest rounds of his majors' career, shooting a 7-under 63 that agonizingly missed becoming the first player ever to shoot 62 in a major (a feat first achieved a decade later by Branden Grace at the 2017 Open). Woods's 15-foot birdie attempt at the 18th looked certain to drop and create history, but the ball violently skirted the cup and defied gravity to pop back out. "The ball was half in at one point," Williams says. Instead, he was the 21st male player to shoot 63 in a major. He led by two after 36 holes.

On day three, playing with Scott Verplank, Woods put the tournament on ice with a 1-under 69. He teed off in 101-degree temperatures (38 Celsius), which climbed higher in the afternoon. By day's end, Woods led by three over Stephen Ames going into Sunday's final round. Almost identically to his iron-play master class at the 2006 Open Championship at Royal Liverpool, Woods had hit driver on only four holes in three rounds. "The ball was just going so far, and that course had so many doglegs with trees in range; we had a game plan and that was backed up with incredible putting," Williams says.

Woods and Ames were set for a 2 P.M. final pairing on Sunday, and the possible tension was not lost on reporters, given the "9 and 8" incident at the 2006 WGC-Match Play. Ames clearly did not want to be asked about it. "Are we at the PGA Championship or at the [2006] Match Play?" Ames said. "I don't know if I want to go there because you [reporters] might take it out of context again. We will leave it at that."

Williams noticed an obvious awkwardness between the two golfers on the first tee on Sunday and knew there was no chance Woods was going to let Ames beat him. "I totally respect every player who gets into contention in a major, but I think Stephen would have preferred to be playing in the group in front," Williams says.

Woods bagged three birdies and a lone bogey to stretch his lead to five shots through eight holes. But he made bogey at No. 9. At the par-3 14th, Woods three-putted for bogey and saw his lead cut to one shot. He then berated himself as he walked off the 14th green. "I could hear him grumbling and yelling into his hand," Williams says. But, true to form, Woods was able to completely reset and birdie No. 15.

That birdie allowed Woods to make three closing pars and shoot 69, and at 8 under par (272), he recorded a two-shot win over Woody Austin, with Ernie Els third at 5 under. Woods had secured his 13th major and fourth PGA Championship. Woods appeared to choke back tears after his winning putt, perhaps feeling the wave of emotion of winning his first major as a father. Usually, Woods would march off the 18th green and see his wife, or his coach, or his manager. Now, he had a daughter to hold in the moments after a win, and Elin had brought Sam Alexis to Southern Hills. "I think he realized he had another loved one who brought a whole new world," Williams says.

Woods had desperately wanted to win the PGA to avoid going into 2008 answering questions about a major-less 2007, which would have only been magnified by sharing second place twice. Winning at Southern Hills ensured Woods maintained a pace of winning one major per year, which after his 10th major win at the 2005 Open at St. Andrews, at the age of 29, was keeping him on track of reaching Nicklaus's record by his late thirties. "Had Tiger ever got to 19, or 21 majors, the 2007 PGA would have been pivotal in my opinion," Williams says.

Woods certainly looked to be on a collision course with Nicklaus. His 13th major win came in his 44th major start as a professional. It took Nicklaus 53 majors to win 13, with his victory at the 1975 Masters. "It's going to take some time; it took Jack 20 years to get [18]," Woods said. "Hopefully, health permitting, and everything goes right, and I keep improving, one day I will surpass that."

Conceding that his fitness would have a say in his ultimate goal felt like a foreshadowing of what was about to come in 2008, and beyond. Williams thought about it in the weeks and tournaments after the 2007 PGA. Woods said he ruptured the anterior cruciate ligament in his left knee while running on the golf course at Isleworth during a workout in the weeks after the Open Championship. He opted not to have surgery and pushed through pain to win four of his next five tournaments, including Southern Hills. "I was aware of the pain in his knee; I could tell by the way he walked sometimes and the treatment he was having, but he never really spoke much about how much pain he was in," Williams recalls.

It was a can Williams was happy to kick down the road while basking in the PGA win. Instead, he read over and over what was arguably the most meaningful message Woods ever wrote to him. It was inked across the 18th green flag from Southern Hills—one of the most captivating in Williams's collection. Southern Hills' pink clock tower, which the club built in time for the 1996 Tour Championship, seemed to pop from its bright yellow background. Beside it, Woods scribbled:

To Stevie,
Thanks for your friendship.

Love always,
Tiger Woods

CHAPTER 13

WHAT WOULD YOU KNOW, YOU SHEEP SHAGGER?

The stratospheric views across the Pacific Ocean, from the emerald-green tee at the 12th hole of the South Course at Torrey Pines in La Jolla, California, were a stunning distraction from one of the most brutal golf holes on the PGA Tour. The 504-yard par 4 lives within the top 20 hardest holes on tour—and rent-free in the minds of average golfers who teed up on the municipal South Course every day.

The 12th hole, which sat at the southern end of the course, closer to San Diego, was dotted with a handful of trees, including some California eucalypts. To the left of the hole, over a fence, was a dirt area that, during the annual PGA Tour event at Torrey Pines, served as a parking lot for officials. One year at the Buick Invitational, play had finished late, and Woods offered Williams a ride down to the lot, given no one was around to shuttle Williams back to his rental car. Woods and Williams arrived at the dirt lot, and the race car driver inside Williams instantly pictured a speedway. There wasn't another soul in sight, so Williams turned on his ignition and told Woods to hop in the passenger seat. He drove in a circular motion to create what saloon car racers call a "cushion," or a mini wall around the boundary. "I was going slow, and it was late with no one around, but we were howling with laughter as dirt flew everywhere," Williams says.

Williams was always in a good mood in San Diego, given the Buick was held in late January and the winter weather was charming. The sun would rise late and warm up the chilly morning temperatures. In the afternoons, a red and orange glow would blanket the entire coastline. Every year, Williams would stay with close friends from New Zealand who lived in a house in the Rancho Santa Fe community, 11 miles from Torrey Pines. He'd go jogging around the hilly neighborhood and marvel at the beautiful houses in Rancho Santa Fe and Del Mar. He felt like he was in Sydney, Australia, with the eucalypts, and seaside villages littered with cafés and bars, like Cardiff-by-the-Sea and Encinitas. It was hard not to be relaxed among cliffs and bluffs that overlooked the ocean.

Torrey Pines was among Woods's most treasured golf courses. He'd fallen in love with Torrey Pines as a child when, at age six, he and Earl hopped in the family car and drove 80 minutes down the I-5 from Cypress to watch the Andy Williams San Diego Open. It was 1982 and the great Johnny Miller, who'd won a U.S. Open and an Open Championship in the '70s, beat Woods's idol, Nicklaus, by one shot to win at Torrey Pines.

Apart from watching the pros each year, Woods couldn't wait to compete at Torrey Pines himself. The Junior World Championships event had made its home in San Diego, and competitors began on a par-3 course in the under-10s category before moving to different courses as they got older. Woods debuted in the under-10s at Presidio Hills, a charming, scruffy par-3 course at the doorstep of Old Town in San Diego, where the longest hole was 110 yards. In 1984, Woods was eight, wearing Coke-bottle glasses, when he defeated 10-year-old Chris Riley by two shots. Riley, who would become a friend of Woods and a PGA Tour pro, saw Woods's real name, Eldrick Woods, and asked, "They call him Tiger?!" Woods won again the following year, as well as the 11/12 category in 1988 at Mission Bay and the 13/14 division in 1989 at Balboa Park. He won the 13/14 again in 1990 at Mission Trails. In 1991, Woods finally got to compete at Torrey Pines South. He was one shot behind Riley with seven holes to play. On that par-4 12th tee, Woods bombed a drive 30 yards past Riley and birdied the hole. He also birdied the 13th, and never looked back.

Like Woods's home course in Cypress, Torrey Pines had a military connection. In a previous life, it was called Camp Callan and was a U.S. Army antiaircraft artillery base during World War II. But the army vacated the site in 1946 and it became a public park. Eventually, it became one of the most famous public golf courses in America. In 2024, Torrey Pines' South Course cost San Diego residents $69 for 18 holes at peak rate.

On October 6, 2002, the USGA had announced Torrey Pines' South Course had been awarded the 2008 U.S. Open, pending approval from the San Diego City Council. The USGA was determined to sustain the momentum from Bethpage Black earlier that summer, which was the first municipal course to host the U.S. Open. The Torrey Pines announcement was years in the making, after San Diego lawyer Jay Rains, president of the nonprofit Century Club that ran the Buick Invitational, formed an alliance called the Friends of Torrey Pines and raised $3.5 million over the summer of 2001 to upgrade the South Course to major-championship quality.

The group hired golf architect Rees Jones and, after USGA inspections of the renovation and positive player feedback at the 2002 Buick, it got the green light.

The news was monumental for Woods. He was a Southern California kid at heart, and now the area would host the U.S. Open for the first time since Riviera Country Club staged the 1948 edition. The U.S. Open had been played in California only nine times.

Woods, from the moment the announcement was made, was obsessed. When he won the Buick Invitational by four shots in 2003, he spent the entire week hounding Williams about how the South Course would set up for the U.S. Open five years later. "Stevie, where do you think the Sunday pin will be on No. 5? What will they do with the fairway on No. 6? Where will they move the tees on No. 13? How wide will the fairway be on No. 18?" Woods asked. Williams recalls Woods peppering him with similar questions in every single edition of the Buick between 2003 and 2008. Williams could not comprehend how one person could be so fixated on an event that was years away. "When he had a chance to win four consecutive majors with the 2001 Masters, that didn't compare to his fascination with Torrey Pines," Williams says.

The stars were aligning in a way only Woods could manifest when he won the Buick at Torrey Pines to open his 2008 season. A week later, in the United Arab Emirates, he captured the Dubai Desert Classic on the European Tour. Three weeks later, he blitzed through the field at WGC-Match Play and in his next start, he registered a fifth career win at Bay Hill. His Arnold Palmer Invitational was one of his most memorable regular wins. After missing all 21 putts from outside 20 feet he faced that week at Bay Hill, Woods made a downhill, breaking 24-foot birdie on the 72nd hole to win by one shot. Just as the ball curled into the hole, Woods walked six steps backward and slammed his hat into the green, with an enormous fist pump. It was his fifth consecutive PGA Tour win, which included his final two starts of 2007. Woods had finally grooved a reliable left-to-right ball flight with his driver. The grueling swing changes were paying dividends. "Tiger was driving the ball the best he had since 2000, and it was really exciting," Williams says.

Woods was listed with incomprehensible odds by the bookmakers for the 2008 Masters, paying 2 to 1 to win a fifth time at Augusta. At the Masters, a lot of the discussion was not only about winning the green jacket, but whether this was the year he could find golf's Holy Grail by winning all four majors. "For most of my career, I've won more than four tournaments in a year; it's just winning the right four," Woods said. At Augusta, Woods hit the ball beautifully but a suspect putting performance in the final round saw Woods finish second to South Africa's Trevor Immelman by three shots.

Two days after the Masters, Woods revealed on his website that he'd undergone arthroscopic surgery on his left knee in Park City, Utah. Doctors had found cartilage damage and, after having his third career procedure on the left knee, Woods would miss at least six weeks. He wrote that he had played through pain since the middle of 2007 and chose the period between the 2008 Masters in April and June's U.S. Open to have the surgery. "I had an idea he might have surgery, from talking with Hank, but I didn't know whether he was going to do it at the end of the year or prior to the U.S. Open," Williams recalls. "But [at Augusta], when the level of pain became extreme, the urgency for surgery was there."

With the cartilage damage, Woods's tibia (shinbone), the adjacent fibula (calf bone) and his femur (thigh bone) all touched each other at the tips around that knee. The pain and swelling were excruciating, which Williams was about to witness firsthand.

During rehabilitation Woods described as "intense," he sustained stress fractures to his left tibia. He skipped his beloved Memorial

Tournament in Ohio and chose to return to competition at the U.S. Open. Williams used Woods's 63-day hiatus to finish his car racing season in New Zealand and enjoy time off with his toddler, Jett, who was born in 2006. "I was just waiting to find out when Tiger would play again and if he would play again in 2008," Williams recalls.

By June, Williams had heard that Woods intended to play through injury and tee up at the U.S. Open at Torrey Pines he had been obsessing over for five years. Woods arrived in Southern California more than a week before the first round. On Wednesday, June 4, Woods rode in a cart with Haney at the course during an 8 A.M. practice round. Fans and media were not allowed on the South Course, but there was a group of TV cameras near the 18th green. Noticing the crew, Woods picked up his ball well before the green at the par 5 and left the course without speaking.

A day later, Williams boarded a Thursday-night flight from Auckland to Los Angeles, unsure if Woods was healthy enough to tee up. He was so doubtful Woods would play, or, if he did, that he'd make the cut, he brought Kirsty and Jett to the U.S. "I thought we could take Jett to Disneyland in Anaheim if Tiger didn't play," Williams recalls. Williams and his family arrived at their Kiwi friends' Rancho Santa Fe house on Friday morning when Haney called Williams to say, "Tiger has no business playing this U.S. Open with his leg the way it is." But Woods was adamant he would compete, so Williams took Jett to Disneyland that day, knowing he was not going to get another free moment for the next 10 days.

Later on Friday, the USGA had added fuel to Woods's motivation when they announced the top three golfers on the world rankings would comprise one of the marquee groups for the first two rounds at Torrey Pines. That happened to be Woods (1), Phil Mickelson (2) and Adam Scott (3). Woods and Mickelson's place in the group was seen as a battle for Southern Californian golf supremacy, and the first time the two had played together in the opening rounds of a major since the 2006 PGA at Medinah. Although Woods was from Cypress, he had dominated the Junior World Championships here. Mickelson, though, was the San Diego hometown hero. He had grown up in San Carlos, on the eastern side of the city, and attended University of San Diego High School, where he became one of the top juniors in the country. Mickelson made his PGA Tour debut at Torrey Pines at age 17, having qualified for the 1988 edition as an amateur. His first win as a pro came at Torrey Pines in 1993. Mickelson *was* Torrey Pines.

The grouping, though, was fortuitous for Woods, and Williams texted Haney to revel in how motivated their man would be. He knew his boss was going to grit his teeth and push through pain to show Mickelson who the king of SoCal was. "I think it was hugely overlooked how significant that grouping was," says Williams. Fans didn't overlook it, though—42,500 tickets were sold for each round. Shuttles from the parking lot at Qualcomm Stadium began at 5:30 A.M., with spectators allowed into Torrey Pines as early as six. Mickelson called it a "once in a lifetime opportunity to compete in the U.S. Open on the course I grew up on in the prime of my career."

On Saturday, Woods played a nine-hole practice round at Big Canyon Country Club with a brace on his leg. The score was never confirmed but it was about 11-over 47—horrific for a pro for nine holes—and he lost approximately five golf balls. Williams spoke to Haney soon after, who urged it wasn't a good idea to play the U.S. Open. "Hank said Tiger's game was completely out of sorts," Williams recalls.

On Sunday, Williams began his work early in the morning, mapping Torrey Pines' South Course before walking with Woods for a nine-hole practice round. Things appeared better early Monday morning when Woods snuck out for a practice round just before seven, with left-hander Bubba Watson and Stanford sophomore Jordan Cox. With about 200 fans and media in the crowd around the first tee, Woods bombed a drive down the fairway.

On Tuesday, Woods conceded in his pretournament press conference that his knee was "probably not fully recovered." As he went to bed on Wednesday night, Williams picked "Right Now" by Van Halen as his motivation to help steer a heavily injured, but emboldened, Woods through a U.S. Open he'd dreamed about for years. Williams felt the lyrics encouraged him and Woods to do something magical: *Hey, c'mon turn, turn this thing around. It means everything.*

Under gray skies and morning fog, Woods began his U.S. Open mission on Thursday, June 12, at 8:06. He had not walked 18 holes of golf since the Masters in April. Haney and Williams warned Woods this would be perhaps his biggest-ever test of patience to not only play, but play *well*.

The galleries had swelled from the 800 people who'd arrived in time for the 7 A.M. first group to 8,000 by the time Woods teed off. The crowd stretched from the first tee to the second green almost 1,000 yards away and was lined 10 to 12 people deep the entire way. A collective groan sounded when Woods hooked his first tee shot into the rough and made a double-bogey 6. But Woods steadied the ship with three birdies before another double-bogey at the 14th, eventually signing for a 1-over 72. On the 18th tee shot, which soared down the fairway, Woods visibly winced for the first time that day, looking down at the ground to try to hide his pain. "For every shot he hit, I was watching his facial expression, and on that tee shot, I thought, *This is ridiculous*. I could see the pain he was in," Williams says.

Woods was in so much pain he skipped post-round practice, telling the team his knee was "killing" him.

Teeing off No. 10 on Friday, it was similarly grim. Woods was sloppy at 2 over for his outward nine, courtesy of four bogeys which soured an eagle at the par-5 13th. His score looked set to worsen when he blocked his tee shot right at the par-4 first, his 10th hole. The ball bounced down a mound in the right rough and settled behind a tree. But Williams was about to witness the most remarkable, and unfathomable, nine-hole performance from a player in his 40 years as a caddie.

Williams looked down at Woods's Nike ball, which was sitting only inches to the right of a cart path. He knew Woods would have to stand on the concrete to hit his approach to the green. With a mixture of dread and shock, which Williams knew was written all over his own face, he kept looking down at Woods's white, black-saddled Nike golf shoes. His eyes darted frantically up the black trousers that encased Woods's heavily injured left knee, and to his spearmint-green golf shirt. Williams was anticipating some kind of tidal wave of pain to travel up Woods's legs and into the knee at impact.

Woods pressed onward with hitting his 7-iron shot from behind the tree, addressing the ball. He took the club back carefully and made a perfect swing with extra-quiet feet during the downswing for extra stability. But milliseconds after Woods struck the ball, his right foot slipped when his spikes didn't get the traction they'd normally have on turf. The awkward move transferred energy into his left knee, forcing Woods to bounce on the left leg. Williams had heard a nauseating crunch in Woods's knee just after the club made contact with the ball. He didn't even watch where the ball had gone. "I could hear the crunch and it made me sick to my stomach," Williams says. "I just looked at his face. He was trying to hide the agony in his knee."

As Woods hopped around, hoping to walk off the pain while heading back over the cart path toward the fairway, Williams chased after him. He begged Woods to consider withdrawing from the tournament. He made what he felt was a compelling argument. "We're only a few hundred yards from the clubhouse, mate," Williams said. Aside from the appeal of an easy exit, Williams also pleaded with Woods to look at the bigger picture; he was going to have plenty more majors in his career if he stayed fit. Did he really want to put his goal of overtaking Nicklaus in jeopardy by one reckless decision at a U.S. Open?

"What would you know, you sheep shagger? I'm f——g winning this tournament," Williams says Woods blurted back at him.

The two were so distracted by the injury they failed to realize the ball had flown beautifully through the air and landed 20 feet right of the hole. Woods then drained the birdie, and it jump-started his fight back. "It seemed Tiger had a sudden realization in the fairway that the most pain he could feel in the knee couldn't stop him from hitting a great shot, and he believed he could bite through and win," Williams says.

Woods added four more birdies on his back nine to fire a 3-under 68 that left him 2 under overall, one off the lead.

The fans were animated. A father and son were arrested for being intoxicated in public by San Diego police after one of the caddies in the Woods-Mickelson-Scott group confronted the two drunk men, accusing them of heckling the golfers. A heated exchange unfolded in the ninth fairway between the men and the caddie.

Williams says that Friday evening brought some much-needed comic relief in the face of Woods's deteriorating knee. In Woods's suite at The Lodge at Torrey Pines, his trainer, Keith Kleven, worked on his client's leg as the 13-time major winner writhed in pain. Williams says Mark Steinberg was yelling, "Keith, you've got to do something!" as Kleven turned a shade of white. Woods, lying on the table, was the one who defused the situation. He urged Steinberg and Kleven to calm down and assured them he would make it through the tournament. "But I don't know if Keith is going to make it," Woods said.

Woods certainly put his team at ease on Saturday in one of the most memorable rounds of his majors' career, which was highlighted by a six-hole stretch for the ages. For his second shot into No. 13, Woods struck an iron shot that nearly bounced in the hole, and rolled up the back of the green, 65 feet from the hole. When he attempted his eagle putt, the ball snaked its way down to the right, then back to the left, and coasted into the hole for an unlikely 3. The crowds erupted, and commentators went wild, knowing what a gift it was, coming during prime-time TV for the East Coast. Woods had changed the course of the U.S. Open. Had the ball not gone in, Williams was sure it would have rolled off the front of the green and 50 yards down the hill into the fairway. Williams felt Woods could have easily made bogey—three shots worse than his miraculous eagle. "It was one of the most important putts of Tiger's career and you could drop 100 balls and not make that putt again," Williams recalls. Woods was on fire, chipping in for birdie from the rough beside the 17th green. He laughed, knowing he'd hit the pitch too hard only for it to crash into the flagstick and drop in. At the par-5 18th, Williams recalls Woods crouching over and grimacing in agony after hitting a fairway wood from 226 yards to the green. "He hit that shot harder, trying to carry it farther than normal because it was into a slight breeze, which made the lower half of his body move quicker. It was worrying seeing him drop down like that," Williams says.

Once on the putting surface, Woods made another dramatic

eagle for a 1-under 70 that gave him the 54-hole lead at 3 under, one ahead of Lee Westwood and two better than Rocco Mediate. It was the 14th occasion where Woods held at least a share of the 54-hole lead at a major. He'd converted the previous 13. "It was the freakiest round I've ever seen," Robert Karlsson, Woods's playing partner that day, said.

The elation of Woods's dramatic third round disintegrated within minutes of his opening tee shot on the final day. His drive on No. 1 sailed way left into the rough and two sloppy shots to escape the rough led to a double-bogey 6. Woods's lead was gone, and he fell further back with a bogey at No. 2. Over a thrilling two hours, the lead exchanged between Mediate, who birdied No. 2 but later fell back with two bogeys, and Woods's playing partner, Westwood. When the Englishman birdied No. 9, he led Woods by one. Woods appeared to seize back control with a birdie at No. 11, but bogeys at the par-5 13th and the 15th led to him standing on the par-5 18th tee trailing Mediate, who finished with a 71, by one shot.

A pulled drive into the fairway bunker, and a sloppy layup that finished in the right rough, led to one of Woods's most dramatic moments, and one of Williams's most important calls.

Williams's heart pounded as he weighed up whether it was the right call. Let Woods hit a 56-degree sand wedge for his third shot from the right rough to the 18th green, which was 105 yards, or engage in a spirited debate to get him to hit a 60-degree wedge? Williams's gut told him the latter was the right choice. Woods needed a final-hole birdie to force a playoff with Mediate, who'd finished at 1 under (283). If Williams chose the path of least resistance and didn't protest the 56-degree sand wedge, he believed the adrenaline coursing through Woods's veins would cause him to hit the ball too hard and over the back of the green. It was a huge risk, especially with grass sitting between the ball and clubface, which would take off spin and add distance. Williams chose to dig his heels in and argue. "Tiger wanted to hit the 56 and hit a flat ball—a lower knuckle shot—and bounce it up short of the green, allowing for it to roll on. But I told him it was an extremely difficult shot with the rough," Williams recalls. Woods eventually relented, grabbed the 60 and asked what the wind was doing. Williams told him it wouldn't affect the ball, to give Woods confidence to make a committed swing, saying the breeze was "barely left to right." Woods took an almighty lash, hoisting the ball high into the air. It bounced with so much spin the ball backtracked toward the cup.

"Don't check out of your hotel, Rocco," commentator Johnny Miller brilliantly joked on the broadcast.

When he got to the green, Woods stalked the putt, analyzing the break with unshakable concentration, and decided it was just outside the right edge. The ball bumped and hopped along the California poa annua grass and snuck in the side door, sending the crowd into a frenzy.

"EXPECT ANYTHING DIFFERENT?" commentator Dan Hicks screamed on the broadcast.

Mediate certainly did not think Woods would miss the birdie putt while watching the broadcast from the scoring area. He yelled, "I knew he'd make it!" Williams also had a hunch that Woods would stand and deliver. "I was already thinking about the Monday playoff pin position on No. 18; I thought it was just Tiger's destiny and I knew he was the best clutch putter who has ever lived," Williams says. Woods had scrapped for a 73 to finish tied with Mediate at 1 under. What was perhaps lost in the furor was that Woods's playing partner on Sunday, Englishman Lee Westwood, missed a birdie putt that would have also given him a 1-under total. "It's sickening not to be in the playoff," Westwood said.

Under USGA rules, the format for the playoff was 18 holes on

Monday, June 16. It was not yet sudden death, rather the lowest round wins. Despite being held on a Monday and featuring just two players, crowds kept flocking to Torrey Pines. It was an encore to one of the greatest spectacles in golf history, a David versus Goliath battle. Mediate was a gregarious Pennsylvania native who was soaking up every moment against a titan who had won 13 majors and dominated golf for 11 years. Mediate, at 45 years and five months, was hoping to become the oldest U.S. Open champion in history.

Adding to the uniqueness of this U.S. Open was Torrey Pines' driving range, which ran adjacent to North Torrey Pines Road. The sidewalk inclined at the northern end of the range, meaning passersby could see through a netted fence when Woods arrived. He wanted privacy at the back end of the range to hit balls toward the clubhouse. It was unlike any other major championship venue, given they were often held at private clubs hidden behind fences and hedges. When a major *did* go to a public course, the range would still be secluded and not visible to the outside world. "The moment we arrived on the range there were people up against the fence trying to get a look," Williams says.

Mediate, ranked 158th in the world and chasing a first major win after an injury-riddled 23 years in golf, had enormous support as the underdog. His journey to this playoff was so unlikely it almost never happened; weeks earlier, Mediate had to progress through a cutthroat round of 36-hole final qualifying for the U.S. Open. At the Columbus, Ohio, site, which was offering 23 spots for Torrey Pines, Mediate opened with a dangerously mediocre 72, but stormed back with a 67 to finish with a score of 139. That put him into a playoff among 11 golfers for seven spots, which he survived just before darkness fell.

At Torrey Pines that Monday, Mediate arrived at the practice fairway ahead of the 9 A.M. playoff wearing a black sweater-vest over a red shirt, in an apparent attempt to mess with Woods, whose trademark final-round colors were red and black. "Can you honestly believe that?" Woods asked Williams. "It's pretty ballsy," Williams responded. Mediate was trying *anything*.

The fashion statement seemed to pay off as Mediate took Woods to task in arguably the most enthralling Monday in professional golf's history. Tens of millions of fans around the world were glued to the TV as the battle boiled over at Torrey Pines. Mediate was three shots down through 10 holes but fought back furiously on the closing eight to hold a one-shot lead when he arrived at the 18th tee. Moments later, Woods then reached that par 5 in two with a pair of brilliant swings, and his eagle putt ran four feet past the hole.

Mediate, who took three shots to the green, could not make the birdie putt that would have won the championship. When Woods and Mediate cleaned up their short putts, the U.S. Open was headed to a 91st hole.

Finally, it was sudden death.

The USGA had selected the par-4 seventh for that extra hole, where Woods hit two perfect shots to the green. Mediate finally caved, driving into a fairway bunker left, then hitting the grandstand with his second, and he eventually made a fatal bogey. Woods's birdie putt stopped just short of the hole and he tapped in for a 14th major win, and a career-defining performance.

Woods couldn't wipe the smile from his face as he shook hands with Mediate, caddies and officials. By the time Woods was congratulated on the seventh green by Mike Davis, the USGA official who oversaw the course setup, Williams had already whipped out the ring spanner and removed the flag. It was only minutes after the U.S. Open had ended, but Williams didn't mess around when it came to the caddie's trophy. It was a deep scarlet cloth with the

USGA logo on the left, the number 7 on the right and "U.S. Open" stitched at the bottom. He walked past Woods and Davis and put the flag-less pin back in the hole. Weeks later, Woods signed his autograph in black ink for his caddie—the only flag Williams had collected from his major wins with Woods that wasn't from an 18th green.

In the moments after accepting the U.S. Open trophy, Woods was asked how he'd managed to put mind over body for 91 holes. Woods answered, "All the people. I could never quit in front of [them]. It wasn't going to happen."

Williams trotted up with the golf bag to Woods's hotel room, where Haney, Kleven, Elin and Kultida were waiting. "There was an excitement in the room that had never really happened after Tiger won a major," Williams recalls. They were all eager to see the champion, who was off with Steinberg fulfilling his winner's obligations, photographs and media commitments. When Woods finally returned to the room, he sat down on the bed and flung himself backward. He had won the first U.S. Open played in Southern California in 60 years.

Williams, after a celebratory beer, told Woods he was driving back to Los Angeles that evening for his late-night flight to New Zealand, which he'd already postponed 24 hours for the playoff. Woods mustered the energy to stand up and say goodbye to his caddie. He complimented Williams for forcing him to hit lob wedge on the 72nd hole. "The hug had a little more meaning to it than most," Williams says. "He said, 'Stevie, you're the best.' I didn't need anything else. It was very powerful. Watching the pain he'd gone through on every shot, the physio treatment he received every night and morning, and the fact he couldn't practice, I believe it was one of the greatest sporting achievements of all time," Williams says.

Woods's victory even earned the admiration of tennis star Rafael Nadal, who watched on TV at home in Mallorca, Spain, resting between the grass court tournament at Queen's Club and the 2008 Wimbledon Championships. "Tiger is probably my idol," Nadal, who himself had battled through injuries, said. "I know how tough it is playing [through] pain."

Williams looks back fondly at the 2008 U.S. Open. He felt Woods was sending a message to Earl: "Almost to say, I'm thinking of you, and here's another win for you at Torrey Pines," Williams says. He will always cherish Torrey Pines as his last major victory working for Woods, although he didn't know that at the time.

All three of Woods's U.S. Open career victories came at publicly accessible courses. Woods had grown up in a modest home in Cypress, for which his parents took out a second mortgage to support his junior golf expenses. He had learned the game at a par-3 course, Heartwell Golf Course, in Long Beach, as a toddler, before playing at the navy golf course in Cypress. Williams observed, over the years, that Woods never forgot his roots, and it was fitting that his boss only won the U.S. Open at courses anyone could play. Two of those, Bethpage Black and Torrey Pines, cost less than $70 for locals to tee up. Pebble Beach was accessible to anyone, although the green fee (in 2024) was $730.

The number of mistakes Woods made that week, but still willed himself to victory, dumbfounded Williams. For four rounds, Woods recorded four double-bogeys, three of them coming on hole No. 1. He also had one three-putt in each round. According to Williams's own statistics, there were only three other majors Williams worked for Woods where he had at least one three-putt every day. Compared to his limited errors in majors from 1999 onward, when Williams joined and started compiling stats, the numbers at the 2008 U.S. Open suggested Woods should not have been remotely close to winning. "U.S. Opens are not about the number of great shots a golfer hits, rather who can hit the least number of bad shots," Williams says.

Williams points to the double-bogeys or worse, and three-putts, that Woods made each year from 1999 through the end of 2007 (all four majors):

1999: 6 double-bogeys, 1 triple-bogey, 15 three-putts.
2000: 2 double-bogeys, 2 triple-bogeys, 10 three-putts.
2001: 4 double-bogeys, 1 triple-bogey, 11 three-putts.
2002: 2 double-bogeys, 8 three-putts.
2003: 4 double-bogeys, 1 triple-bogey, 5 three-putts, 2 four-putts.
2004: 6 double-bogeys, 8 three-putts.
2005: 1 double-bogey, 16 three-putts.
2006: 4 double-bogeys, 15 three-putts.
2007: 2 double-bogeys, 5 three-putts.

"Tiger had twice as many double-bogeys at the 2008 U.S. Open as he had in all four majors in his incredible 2000 and 2002 seasons," Williams says.

* * *

The comedown, for Williams, was steep. Woods called later that week, once Williams was back in New Zealand, and said he was having knee surgery, which didn't come as much of a surprise. Woods would reveal on his website he had played the U.S. Open with a torn anterior cruciate ligament as well as a double stress fracture in his left tibia. He underwent reconstructive surgery on the damaged ACL the following week in Park City, Utah. Woods missed the remainder of the 2008 season, cutting his season short by almost five months.

"I experienced a low point in my time with Tiger, with the uncertainty about when he would come back and whether his knee would ever be as healthy again," Williams says. Williams spent the next six months at home in New Zealand, and for the first time in almost 30 years, he was able to stay put in his home country for a long stretch. He was a dad around the house, mowing the lawn, racing saloon cars and playing golf. Williams didn't know it at the time, but he needed a mental break from caddying for the world's most famous athlete. "It was nice to live a normal life for a while," he says.

Somewhat normal. After the 2008 U.S. Open, Woods was so chuffed with his caddie's performance, he told him to take his 155-foot yacht, *Privacy*, for a week, anywhere in the world he wanted. Williams was floored by the gesture. Yes, he'd stayed on the yacht multiple times, during tournaments near port cities, but now he had the pleasure of enjoying *Privacy*, which could travel up to 4,000 nautical miles, outside of work and with his family. Woods had paid $20 million for the vessel in 2004. It had three levels—a main deck, a second level and an observation deck. It had five bedrooms, which didn't include the quarters for the yacht's crew. It had a Jacuzzi, a gym and a decompression chamber for scuba diving.

Williams took Kirsty and Jett, as well as Kirsty's parents and Williams's mother, around the Caribbean for seven days, stopping in at different islands. But it wasn't the lavish trip that was most meaningful to Williams, rather how Woods told him he could borrow it.

"Stevie, you helped pay for it," Woods said.

Woods did not compete for 253 days while recovering from the surgery. In February 2009, Woods and Elin welcomed their second child, a boy they named Charlie Axel Woods. Charlie arrived on Sunday, February 8—the same day as the final round of the PGA Buick Invitational at Torrey Pines, a tournament Woods had won six times.

Woods returned to golf at the WGC-Match Play event in Arizona in March 2009.

His reception at the Ritz-Carlton course at Dove Mountain, in Marana, was epic. Fans packed around the first tee and down the entire hole. They cheered so heavily as Woods was introduced that Williams advised him to back off his opening tee shot, which he did, before regathering and blasting his ball down the fairway. "You are *BACK*!" Williams recalls one fan screaming after the tee shot. He began his head-to-head match against Australian Brendan Jones with a birdie and an eagle in the first two holes. He eventually defeated Jones, but lost in the second round to South African Tim Clark.

Woods had indeed returned to his kingdom, and 2009 looked set to yield more victories. But it was also going to be one of the wildest years in professional golf's history. One that would ultimately spell the beginning of the end of Williams and Woods's relationship.

CHAPTER 14

END OF AN ERA

Williams moved through one of the paddocks at his Huapai home, west of Auckland, cutting the grass with a slasher on Friday afternoon, November 27, 2009. His headphones were in, listening to a New Zealand national radio station when breaking news came through the wire: Woods, in the U.S., had been rushed to an Orlando hospital after crashing an SUV into a fire hydrant and then into a tree near his home at Isleworth.

"What the f——k?" Williams shouted over the slasher.

At the end of 2009, Woods was embroiled in an off-course, extramarital scandal that engulfed his personal life, career and global news headlines for months on end. It also significantly impacted the nature of his working relationship with Williams and ultimately fast-tracked the end of their incredible partnership. Perhaps the most peculiar aspect of Woods's 2009 season was the auspicious start to it. For a while, it appeared Woods would brush aside the eight months he lost to knee surgery and continue the soaring trajectory of his quest for major championship wins.

In late March, four weeks after his return to golf, Woods won at Bay Hill for the sixth time, and then contended at the Masters, where he tied sixth. He also collected victories at the Memorial, for a fourth time, in June, as well as the AT&T National, the Buick Open, the WGC Invitational at Firestone Country Club, the BMW Championship and the Australian Masters at the revered Kingston Heath course in Melbourne in November. In all, Woods's 2009 season included seven victories and three second-place finishes from 19 official events—a mind-boggling year of results considering what was happening away from golf.

In mid-November, U.S. tabloid the *National Enquirer* had been trailing a story that claimed Woods was having an affair with New York nightclub hostess Rachel Uchitel. The newspaper had followed Woods to Melbourne because reporters had learned Uchitel had also traveled to Australia. Woods won the Masters on November 15. That afternoon, he curiously changed plans and told Williams he would be getting a helicopter out of the course and would be on a plane back to the U.S. immediately. Williams would have to find his own way back to the hotel. Mark Steinberg then texted Williams, alerting him that a story would be coming out, but offered little details.

Ten days later, on November 25, the *National Enquirer* story was published, but it gained little traction. Many thought it to be tabloid waffle. But early on Friday morning, November 27, Woods crashed his SUV. That breaking news story was followed by silence and mystery as to the cause of the crash, and it kicked off the entire scandal. One by one, women came forward alleging they'd had affairs with Woods. From Thanksgiving night onward, Woods was embroiled in one of the most publicized scandals in sports history.

Williams did not find out until after the SUV crash, but he was not worried about any of the details of the scandal.

"Firstly, I was concerned for my friend; I could not have cared less about any of the details other than his well-being," Williams says. As anxious as he was for Woods's health, Williams knew his world would have been spiraling downward. He waited to hear from Woods rather than reach out and a few days went by before he received an email from the embattled superstar. "Tiger described that he was going through a tough situation and that he'd soon be in touch," Williams recalls. But four months went by before Williams heard from him again. Still, he was a friend. Despite being upset at what he'd put Elin through, Williams was going to stick by a friend who needed help.

In the meantime, Williams was hounded by media relentlessly—both international and local New Zealand press—about his supposed involvement. Williams's family was hassled by phone, text and email. At times, he would go to the grocery store and random people would wrongly accuse him of being a liar or an enabler. At one of Williams's race car meets at his local speedway in Auckland, he was booed by the crowd during a celebration for national saloon car champions while Jett, four at the time, sat next to him. Jett also came home from school one day and asked his father why he was on the news so often. During a family holiday to Australia in February 2010, Williams was harassed by media at the beach and a subsequent photo of him walking across the road, shirtless after a swim, appeared in a newspaper the following day.

"I could understand how people thought I was involved because of the time I spent with Tiger, but I never heard anything about his private life outside of his marriage and kids," Williams says. Woods knew precisely how old-school Williams's values were; he knew his caddie would have been repulsed at what had been going on. Williams was glad that at least Kirsty and Elin supported him throughout the saga. "Both Elin and I understood that Tiger knew very well Steve was the kind of guy who would have told Elin if he had known," Kirsty said. Williams's lack of knowledge on the subject was obvious in Steinberg's text to Williams after the final round of the Australian Masters, which read "There is a story coming out tomorrow. Absolutely no truth to it. Don't speak to anybody." If Williams had prior knowledge, it's hard to imagine that would not have been reflected in the content of the text message.

Robert Allenby, Woods's Isleworth neighbor who was spending extra time in his hometown of Melbourne after the Australian Masters before returning to the U.S., says Williams was blindsided. He called Allenby, who was at the Melbourne Zoo with his son, Harry, and daughter, Lily. Williams asked Allenby, the four-time PGA Tour winner, whether he had any idea of the affairs. Allenby said no. "I never knew that part of him and I guarantee Stevie didn't know, either," Allenby says.

One woman claimed to have met Williams in Las Vegas, where she had allegedly been with Woods. That story was picked up by radio stations in New Zealand. "I'd only ever been to Vegas twice, once to caddie in a tournament for Tiger and another to support his Tiger Jam [charity] event. I'd never met any woman claiming to be with Tiger," Williams says. Williams wanted Woods's management to issue a statement absolving the caddie of any knowledge, but they wouldn't single out one person from the team as innocent. Williams believed that was because it would prompt follow-up questions about whether any of the team *did* know. He felt humiliated and as though Woods's management team had hung him out to dry. "It was an extremely tough time for me and my family," Williams says.

Several of Woods's major sponsors, including AT&T, Gatorade

and Accenture, ended their business relationships with Woods. Nike stuck with him. Woods took an indefinite break from golf on December 11, and in February 2010 he delivered an apology at PGA Tour headquarters at Ponte Vedra Beach. It was a surreal scene, with Woods reading a 13.5-minute speech at a podium in front of a presidential-blue backdrop and a quiet room of associates. "What I did was not acceptable," a somber Woods said.

On Friday, April 2, 2010, Williams boarded a plane from Auckland to the U.S., returning to work as Woods's caddie for the first time in five months. He worried that the job would never be the same. Over the first weekend in Orlando, Williams watched Woods practice at Isleworth ahead of the 2010 Masters. Although Williams and Woods had written over email, and then spoke on the phone on March 23, this was the first time they'd seen each other in person since the Australian Masters. "He was hitting the ball well; it was clear he'd been practicing hard," Williams recalls. Woods seemed his ordinary self, and there was no discussion of what had happened.

Williams had been saving several issues to raise with Woods but the opportunity to talk privately did not arrive until they drove from Isleworth to the Orlando airport on Sunday, April 4, to fly to Augusta.

Williams let Woods have it.

He laid down the law, wanting to convey what it was like to be connected to the subject. "Some people might not have had that talk with Tiger; it was deep and there were some pretty strong words exchanged," Williams says. He described what had occurred in New Zealand and how humiliating it had been. "Tiger's reaction was simply to listen and he was a little downtrodden because I think he appreciated the honesty, but when I look back all these years later, maybe I was too hard on him," Williams says. After all,

Woods's family had also been through a lot. They'd watched as his scandal appeared on the front cover of the *New York Post* for 21 consecutive days and as he'd entered a rehabilitation center in Mississippi after Christmas. Elin and the children had moved into another home near Isleworth. After the car ride, Woods and Williams closed that topic.

They arrived in Augusta for the 2010 Masters, Woods's first competitive appearance in 145 days. The world's attention was fixed firmly on the superstar's first tournament since the scandal. "Tiger's game was looking very good, but I didn't know if he would be ready for the mental challenge," Williams says. Woods was subjected to a perplexing speech by then Augusta National chairman Billy Payne, at his pretournament address to the media, which included lines such as "Our hero did not live up to the expectations of the role model we saw for our children."

Williams could sense Woods was anxious about how fans would receive him, but the galleries at Augusta National were forgiving. "Other than a few negative comments, the fans were supportive," Williams says. The Masters patrons were able to separate Woods's private life from the champion golfer on the course.

Woods opened with one of his lowest-ever first rounds at the Masters, a 68, and followed that with 70. Williams was reminded how Woods was exceptional at compartmentalizing his life. He was also warm with fans, other players and media for the first two rounds. But after Friday's second round, Woods and Williams were on a golf cart shuttle from the Press Building to the driving range when Steinberg said to Woods he had to stop being so nice—and revert to his ruthless side—if he wanted to win the tournament. "It was very disappointing because I felt Tiger had a wonderful opportunity to show the infectious and warm personality that I knew he had; he was talented enough to keep winning as the nice guy he is," Williams says. Woods tied for fourth at the Masters, while Phil Mickelson won his fourth major and third Masters title—rubbing salt into Woods's wounds.

Williams felt a paradigm shift in 2010 in his working relationship with Woods at Augusta and the weeks after it. "As much as I tried to see Tiger as the same person and put everything behind us, I guess we were never quite on the same page again," Williams says. While Woods had taken a break from the game to address his personal life, Williams realized that when he did go back to work, their relationship would be drastically different. There had been too much emotional turbulence to just pick up where they had left off. Still, Williams had said his piece and moved on. The reaction to, and comeback from, the scandal by Woods, and his management team, was what most disappointed Williams. Woods missed the cut in his next start at Quail Hollow, where Williams felt there was a significant shift in Woods's attitude toward him. He was short and irritable with his caddie and Williams could sense it was only a matter of time before they'd part ways. At the Players Championship, Woods walked off the course on the seventh hole of the final round with a neck injury at TPC Sawgrass. Days later, an MRI scan revealed an inflamed neck joint.

Driving that disconnect between Woods and Williams was the end goal of surpassing Nicklaus's 18 majors. It had completely unraveled. Until 2010, Williams's daydream of standing on the 18th green of a major championship as Woods took a trophy for his 19th, and later 21st, major win inspired him every day, week and month. After 2010, that thought was shattered. "I couldn't see that picture anymore and I didn't have that same drive and desire to caddie towards that 21st major," he says.

There were still moments of pride and success. There was another T4 at a major, at the 2010 U.S. Open at Pebble Beach. At the 2010 Ryder Cup, which was a rain-soaked mess at Celtic Manor in

Wales, Woods had been eviscerated on the Sunday TV coverage by a commentator who questioned Woods's desire to play for the U.S. team, despite partnering with Steve Stricker to win two points from his three matches. The inclement weather forced a Monday finish to the cup, which meant Williams was not able to caddie in the singles matches because he had to fly back to New Zealand for a personal matter. He called Woods to relay the TV criticism and after hearing Woods's disappointment, he decided to stay and caddie in the finale. "Tiger was fired up," Williams says. Woods went out and beat Italy's Francesco Molinari, 4 and 3. "It was a satisfying moment in an otherwise tough year," Williams says.

2010 ended on a positive note between them when Williams was astounded by a generous act from his boss. In late November, Williams was in New Zealand on the South Island for seven days of consecutive racing. One of the races was scheduled for the town of Greymouth, but an incident called the Pike River Mine disaster rocked the town and the nation. A coal mine explosion resulted in the tragic deaths of 29 miners. Williams passed a donations bucket around the crowds at four of the remaining races, where more than $16,000 was collected. He also held an impromptu race called the Pike River Memorial 29 Lapper to raise extra money. Williams later presented a check to the mayor of Greymouth, who was emotional at the gesture. Days later, Woods called Williams to catch up and when the caddie filled him in on the tragedy, Woods said, "Give me the banking details for the [Pike River donations] relief efforts and I'll donate some money straightaway."

* * *

The first six months of 2011 showed flashes of Woods's former brilliance, but he was hampered by injuries. During the Masters, where he tied for fourth, Woods suffered an Achilles tendon strain. That forced his withdrawal from the PGA Tour event at Quail Hollow, and weeks later, Woods walked off after just nine holes of the Players Championship citing knee pain. Carrying a pronounced limp, he shot 42 on the front nine at TPC Sawgrass.

Meanwhile, Williams was at his home in Sunriver, Oregon, in early June. His father-in-law, Ian Miller, a builder by trade, was there to help with renovations to the house. The two were to be joined by a friend from Oregon and the trio would take a trip to the East Coast, which was planned almost two years in advance. The two were set to join Williams at the 2011 U.S. Open at Congressional, a golf course in Bethesda, Maryland, frequently played by politicians from nearby Washington, D.C. After the U.S. Open, Williams's friends would follow him to the AT&T National, a tournament hosted by Woods at the historic Aronimink Golf Club in Newtown Square, a lush, green and hilly area 30 minutes northwest of Philadelphia. Williams's crew were also scheduled to watch car races at the Williams Grove Speedway and Lincoln Speedway. But on June 8, Woods released a statement saying that, due to a left knee and Achilles injury suffered during the 2011 Masters, he would have to sit out the U.S. Open.

Australian golfer Adam Scott was quickly on the phone to Williams, asking him to caddie as a one-off at Congressional. Williams had given Scott a stirring pep talk before the final round at the Masters two months earlier, which had clearly resonated. Scott was well in contention going into the final round at Augusta when Williams spotted him alone on the practice putting green. Williams was waiting for Woods to arrive from the locker room. As a longtime admirer of Scott's talent, Williams approached the affable Aussie with a sudden urge to boost his confidence enough to win a maiden major title. "Adam, you have to believe you're the best f——ng player in the world today because you are! It's your day and it's your time to win one of these," Williams said. Williams could sense, deep down, that his working relationship with Woods was nearing its end. Helping out Scott was, in a way, creating a future opportunity. But he also felt it was the right thing to do for a player he considered a friend and one of the true gentlemen in pro golf. It almost worked that day. Scott later said he'd never heard a speech like it and shot 67, enough to share second place behind South African winner Charl Schwartzel. In June, when Scott called, Williams says he ran the idea of caddying for Scott at the U.S. Open past Woods. Woods didn't immediately see an issue and allowed it. But Steinberg called Williams and asked, "Do you really think it's a good idea to caddie for Adam?" Williams did go on to caddie for Scott, who missed the cut.

On June 23, Woods announced he would not play in the AT&T National based on "doctor's orders." Again, Scott called Williams and again, the caddie ran it by Woods. Woods offered an alternative to Williams: they could travel to Aronimink together and he and Williams could watch the tournament together, with Williams's guests. Williams rejected the offer. He wanted his friends to see him caddie in person. Woods eventually agreed, but soon called Williams back and said, "Actually, I'd rather you didn't caddie for Adam." It left Williams furious.

Williams recalls that Kirsty condemned the idea of caddying for Scott. She believed it would indeed trigger Woods to fire him. But Williams didn't think the matter was serious enough for that. He then had a back-and-forth conversation with Steinberg, who reiterated that "Tiger is going to be disappointed if you caddie for Adam" in Philadelphia. Although Steinberg didn't explicitly say the words, it became obvious to Williams he would be sacked. Bitter and stubborn about the saga, Williams decided to caddie for Scott anyway, who tied third.

On Sunday, July 3, Woods was on the grounds at Aronimink, attending as tournament host but not playing. Steinberg approached Williams, who came off the course after Scott shot 68 to tie for third. Steinberg asked Williams to meet Woods in the boardroom to talk.

Williams walked to the boardroom, running his list of grievances over and over in his mind so he could verbalize them concisely and impactfully. He felt Woods was being selfish by trying to stop him from caddying while he was out injured. As Williams opened the door to the stately room, he saw Woods leaned back in a chair. His body language, Williams felt, was aloof and dismissive. Williams instantly decided he wasn't going to argue with Woods and bit his tongue. He felt Woods was also holding back, telling Williams that, because he'd disregarded his wishes, he was letting him go. He wished him luck. Williams walked over and shook Woods's hand awkwardly. Woods ended the exchange by noting he was going to skip the Open Championship, due to injury, and that he wouldn't make a statement about their split until after the U.K. major to avoid throwing Scott into a storm of questions. Williams spun around and walked out of the boardroom. He was angry and felt a lack of closure, as though things were still bottled up. It was a bitter pill for Williams to swallow, after investing so much of his life into working for the star for 12 years. "Even though I knew it was coming, it was devastating," Williams says. "We both had a goal and we lived and breathed it. I thought about that goal every day. It was disappointing because I was not going to be part of that pinnacle if he went on to achieve it."

Williams began working permanently for Scott, and at the Open at Royal St. George's, Scott tied 25th. "I'm someone who is always on to the next thing, so I launched into helping Adam reach his potential," Williams says. But as much as Williams was trying to focus on his new boss, he was still hurting from splitting with Woods. During the Open, Williams stopped by O'Meara's rented house for some advice. O'Meara said he didn't know how the split was going to play out, but praised Williams for being like an older brother to Woods and helping nurture his talent. "Whatever happens, you should take the high road in life and throw praise on him," O'Meara recalls telling Williams.

The emotion was reflected in Williams's statement about the split, which followed Woods's revelation on his own website. "I want to express my deepest gratitude to Stevie for all his help, but I think it's time for a change," Woods wrote. Williams's statement read: "Following the AT&T National, I am no longer caddying for Tiger . . . Needless to say this came as a shock. I am very disappointed to end our very successful partnership."

Despite O'Meara's advice, Williams missed the high road completely when he and Scott recorded their first victory together at the World Golf Championships-Bridgestone event at Firestone Country Club a month later.

The Akron, Ohio, fans had grown to love Williams while Woods had dominated the event for 11 years. Now on Scott's bag, Williams was cheered by name as he walked alongside the Australian golfer down the 18th at Firestone. In a postgame interview with then CBS commentator David Feherty, an emotional Williams said, "Honestly, that's the best week of my life. I've caddied for 33 years, 145 wins now, and that's the best win I've ever had."

The remarks were taken as a slap in the face to Woods, whom Williams had worked for in 73 wins across the PGA, European,

Japan, Asian and Australian tours. The comments also drew criticism on social media from former major winner Paul Azinger and even tennis star Andy Roddick, who posted, "Am I missing something? Was Steve the one actually playing?" The following week, on August 11, Williams posted an apology to his website. "My emotions following Adam's victory were running very high and at the time I felt like my emotions poured out and got the better of me. I apologize to my fellow caddies and professionals for failing to mention Adam's outstanding performance." Woods was asked about the gaffe the following week at the PGA Championship and replied that while he was not going to speculate on Williams's statement, they were "his feelings and emotions."

Williams was regretful, but felt he was taken advantage of. "No question, I should never have said what I did," Williams says. He was in the heat of an intense moment, and part of him was eager to prove a point to Woods. But Williams was adamant he should not have been in that situation, when he was approached for a comment. "When has a TV commentator ever come onto the 18th green to ask the winning caddie a question? I think they [CBS] knew what they were doing."

Things got worse for Williams in 2011. Much worse. On Friday, November 4, he was attending a Caddie of the Year dinner at the European Tour's World Golf Championships-HSBC Champions event in Shanghai. Williams found himself at the center of a racial controversy after making regrettable remarks about Woods.

The event was described by organizers as "private," and "off the record." It was held at the players' hotel and the atmosphere was considered a night of lowbrow, locker-room talk. Caddies roasted their bosses in outrageous ways. Williams was given an award for Celebration of the Year, an ironic gong, given his comments after

Scott's win in Ohio. Williams was asked why he was so animated at the WGC-Bridgestone, to which he answered, "I wanted to shove it up his Black arse."

The fallout was monumental and became one of the unfortunate sports stories of the year. Williams was accused, in global headlines, of calling Woods "a Black asshole," which he says changed the meaning entirely of comments that were already reprehensible.

Williams, to this day, regrets his remarks. "I shouldn't have said it, it was deeply wrong and I'm still apologetic," he says. He wrote an apology on his website at the time, addressing remorse to Woods and people he had offended. Pro golfers, such as Northern Irish star and 2010 U.S. Open winner, Graeme McDowell, were asked about the incident. "I don't think Stevie Williams was trying to be racial," McDowell said. "I don't think it was a racial comment; I think he was trying to be funny." McDowell's fellow U.S. Open champion Rory McIlroy (2011) also said at the time that Williams's apology was all that was necessary. "I've heard that, since then, Stevie has apologized for his comments, and I think now that he's done that everyone can just move on." Scott, when asked about the future of his bagman, said, "I disagree that he should be sacked."

As he reflects on the incident, Williams remains disappointed with himself. The function was supposed to be funny but his own choice of words, and how they were reported, still hurt. "Being called a racist was devastating because it's not who I am and I'm also part Maori," Williams says. "With the split from Tiger, and everything that followed, 2011 was very tough overall."

As for what Woods thought of his comments, Williams would find out the following week in Australia.

The trip Down Under began with an enormous pack of TV cameras and reporters, who wanted more answers, meeting Williams at the Sydney airport ahead of the Australian Open at The Lakes

Golf Club. Woods and Williams met the following morning, Tuesday, November 8, at a player hotel used for the tournament. They went to Woods's room and cleared the air. Williams apologized and told Woods he regretted the remarks. "Tiger knew the whole situation; I didn't even need to explain it," Williams says. "Mark Steinberg had contacted me, and I told him exactly what happened. There were no ill feelings among anybody." Later, Woods told a press conference, "Stevie's certainly not a racist. There's no doubt about that. It was a comment that shouldn't have been made and was certainly one that he wished he didn't make."

Williams was moved that when Woods had a chance to publicly scold his former caddie, he took the high road.

CHAPTER 15

THE BOYS OF SUMMER

The driveway at the Fairmont Miramar in Santa Monica, California, is just under 100 yards long and peels off Wilshire Boulevard, right where it meets the famous Ocean Avenue. During the daytime, sweeping views of the Pacific Ocean greet Fairmont guests as they exit the lobby. But at 6 P.M. on February 15, 2023, it was too dark for Williams to take in the scenery. He was well acquainted with Santa Monica, anyway, having caddied at the PGA Tour's Los Angeles Open for decades. There was no need to gaze at the shimmering lights of the Pacific Wheel, the world's only solar-powered Ferris wheel, down on the Santa Monica Pier. Instead, Williams parked his rental car and began the walk across the driveway on a crisp winter night in Los Angeles.

Williams had just arrived after an 11-hour flight from Auckland, where a cyclone had delayed his Monday departure by two days. At last, he was in L.A. But there was no downtime; he had to start work the next morning caddying for Adam Scott at the Genesis Invitational and he needed to pick up a yardage book from the

Australian at the player hotel. The tournament host course, Riviera Country Club, had seen some minor changes since his last visit and Williams needed to study them. As he entered the lobby, though, he saw a familiar figure: Woods.

Woods, 47, was in town from Florida to host the Genesis, a sponsored and renamed version of the Los Angeles Open and a prestigious tournament which benefits his TGR Foundation. It's held annually at Riviera, a historic course in the lavish neighborhood of Pacific Palisades. Woods had made his PGA Tour debut at the Los Angeles Open at Riviera as a 16-year-old amateur in 1992, to enormous fanfare and media, although in his prime he never won the event, nor had any real success there.

Williams and Woods had not spoken in 12 years, since the aftermath of their messy split in 2011. In fact, the last time they'd seen each other was at the 2019 U.S. Open at Pebble Beach and it was not a friendly encounter. Williams had come out of semiretirement to briefly work for former world number one Jason Day, a talented Australian who'd won one major, the 2015 PGA Championship. Williams and Woods crossed paths at the practice area at Pebble Beach as he walked his new boss's golf bag to the driving range on the Saturday before the championship started. "The only person there was Tiger. I was uncomfortable, and I could tell he was uncomfortable," Williams says. Williams felt deflated and longed for the feud to be over. But in that moment, it didn't feel like the right time to say anything. "Perhaps not enough time had passed," Williams speculates.

But outside the Fairmont, it was time to talk. Woods and Williams approached the door from opposite sides and could not avoid crossing paths. Outside, on the sidewalk, Woods grinned.

"Stevie, how are you, mate?" Woods asked. "I didn't know I'd run into you here."

"I didn't think I'd run into you, either, mate," Williams responded with a nervous laugh.

Woods had known his former caddie for three habits: an unwavering attention to detail; a steely conviction when offering advice on a shot; and always wearing the minimal amount of clothing in his spare time. The last one Woods found particularly funny; when Williams wasn't wearing a caddie bib and golf clothes, his usual outfit was a tank top and shorts. Woods looked down and saw Williams's airplane attire was a T-shirt, shorts and sneakers. Woods was rugged up in a Nike hoodie. It was 50 degrees out.

"It's freezing and you're hardly wearing any clothes, so nothing's changed," Woods joked. "What are you doing in Santa Monica?"

"I'm just passing through L.A., mate. How've you been?" Williams responded.

Williams, 59, was caught off guard by the unexpected reunion and didn't think to tell Woods he was actually in L.A. to caddie for Scott at the Genesis Invitational. He was relieved at how warm the conversation was. Woods—now a 15-time major winner, having stunned the world with a comeback victory at the 2019 Masters—asked how Williams's teenage son, Jett, was doing. Jett was born in 2006, at the height of Woods's powers and not long after Williams's wedding. "Jett is a professional scooter rider now," Williams said. "He travels the world competing at big events at skate parks. It's really cool." Woods agreed; Jett's career path sounded fun and unique. Woods had always liked Jett. During a practice round at Tiger's epic 2008 U.S. Open win at Torrey Pines, a two-and-a-half-year-old Jett ran underneath the ropes and into the fairway to hug Woods.

Williams told Woods his son researched different GOATs—the Greatest of all Time—from various sports, trying to emulate qualities that made them successful. The list included Tom Brady, Michael Jordan and, of course, Woods. Williams explained that Jett would love to ask Woods a couple of questions one day. "Totally, I'd be happy to," Woods said. The conversation only lasted another minute or so before Woods was swarmed with requests for selfies and the two said their goodbyes.

Fortuitously, the Fairmont encounter broke the ice for another run-in, 24 hours later, in the locker room at Riviera. Woods, who was competing in addition to his tournament host duties, shot a 2-under-par 69 in the first round to be in contention. Woods's locker was near Scott's and the two saw each other again. "I thought you were just passing through L.A.?" Woods laughed. Williams revealed he was actually caddying for Scott again, part-time. "It was really nice to have a joke together after all these years," Williams says.

A month later, Williams caddied for Scott at the 2023 Masters and conceded it might have been his last time in the club's white caddie overalls. Woods was also at Augusta, and in just his second tournament in eight months made the cut despite nursing a severe limp due to plantar fasciitis, an injury related to a single-car accident Woods had in Los Angeles in 2021. Woods, however, withdrew before the final round due to the pain in his foot. He tied the record for 23 consecutive cuts made at Augusta; a year later, he earned it outright with 24.

Williams was proud of Woods. Even when he started caddying for Scott in 2011, and when he retired from full-time caddying in 2017, he was always privately cheering for his former boss, who went on to have great success with caddie Joe LaCava, a kind but hard-nosed Connecticut native. In 2013, Woods won five times, at Torrey Pines, Doral, Bay Hill, TPC Sawgrass and Firestone. In all, he won 11 PGA Tour titles with LaCava, including the 2019 Masters. Woods was also in contention to win the Open Championship three times: in 2012, 2013 and 2018. He was also right in the hunt at the 2013 Masters when Williams helped Scott to win. "I still hoped Tiger was going to get back on the horse and get 18 or 19 or 21 majors. I wanted that for him," Williams says.

The 2019 Masters—when Woods came from two shots behind and stole the lead on the final day to win by one—was among the two or three tournaments Williams has ever watched on TV. He can't stand watching professional golf from afar. It was also the first time since the 1997 Masters that Woods won a major without Williams on the bag. His return to glory also ended an 11-year drought at the majors, stretching back to the 2008 U.S. Open. Williams sat and watched the entire Sunday back nine. "The excitement of helping your player in the hunt on the back nine at Augusta, there's no adrenaline rush like it in golf," Williams says.

Williams pinpointed the moment he knew Woods had demoralized his final group playing partners, Francesco Molinari, the reigning British Open champion, and Tony Finau. At the famous par-3 12th, Molinari was leading but hit his tee shot in the water. Woods then played a very conservative tee shot to the middle left of the green. He knew how important, psychologically, it was to have a putt for birdie, regardless of where it was from. While Molinari walked to the drop zone to take a penalty stroke, Woods walked ahead and stood on the green to look back at Molinari—to remind him Woods was safely on the green and about to take advantage. "That was vintage Tiger, and I knew, even with six holes remaining, he was going to win," Williams says.

Woods had engineered the most miraculous comeback after battling injuries, the chipping yips, a highly publicized DUI in Florida in 2017 and a back injury that he told fellow players was going to force his retirement. Woods rolled the dice with spinal fusion surgery that made it possible to turn back the clock in 2018 and 2019.

In 2018, Woods gave Brooks Koepka a serious run at the PGA Championship at Bellerive Country Club in St. Louis, finishing second. A month later, he made global headlines by winning the Tour Championship in Atlanta for his 80th PGA Tour win, and first in five years. The next year, he made the final eight of the WGC-Match Play weeks before winning the 2019 Masters. After that, he overcame further injuries that contributed to missed cuts in two majors. In October, Woods won a record-equaling 82nd PGA Tour title at the Zozo Championship outside Tokyo.

Perhaps it was fitting that what was likely Woods's last career victory on the PGA Tour came outside the United States—and under magical circumstances. The Rugby World Cup was being held in Japan and the country was buzzing. There was also an enthronement ceremony held for Emperor Naruhito in the Imperial Palace in Tokyo on Tuesday, October 22, 2019. It shut down the entire city. Torrential rain forced the golf tournament, which started on Thursday, into a Monday finish. Woods defeated homegrown superstar Hideki Matsuyama by three shots. Woods had his own enthronement ceremony, of sorts—he joined Sam Snead on top of the all-time list for most PGA Tour victories. "If that was to be Tiger's last PGA Tour win, it was special it came in Japan, a country he loved," Williams says. Woods prided himself on playing well overseas; whenever he received an appearance fee to play outside the U.S., he never finished outside the top 10 while Williams worked for him.

* * *

On a cold, windy afternoon in early May 2024, Williams walks around the man cave he's made from the bar inside his house in Auckland. It's a long, rectangular room with timber flooring and a stately whiskey bar at one end. There's a pool table in the center, and a series of 12-panel windows that look out over his manicured tree-lined paddocks. There's a rustic fireplace, which sits under an aged oak shelf, at the far end. The warm, inviting space feels like the billiards room at a luxury hinterland lodge resort.

Two vintage golf bags sit on each side of the fireplace. On the left is Woods's original Titleist bag from early 1999, with his signature splashed across its front pocket. Then there's a newer-looking golf bag from the mid-2000s with Williams's name on it. To the right of the fireplace are two more bags: Woods's first-ever Buick golf bag. It's made of black leather, but with large white panels and red trimming on its side. There's also a curious gold plate at shoe level that is heavily dented, appearing to have been kicked, in frustration, on occasion. There's also an ageing red Spalding bag from the 1980s bearing the name Greg Norman and the former world number one's then sponsor, Australian airline Qantas.

The room is essentially a golf museum. Williams has fashioned the flags he took from the final hole at all 13 of the majors Woods won with him into an L-shaped Perspex glass shrine that wraps around the lower part of the wall, just above the skirting boards. Many of the flags have a signature from Woods and a message of thanks to his caddie. There's the 18th green flag from the 1999 PGA at Medinah, the first major they won together. There's the flag from the 2000 Open at St. Andrews, where Woods became the fifth, and most recent, golfer in history to complete the career grand slam, and only a few flags to the right is that from the 2005 Masters. There's also a flag from their final major win together, the 2008 U.S. Open, which ended on the par-4 seventh at Torrey Pines South due to a playoff. It's the only flag Williams has mounted that isn't from an 18th hole.

Gazing around at the memorabilia, it's glaringly obvious that

Woods truly cared about Williams as a friend, and the contribution the Kiwi made to his golfing legacy. O'Meara says Woods and Williams's partnership was unlike any other in golf history. "Winning 13 majors together is incredible. Tiger and Stevie were so similar in certain ways, with their competitive drive. They wanted to be the best. But they were different in other ways, too. They were a perfect match."

On the wall left of the pool table, there's a photo of the pair trudging through long, wispy grass at a British Open in the early 2000s. Woods wrote a message:

To Stevie,
As always, it's just you and me!!!
Your buddy,
Tiger Woods

There's also a framed collage of the 2006 Open at Hoylake, where Woods had written a personal note:

To Stevie,
Thanks for just an unbelievable week!! It's a week I will never, ever forget. You're the best, my friend.
Tiger Woods

The warmth and respect captured in memories on these walls seems sharply at odds with the difficult circumstances surrounding their split. Williams knew he had no hard feelings, even though he made emotional, and, at times, reprehensible comments about his former boss. They were projections of the hurt he felt inside at the meaningless way their partnership ended. He wondered whether Woods would also get past that chapter, and if they'd get back on friendly terms. Their brief chat in 2023 confirmed that, one day, it was possible.

Williams still has brotherly love for Woods. "Absolutely, how could you not?" he asks, looking around the room, arms crossed and deep in thought. "Working with Tiger, everything went by in lightning speed. Anytime I come into this room, it's humbling to know that I was a part of history and that we'll always have that chapter together." Williams is eternally grateful he was a part of, and contributed to, one of the most remarkable stretches in any sport. He carried the clubs for Woods during 13 major wins and six second-place finishes on golf's biggest stage. There were also 63 PGA Tour wins in their partnership, 16 of which were elite World Golf Championships, as well as seven European Tour titles. "A lot of Tiger's accomplishments are never going to be repeated; I don't think we'll ever see a player like Tiger again," Williams says. "He didn't reach his ultimate goal of surpassing Jack, but he's a close second on that majors record and I don't see anyone ever surpassing Tiger in that spot."

Williams also can't help but think of the runner-up results where Woods could have easily won three additional majors had it been for a different bounce here or there. Woods had six runner-up results at the majors, but three stand out that are obvious when thinking about the championships that cost him a shot at equaling Nicklaus's record.

The first that comes to mind, for Williams, is Woods's second place at the 2005 U.S. Open at Pinehurst, when he was defeated by New Zealander Michael Campbell by two shots. Specifically, Williams still thinks about a bump-and-run chip shot that Woods misjudged on the 16th hole, causing it to leak right. He made bogey.

"It was such a straightforward chip for any pro, and 'Cambo' could hear that Tiger dropped a shot, and I think that gave him a monumental boost, like, *I can beat this guy now*. Had Tiger not bogeyed that hole, the outcome could have been so different. That's one major where I felt the tournament was in his hands." At No. 17, Woods three-putted for another bogey and allowed Campbell to stroll to victory.

Then there was the 2007 U.S. Open at Oakmont Country Club, near Pittsburgh, when Woods could have tied the lead with a birdie at the short par-4 17th. Woods pushed his 3-wood tee shot into the greenside bunker and caught his sand shot with a touch too much sand, causing the ball to release and roll past the hole and off the green. He made par instead. Argentine Angel Cabrera won his first major, with Woods and Jim Furyk tied second, one shot behind. "Tiger was in incredible form in 2007, and on Sunday at Oakmont, he was really up for the task," Williams says. "He loved Oakmont. His tee shot on No. 17 just didn't draw enough, and his bunker shot just rolled a few inches too much. A birdie on No. 17 could have changed everything."

The third moment was more the golf course, Hazeltine, where Woods had two golden opportunities to win PGA Championship titles in 2002 and 2009. Both times, he finished second to unheralded players. In 2002, in the final round, Woods three-putted No. 13 for bogey and dropped another shot on the short 14th, after missing the fairway with his tee shot with a 4-iron. Despite Woods birdieing the last four holes, Beem won by a shot. In 2009, another year in which Woods was playing sensational golf, Woods posted an uncharacteristic final round of 75 to lose to Korea's Y.E. Yang, who shot 70 to win by three shots. It muddied the image of Woods as a ruthless closer; he was 14–0 when leading a major after 54 holes. He hadn't lost a tournament anywhere in the world in over nine years when he'd held a two-shot lead going into the final round.

"I think that was probably the [runner-up] that disappointed Tiger the most . . . Y.E. Yang played unbelievably well that Sunday, but he really had no experience leading in the final moments of a major championship and Tiger had it all," Williams recalls. "Tiger believed that if he had put a bit more pressure on Yang, he would have won."

Critics of Williams, or caddies in general, may wonder if it mattered who carried Woods's clubs from 1999 to 2011. His talent was so sublime that Williams's true contribution isn't easily quantified. But O'Meara and Baker-Finch are among a series of golf greats who argue Williams unequivocally improved Woods's performance and added to his majors tally. "Certainly, Tiger hit the shots and would still have had *a lot* of success, but I'm not sure it'd be exactly the same amount of success if Stevie was not on his bag," O'Meara says. Adds Baker-Finch, "I think he was a big part of Tiger's performance; he needed someone as strong and instinctive as Steve."

As a father, Williams also appreciates the lessons he learned from Woods as an athlete and a person. As a lover of sport, Williams admires Woods for demonstrating that any level of athlete, amateur or professional, can always push their own perceived physical limits. "I considered myself fit, but Tiger's idea of being fit was a real eye-opener and he pushed me into running 10 kilometers at a pace I didn't think I could," he says. Williams also appreciates that Woods never checked the prize money sheet for players at a tournament. That's despite the fact prize purses soared in professional golf between 1999 and 2011 as a direct result of Woods's popularity. "At the completion of a tournament, there was always a sheet with the prize money allocation for each placing," Williams says. "Tiger never looked at that. Not once. He played to win trophies and create records." Working with Woods also made Williams believe that anything in life is possible with hard work.

Williams developed a belief that, in a team environment, trust bred confidence. Williams never feared losing his job for a bad call, because Woods had the perfect blend of accountability—blaming himself for bad results when it could have been pinned on poor caddie advice—and self-belief. He had an inner confidence and that projected onto Williams. "I never doubted myself because he trusted me to do my job," Williams says.

The trait that astounded Williams the most, though, was the prolonged intensity he saw from Woods. He wondered if any athlete in history could compare with Woods's insatiable hunger to perform, which lasted decades. Golf tournaments at the elite level can be a marathon of the mind, where the world's best players spend four days trying to limit the number of mistakes, which are unavoidable when hitting a golf ball between 260 and 280 times while millions of dollars are on the line. Woods put his entire life into four majors a year, knowing they would ultimately define him as a golfer. Yet after the final major every year, which for a long time was the PGA Championship in August, Woods rarely took his foot off the gas. During the 12 and a half seasons Williams caddied for him, Woods won at least one tournament after the PGA in almost every season except 2008—when surgery ruled out the second half of the year—and 2010, the year after the scandal. Often, those wins came months after August and, on several occasions, he won his very last official start of the year in another country. In 2000, he won his last official start in Thailand. In 2004 and 2005, he won in Japan to end the year. He capped off 2007 with a Tour Championship victory in Atlanta. In 2009 and 2011, he closed the year with wins in Australia and the Bahamas, respectively. Williams doesn't think modern golf will ever see that hunger from one player again. On the PGA Tour, there are a series of tournaments with $20 million prize purses, while the financial windfall for winning a major is so lucrative that most players can't help but relax after a big win, or after a purple patch. "These days, often a guy will win one week and miss the cut the next week, or he'll win a major and not contend in majors for quite some time," Williams says. "Tiger winning an event in October or November, when he'd won a major or two that year, was unlike anything I'd ever seen."

Williams feels at peace with his relationship with Woods, even if his chance meeting with Woods in 2023 was too brief for his liking. "Eventually, I would love to sit down with Tiger, just him and I, and talk over lunch," Williams says. The pair could have done so if Williams was still caddying, but he's happily retired in New Zealand, where he can retreat to his man cave, or take an entire day to mow the lawn, or wash his cars or prepare Jett for his next tournament. He admits that, apart from that welcome idea of lunch, it's unlikely he'll run into Woods again. "But it's special to know that what possibly could have been the final time I'll see him, it was like the good old days."

As always, Williams uses classic rock ballads from the 1980s to make sense of everything. The song he feels sums up his whirlwind 12 years with Woods is "The Boys of Summer" by Don Henley. It's fitting, considering Henley was the drummer and co-vocalist of The Eagles, who formed in Los Angeles near where Woods grew up. Williams felt he and Woods *were* the boys of summer, given they worked most of the year at tournaments in warm weather—from Florida and parts of the American South in the spring, to the drowning humidity of the Midwest and Northeast, and even the U.K., in the summertime, before retreating to their respective homes briefly every winter. Several one-liners within the lyrics of "Boys of Summer" help Williams reconcile the enormity of their partnership and how it came to an end:

A little voice inside my head said,
Don't look back, you can never look back.

For years, Williams was too disappointed to reflect on his time with Woods. He'd also look at the line *Those days are gone forever, I should just let them go*, and feel he was doing the right thing by burying the past and focusing on caddying for other players. But as he got into his late fifties and early sixties, and retired from almost five decades of caddying, he reflected on those 12 years with Woods with only nostalgia. It's what compelled him to share his once-in-a-lifetime stories with the world. "I'll always consider him a great mate and we'll always be those boys of summer who were chasing a goal," says Williams. As for the line that stands out the most, he points to the moment Henley sings, *I wonder if it was a dream*. Because Williams, to this day, wonders if it was.

ACKNOWLEDGMENTS

Together We Roared would not exist without the patience, commitment and generosity of Steve Williams. He sat down, twice a week, for interviews over a six-month period. During those sessions, his memory was absolutely astounding. I could only imagine how difficult it would have been to recall the moments my ultra-specific questions were pressing on. Often, they were 25 years after the fact. Steve, to his credit, appreciated what we had both been tasked with as coauthors—extracting the most vivid pictures of his and Tiger Woods's partnership and organizing them in a definitive, compelling, accurate and respectful way. With each year that passes since Woods's historic achievements of the late 1990s and throughout the 2000s, it becomes more important to capture those reflections. Steve also opened his home to this book, sharing never-before-seen flags and photographs, as well as gifts and handwritten messages from Woods. An enormous note of thanks must also go to Steve's wife, Kirsty, who helped him recall so many of the moments and emotions, as well as their dates and locations. Kirsty also kept Steve on track to meet deadlines for *Together We Roared*. The book would not have gone ahead without her. I hope that golf fans, and sports lovers in general, are as grateful as I am that Steve was willing to open up about the position he occupied in history.

Balancing the interviews, research and writing was only possible because of the support, proofreading and unrelenting optimism of my partner, Laura.

Steve and I would also like to thank, from the bottom of our hearts, the players, caddies, reporters and others who generously gave up their time when they didn't have to. The great Mark O'Meara was gracious and did not think twice about helping out a project his old friend "Stevie" was involved in. Chris DiMarco, too, was generous in jumping on the phone and describing what it was like to go head-to-head with a legend of the game so many times. More than two decades later, DiMarco is probably asked about Woods's chip-in on the 16th at Augusta National in 2005 more than Woods himself, but he gave such thoughtful insights and context into not only the chip, but how he controlled *his* emotions after it and managed to force a playoff. Stuart Appleby, a nine-time PGA Tour winner and, for a while, Woods's Isleworth neighbor, was fantastic in offering detail about how underappreciated Woods's trips to Ireland were during the week before several Open Championships, and the private jet ride home from Scotland in 2000 after Woods at St. Andrews. Another Orlando resident in Woods's prime, Robert Allenby, shed more light into how Woods played and practiced around Isleworth. Adam Scott told several hilarious anecdotes about what young professionals were feeling when they arrived onto the professional scene as Woods was in his most dominant form. Scott and Williams also teamed up for over six years as player and caddie, winning the 2013 Masters together. Mike "Sponge" Waite gave rich detail about his close friend, Williams, and how other caddies saw him. Sponge also told stories about the lighter side of Woods behind the scenes and how he loved to banter with foreign caddies through jokes they'd understand.

It's deeply important to note the role that golf writers played throughout Woods's golden years. Before social media, and outside of the TV broadcast windows, golf scribes from all around the U.S., and the world, were responsible for capturing details not seen on telecasts. Those reporters were documenting sports history. Their efforts to ask Woods, Williams and others involved in professional golf the right questions are why books, magazines, podcasts and documentaries can be made. Members of all forms of modern media are forever in debt to them and the stories they originally chronicled. There are too many to name, but they know who they are. Thank you.

Together We Roared was also possible because of our incredible agent, Nena Madonia Oshman, who immediately understood the vision and importance of sharing Steve's stories with the world. So, too, did the wonderful team at HarperCollins: Mauro DiPreta and Allie Johnston were a dream to work with.

And lastly, the best fact-checker this book could have asked for, Ben Everill. Benny went above and beyond, had many a late night in Los Angeles, verifying absolutely everything among the 95,000 words we threw at him. His gift with numbers, scrupulous approach to every sentence and talent as a golf writer helped *Together We Roared* more than he knows.

PHOTO CREDITS

Grateful acknowledgment is made to the following for the use of the photographs that appear in the photo insert:

Page 1, top right: Evin Priest/Steve Williams

Page 1, middle right: Jon Ferry/Allsport

Page 1, middle left: Craig Jones/Allsport

Page 1, bottom right: Michael Joy/R&A/R&A via Getty Images

Page 2, all: Evin Priest/Steve Williams

Page 3, top: Simon Bruty/Anychance/Getty Images

Page 3, middle: Ross Land/Getty Images

Page 3, bottom: Evin Priest/Steve Williams

Page 4, top: Steve Williams

Page 4, middle: Scott Halleran/Getty Images

Page 4, bottom: Chris DiMarco

Page 5, top: JEFF HAYNES/AFP via Getty Images

Page 5, middle: Sandra Mu/Getty Images

Page 5, bottom: Steve Williams

Page 6, all: Steve Williams

Page 7, top: Steve Williams

Page 7, bottom: Dave Pinegar/The Golf Picture Library

Page 8, all: Matthew Harris/The Golf Picture Library